BIG GIRL

BIG GIRL

How I Gave Up Dieting and Got a Life

Kelsey Miller

GRAND CENTRAL
PUBLISHING

New York Boston

Grand Central Publishing
Hachette Book Group
1290 Avenue of the Americas
New York, NY 10104

HachetteBookGroup.com

Printed in the United States of America

RRD-C

First Edition: January 2016

10 9 8 7 6 5 4 3 2 1

Grand Central Publishing is a division of Hachette Book Group, Inc.
The Grand Central Publishing name and logo is a trademark of Hachette Book Group, Inc.

The Hachette Speakers Bureau provides a wide range of authors for speaking events. To find out more, go to www.hachettespeakersbureau.com or call (866) 376-6591.

The publisher is not responsible for websites (or their content) that are not owned by the publisher.

Library of Congress Control Number: 2015953992

ISBN: 978-1-4555-3263-6

For Momor

Contents

A Note from the Author   ix

A Beginning   1

Two Bottoms   *   6

The Final Pig-Out   *   12

Embracing the Plate   *   19

The Part Where I Blame My Parents   *   28

The New Diet Buzz   *   48

A Brief History of Things I Haven't Eaten   *   65

Carbs!   *   86

The Cool Table   *   93

The Gun on the Wall   *   105

Reruns   *   113

Telling   *   122

The Mushy Stuff   *   132

Hurricane Sex(ually Transmitted Infection)   *   146

On Dumplings   *   153

Once More, Into the Suburbs   *   167

"Your Image"   *   183

Someone Else's Story   *   208

The Truer Version   *   214

Thirty   *   222

Still Thirty   *   228

The End (Just Kidding)   *   235

The Sucker Punch   *   245

Ice Cream Revisited   *   256

Another End   270

Discussion Questions   274

Many Thanks   276

A Note from the Author

One of my greatest lifelong goals has been to ensure that absolutely everyone likes me and no one is mad at me, ever. Unfortunately, my other goal has been to be a writer.

In writing this book, I have come to realize that some people will be mad and others may not like me—and that's a fair price to pay for the great privilege I have to tell my story. I have made every attempt to recount the events included accurately and portray those involved with honesty and compassion. But I do recognize the inherent selfishness in writing a memoir: These are the stories and memories that make up my journey, and yet there were dozens of other people along for the ride. I'm sure some of them would tell their version differently, look back with more fondness or vitriol.

In respect to those people and their privacy, I have changed many names and some identifying characteristics in this book. In one scene I simply smushed two people into one because their appearance was brief and minimal. Internet comments are mostly paraphrased and usernames have been changed, because even jerks on the Internet deserve their privacy (and because many of them have since been blocked and deleted for aforementioned jerkiness). One person I carefully labored over to make entirely anonymous for reasons I've made clear in context. But in writing this book, I set forth to tell the truth, no matter how painful or complex. We all have a right to our stories, me included.

I'd also like to acknowledge that this memoir is by no means my entire life's history. I had to compress or skip over many events and people, which are deeply important to me but didn't necessarily fit into this text. I had to remind myself that this is not a book about being a celebrity's assistant or going to musical theater boarding school, but my fucked-up relationship to food and my body. Those other topics played into it, but they're not the central theme. On the one hand, it's a bummer. On the other, it means I have more to write about.

Finally, I'd like to add that I'm not exactly the same person I was when I began *BIG GIRL*. People grow and relationships evolve (thank *God*). In one way, this book is a snapshot of a wild, precious year of my life. If I were to sit down and write this from the beginning, it would be with the perspective of Kelsey: Summer 2015 Edition. It might come out a little less raw, perhaps a little more smart than smart-mouth. But maybe I'm kidding myself with all this talk of grand maturity, and the words would come out just as they are now. All I can say is I did my best. Anyway, I'm not starting over now. I have more stories to tell.

Kelsey Miller
May 30, 2015
Brooklyn, NY

A Beginning

October 2013

I'm not special. Not that you thought I was, but let's just be clear that being a twenty-first-century woman with a messed-up relationship to food does not make me a beautiful and unique snowflake.

My story started like that of a million other snowflakes: I'd been wrestling with my chubby body for my entire conscious life, doing anything I could to make it small. I tried every mainstream weight-loss fad and nutrition plan. I'd worked with dietitians and doctors, all of whom added more foods to my Bad list until there was little left on the Good. Every time, it worked. And, every time, it then stopped working. Inevitably, I tired of hunting for low-carb sandwich wraps or could no longer stomach the flavor of fat-free, sugar-free yogurt with absolutely no fruit on the bottom. Each attempt petered out and the same old weight bloomed anew around my hips and beneath my chin, along with an extra ten pounds. But no matter. All I needed was a fresh start.

I don't believe in fresh starts anymore. I see them happening all around me, but I'm not buying it. You break up with your lover and move to a new apartment that doesn't smell like him. You have a lousy day at work and decide it's time to go back to grad school. You take the job in San Francisco, thinking, *I'll become a California person who makes homemade jam and jogs.* But in the end, you're still the same old jelly buyer.

Of course, it's easy for me to judge, because I never cared about any of that. I just wanted to be skinny. At least, I wanted to be not fat. I wanted to start over and learn how to eat less, how to dislike brownies, how to *want* to wake up for a 6 a.m. workout every day, forever. You don't need grad school for that. You just need a diet. The real-life version of a fairy godmother, every diet on earth promises one thing: You will be different. This is the trick. This is the magic that will finally transform you, thirty pounds in thirty days. We'll take care of the fairy dust; you just have to believe.

I was twenty-nine when the spell finally broke.

I started my last diet at the age of twenty-seven. Up until then, I'd been in limbo. I'd spent most of my twenties watching as friends blossomed into adulthood while I watched reruns. I wanted a life, too. I wanted to be a writer, have a relationship, or even just have sex. But I just wasn't ready, and I definitely wasn't thin enough. So I signed up for Weight Watchers for the fourth time believing without a doubt that this was it—the final, freshest fresh start.

I spent a year counting Weight Watchers Points and power-walking to yoga class at 7 a.m. and hitting the gym every night. Lo and behold, it worked. My weight dropped from the 200s to the 160s; I wasn't thin but I wasn't quite so monstrous. The villagers wouldn't light torches if I went outside. Anyway, I'd lose the remaining thirty pounds (maybe forty pounds?) soon enough. Armored in my new skinnyish clothes, I nudged my way out of the comfort zone, e-mailing editors with my little humor essay pitches and wading into the world of online dating (with a profile full of new, not-fat photos).

Nudge turned to push and suddenly I got a writing gig, and then another. I met a guy, and then another. I found I kind of liked this whole doing-something-with-my-life thing. Another year went by, and now I had a full-time job on an editorial staff. Plus, I was bonkers in love with a guy who loved me back, from head to toe. It was scary and new, but all of a sudden, I was out in the world, doing stuff I'd only seen in movies—like dating and leaving the house.

Things would have been almost perfect, had it not been for one large and growing issue: me.

Suddenly, I was too occupied with my job for twice-a-day workouts. I wanted to hit the office early, a new idea itching in my fingers, so I scavenged a breakfast of stale cereal and those pretzels I left in my desk last week. Once, I'd spent each Sunday making giant pots of fat-free soup, then going to yoga, then going to bed. Now, Sundays were for lazy mornings talking in bed with my boyfriend, then possibly dragging him to yoga, but probably just having sex instead. Besotted as I was with my new job and relationship, I'd never be the kind of person who vanished on her friends, and so I made a point of scheduling dinners, brunches, and other excuses to sit around and talk over a plate of something—regardless of how many Points I had left.

I had traded human relationships for the one I'd previously had with my scale, and so, slow and steady, the pounds crept back on. A few months after my twenty-ninth birthday, I went for an annual physical and stared in familiar horror as the scale topped out at 221 pounds. Dr. Payne had noted the number in a neutral, no-judgment tone, but I felt the numbing shiver of shame, panic, and helplessness settle over me like the opposite of an invisibility cloak. It was an everyone-can-see-you cloak.

I left the doctor's office and spent the rest of the afternoon online, searching for the next book that would fix me, for real this time, and once again saw the title *Intuitive Eating* pop up in my suggestions. "Customers who bought *Skinny Bitch Deluxe Edition* also bought *Intuitive Eating, 3rd Edition*." But I wasn't going to. Why buy something that sounded so vague and complex as "intuitive eating"? I didn't want to intuit or eat anything. I just wanted to be a deluxe-edition skinny bitch.

I clicked anyway, curious as to why the Internet kept shoving this particular diet book down my throat. Written by two nutritionists, *Intuitive Eating* was described as "the go-to book on rebuilding a healthy body image and making peace with food." Aw, that's precious but—next! That book made no promises about guaranteed weight loss. It didn't tout the evils of carbs and the virtues of raw leafy greens. This book talked about "honoring hunger" and "achieving a safe relationship with food." *Intuitive Eating* sounded like a great idea that I should try someday, but not today—like meditating. I'd buy the book just as soon as I lost, say, a hundred pounds. I could heal my relationship with food once I stopped eating so much of it, once and for all. I'd shed a hundred pounds off my body—hell, even just eighty!—and then I could work on the mind. And I would totally meditate, too.

But first things first, and so each month, I let Weight Watchers automatically deduct $17.95 from my bank account, because I was definitely going to start doing it for real again on Monday. No, after the holiday weekend. The digital scale lurked under my bedroom dresser, resentfully gathering dust. Maybe I should just buy a new one, and *then* restart Weight Watchers. (Or maybe I should try that four-hour body thing? Do you only have to do it for four hours?) Meanwhile, I'd just lie on the floor and suck in my gut, then try the zipper on my jeans again. See? Done! I can so breathe!

I didn't know how to stop it without a diet, and I didn't know how to diet and live my life.

I carefully got up off the floor, feeling the rough edge of denim dig into my hips, and opened my closet door. It was October 2013 and I had a work trip to pack for. Digging through a jam-packed rack of hangers, I pushed past dozens of too-tight blouses and ill-fitting skirts, all purchased with the hope of thinner days to come. With every diet came new clothes, and after every failure they lingered in my closet like a gathering of ghosts, sized 8 to 12.

Staring at it, I realized that wardrobe held the last twenty years of my life. And not a single thing fit.

Chapter 1

Two Bottoms

You sure? It's really not much longer." The trainer held my gaze, running in place like an overstimulated third grader. He was disappointed in me.

I looked down at my feet, my beat-up sneakers smacked with wet leaves. At that moment I regretted every decision in life that had led me to this place: running through the woods of East Hampton before 8 a.m. in yoga pants and a pajama top. My lungs stung with chilly air and I wheezed into his face.

"C'mon. You got this!"

But I didn't got this, and he knew it. He was just one of a long line of trainers, gym teachers, and other people in shiny track pants whom I'd disappointed over the years. Seeing as I'd known him for all of twenty minutes, though, I decided I could live with the shame of letting him see my true self: unfit, unenthusiastic, and really, really done with this run. All at once, I knew it. I'd hit bottom.

It wasn't as cinematic as I'd imagined. No interventions or hysterical tears. Just the two of us: a trainer hired for a two-hour workout gig and a twenty-nine-year-old woman having an unplanned epiphany in front of him. I didn't feel tearful or anxious. I didn't feel much of anything so much as finished. I'd come to the abrupt end of a story that had defined my entire life thus far. I was so done being the fat girl.

I looked down the trail where Janet, a sixty-two-year-old grandmother of four, sailed confidently toward the end with the rest of our small group. She didn't even need this beefy baseball-cap of a man to chase after her, demanding she pick up the pace. I was a fucking millennial and had nearly collapsed after four whole minutes of zero-incline jogging. I was definitively out of shape, miserable, and ashamed—a grown woman still failing middle school gym class.

Had I been able to speak, I might have told all that to the trainer, the man who changed my life but whose name I can't now remember. As it was, I just shook my head and plonked down on the damp ground, heaving for air. That's how done I was.

Watching him run on ahead to catch up with Janet and the others, I realized something else. I wasn't just done being the fat girl. I was done with dieting. An alarming discovery, like sitting on the edge of the bathtub and watching a plus sign emerge on the pregnancy test, discovering I'd come to the end of my dieting days left me feeling instantly unmoored. And yet, the plus sign appeared, irrefutable. There was no unseeing it.

I waited until the trainer was out of sight, probably high-fiving Janet and doing a celebratory round of push-ups or whatever it was fitness people did to celebrate. Then I dragged myself up off the ground, both hot and clammy from the early-morning chill, and headed back up to the house, settling into my newfound doneness.

How humiliating. I'd considered myself such a success, what with my healthy relationship and cool-girl career. I was in East Hampton on a *Thursday*, for God's sake. I'd finally gotten my shit together, except for the one unfixable thing that seemed to prove just how untogether my shit really was.

All my personal and professional progress seemed faint and ephemeral when compared to the permanent record of stretch marks and cellulite I lived inside. All I knew for certain was that I was fat again, moping around in my yoga pants. I wanted this taken care of and behind me once and for all, so I could quit wasting brainpower weighing the pros and cons of eating a banana.

"How was the run?" Olivia asked as she set coffee mugs out on a marble kitchen island. I gave her a thumbs-up, catching sight of my purpled face in the high-shine surface of the fridge. She was one of our hosts on this small press trip for food and fitness writers (guess which one I was). Getting to head out of town and test kitchen products for the weekend was one of the greatest perks of my job at Refinery29, a popular women's fashion and lifestyle website.

Olivia was a friendly, whip-thin woman, so small and bouncy that even her voice sounded low fat. She munched on a rice cake lightly smeared with almond butter, which had recently become a thing in the health-food zeitgeist. Like chia seeds and coconut water, almond butter was one of those foods everyone was supposed to like but no one really knew why. It was like the invisible nerd girl who showed up at school with a makeover, and then suddenly everyone claimed to have been friends with almond butter before she was hot.

I poured a sample of flavored Starbucks creamer into my coffee as we talked about bus schedules back to the city. Olivia tilted her head, all sad-to-say-good-bye.

"Well, we just loved having you here."

"Well, thanks so much for including me. Anytime you need someone to drink coffee creamer in the Hamptons..."

She chirped a laugh.

"I know, right?!" She tilted her head again, somehow differently. Tiltier. "And, can I just say, I think it's great that someone like you works at a fashion website? I just think it's *so* wonderful."

I blinked into my cup, just a slight pause. If this were the first time I'd heard it, I might have done a spit take, but it was more like the seventh. Though, I still needed to work on my comeback:

"Oh, yeah."

It went without saying that "someone like you" meant "fat girl." And that I was, irrefutably. I was not round or curvy or any of those euphemisms we prefer to use, rather than "clinically obese." No one wants to shop the "clinically obese" section. As I packed up my overnight bag to head back to New York, the same thought emerged over and over again: *Surely, some people manage to have a life, a job, and dinner without gaining fifty pounds, right? Maybe?*

I thought of that old book title that kept popping up online during my desperate new-diet searches. If I was truly through with dieting, then maybe it was time to give *Intuitive Eating* a shot. But I couldn't just do it myself with a book. Books could be put down. If I didn't get some real guidance then I'd just end up eating pizza all day, every day. I made the first decision: I'd ask for help.

Fuck.

One of the best things about diets is that you don't usually need to rely on anyone else. Asking others for help was not my favorite thing, but I knew from experience that damn it, it worked. I'd been in therapy for, oh, ever—so, why not find a food shrink of sorts? New York had every possible kind of therapist imaginable. If there were therapists for traumatized parakeets, I could find one that specialized in this method. I'd reach out to an intuitive eating coach and throw myself upon his or her mercy as a chronic case. A real live person would keep me accountable. And that way there would be someone to dial 911 if I actually did overdose on Domino's.

An hour later, Olivia dropped me off at the bus stop, a little white bench in front of an actual picket fence, where my picturesque epiphany continued. As I waited for the Hampton Jitney, my bags heavy with painfully symbolic food products and kitchenware, I thought of another element of the plan. It was a plan now.

This wasn't just about food. I'd spent my life swinging between two distinct phases: obsessive exercise or high-intensity sloth. I'd go through months of morning yoga, evening cardio, and walking miles out of my way just so I could calculate the calories burned. I hated every second of it, but that was the point of exercise, right?

To absolutely no one's surprise, these spurts of mania always flamed out fast. Sometimes I'd quit because of injury—a sprained back or a torn ligament, all in a day's workout when you're a lunatic. Other times, simple boredom brought me to a halt. Thus the lazy phase would begin again and I'd spend a year taking cabs and sleeping in.

The second decision: I would find a trainer. There had to be a way to integrate fitness into my life without letting it take over. I still suspected that a workout didn't really count unless it bordered on self-harm, but I was willing to be proven wrong. I knew I couldn't afford a lifetime of personal training, but I also knew I needed someone to set me straight, at least in the beginning. I promised myself I'd go in with no judgment. As long as he or she didn't make me run or spin or do anything I didn't want to do, I'd do it. I would find a trainer and be honest with him or her: "Nice to meet you. I don't know what the hell I'm doing."

There's nothing quite like a solo bus ride for personal introspection. Put on some old U2 and you're halfway to a montage; you're the lead character in a movie about a girl who tries to leave her troubled past behind, but guess what, she can't. I keep a playlist for just these kinds of road trips, so when the bus arrived, I cued it up and settled into an empty window seat, one of two passengers on the Jitney at 4 p.m. on a Thursday. I looked back at my fellow rider, barking instructions into her phone and hoped she could wrap it up quick. *Can't you see I'm in the middle of an epiphany?*

There was a third decision knocking around in my head, though I hesitated to make it. But since the idea first emerged that morning as I sat on a pile of dead leaves, this part was a foregone conclusion. I pulled out my phone and began an e-mail to my editor in chief, the subject line reading: "New column idea."

I had to write about it. Good, bad, and probably ugly.

I needed to chronicle the journey publicly, and not just because I knew there would be others who could relate to being trapped in their own bodies, waiting for life to begin thirty pounds from now. That was the story *I* wanted to see each time I opened a magazine or clicked on a website proclaiming to speak to women. Instead, I got "Why Your Diet Failed Again, Asshole" and "30 Ways to Stop Being So Disgusting Starting with Your Upper Arms, Ew!" I wanted to write a big, beautiful fuck-you to those stories while giving people like me something better—or, at least, something different. But while I relished the thought of starting an Internet crusade in the name of the not-skinny, I knew I needed them more than they needed me.

If I was going to write all this down and blast it out into the chattering void, I would need to hear a voice echo back, saying, "Me too." Two things I knew about myself, for sure: I was a writer and I was a show-off, for better or worse. So, why not make use of the tools I had when I was lacking so many others? If I had an audience available I'd never disappoint those faceless millions, or even faceless dozens.

Maybe it wasn't the healthiest impulse, but that was another issue for another bus ride. For now, I needed others to be honest with and accountable to. I wasn't yet able to be accountable to myself alone, and if that made me less than perfect, too bad. Perfect hadn't worked out so great, thus far.

Chapter 2

The Final Pig-Out

The Jitney dropped me off in the middle of Midtown, and I inched the rest of the way home in a rush-hour cab ride, vibrating with anticipation. Flying up the stairs of my building, I plopped down my bags, kicked off my sneakers in a little performance of glee, and dug out my laptop. In just a few weeks the first snow would arrive, sealing the city in a frozen crust, but that evening my bedroom was hot with autumn sun and I shoved a window open. The ice cream truck was parked downstairs playing an off-brand version of "Turkey in the Straw" but for once I didn't wish for an assault rifle. I had books to order and people to call and then: the Final Pig-Out!

I'd been in Williamsburg for seven years, but not fancy Williamsburg. Not the part historically identified as the source of all insufferableness and mustaches. Considering my yoga-pants-based wardrobe and abiding love of musical theater, I was never in the running for true hipsterdom, nor have I ever lived in one of those luxury buildings that comes with a meditation studio. I shared a long, narrow fourth-floor walk-up with a roommate I met on Craigslist a few years prior. The block was loud, and the living space was small, but the bedrooms were big and airy, and when I woke up in the morning I could lie in bed and watch the J train chug by in the distance, heading over the Williamsburg Bridge. I got a constant, geeky thrill knowing that I lived in the same neighborhood as Francie Nolan, the heroine of *A Tree Grows in Brooklyn*. Who cared about its reputation when I got to live in the setting of my favorite childhood book—even if I did have to call 911 to report gunfire every now and then?

Sprawled across the unmade heap of rose print sheets on my bed, I flipped open my laptop and immediately ordered *Intuitive Eating*, using my boyfriend's account to exploit his free-shipping perk (all couples do this, yes?). Harry lived in Park Slope, an actual fancy neighborhood in Brooklyn, ten subway stops away from me. We'd been together for over a year, and though most of our coupled friends were somewhere between the moving-in and planning-babies phases, we just weren't there yet. In fact, *I* just wasn't there yet, and Harry, my sweet and patient first love, gave me the space to not be. It was typical of our dynamic, him being boundlessly generous and me requiring boundless generosity. Things weren't entirely one-sided, but it was pretty clear which one of us was the designated freak-er out-er.

I hit "Confirm" on the order and texted him to send me the confirmation e-mail IMMEDIATELY, please, love you.

Hey there, he replied. *Are you back?*

Yes! Can you send?

Yeah, forwarding now. How was the trip?

AMAZING.

Are you up for dinner or are you beat?

Too beat, need an early night. Call you in a bit?

I *was* beat, but I was pumped, too. I was up, up, up, with adrenaline and nerves and then worn out by adrenaline and nerves. Plus, I had dinner plans already—and no one was invited.

Along with Harry's forwarded e-mail, there was another message in my inbox. My editor in chief had approved the column idea with a big, exclamation-pointed "Yes!" It was official. Not only would I change my life, but I would also do it in public. I would name it. It was all new, newer than any new diet because, for once, it was *actually* new. Adrenaline, nerves, sleepy, adrenaline, nerves, anxiety, panic, thrill, wonder, hope, hope, hope, anticipation, excitement: time for food.

I knew this wasn't a diet I was starting. I remained firm in my done-ness, and yet the excitement and thrill of the new plan was still there, urging me to go all out. Despite the fact that I wasn't going to be starting Jenny Craig or CalorieKing tomorrow, there was a "tomorrow" to look forward to. And I wanted to have my night before. I wanted my Final Pig-Out.

I don't know what you call the night-before-new-diet ritual, but for any dieter, there is one—and those are the best nights of our lives. For a brief window, there are no rules. The idea is actually to break all the rules at once. You order a pizza or greasy Chinese. You buy a tube of cookie dough and maybe some wine. If you do it alone, you put on the junkiest TV you can find, because no one wants to watch *Charlie Rose* while they're eating chicken wings and pudding out of a mixing bowl. If you do it with a friend, then the friend becomes your partner, goading you on and nodding with real and gleeful horror when you say, "Fuck it, mozzarella sticks, too."

It's a last hurrah, and in a way it works. You wake up the next day bloated and ashamed, and the idea of living on green juice forever sounds just about right. But that feeling lifts somewhere around noon when somehow you're hungry again, and suddenly you have to tangle with food on a diet rather than food on a binge. By then you're riding high on the New Diet Buzz, and that carries you through the early days until you plateau—then you stumble, then you fall. Then it's time to start over again, and that means calling the pizza place.

*

I'd been Final Pigging-Out since my first diet, but I didn't have a name for it until somewhere around my twentieth. During our senior year of high school, my friend Sydney and I planned to start a low-carb regime right before graduation. This was the spring of 2002 and you'd be hard-pressed to find anything as universally reviled as a basic carbohydrate, except *maybe* Osama bin Laden. I was irrefutably fat, while Sydney was of completely average weight, but she was heading to a summer theater and dance intensive, and I was going to be a production intern at *Sex and the City,* so both of us needed to lose a million pounds ASAP.

"Should we go downtown for dinner, then?" Sydney asked as we plotted skinny-girl plans in her room. She lived in a dorm across campus from mine on the cozy grounds of our small boarding school. It was May and hot as actual hell in every room of the old New England buildings.

"China Village?" I asked hopefully.

China Village was the gross but good place that almost no one ordered from. If you wanted Asian food, you got take-out from Da Mei, the Thai/Vietnamese/sushi restaurant with cloth napkins and lacquered chairs. If you ordered from China Village, the place with sticky floors and a bench outside, you'd better have had some kind of severe PMS-breakup-college-rejection excuse. But the lo mein was outrageous and, after all, Sydney and I were going off all carbs (and most fat, we decided at the last second) first thing tomorrow. So, one way or another I was going to get some outrageous lo mein in my face, plus dumplings and General Tso's.

Sydney barely hesitated: "YES. Lo mein. Now." She was my partner. We bounced down the hill and into town, high on the thrill of badness.

Over dinner on the bench, we talked about how amazing this diet was going to be for our summer plans, and eventually our college experiences and lives in general. Low-carb was the way to go. Our bodies didn't want all this (OMG, delicious) processed garbage. Our bodies wanted to go into ketosis and burn fat and protein, or something like that. It would feel *so* good. I don't recall exactly what we ate that night, only that we ate everything. Years later, when we were postcollege roommates, Sydney would ask, "Remember the time we ate an entire Chinese restaurant?" I laughed and nodded. I did remember. "The final pig-out," one of us had declared, surveying our heap of empty aluminum containers. And I thought of how we crossed the park afterward, stuffed and lethargic, to order ice cream sundaes at the Candy Cone.

Sydney and I made the low-carb thing happen for a week or so, but graduation excitement soon trumped all concerns of skinny days to come. There were midnight walks to Dunkin' Donuts and tearful good-bye dinners. Nobody wants to hear "I need dressing on the side" in those moments, nor do you want to waste your breath on dressing instructions. You've got song lyrics to quote.

Lying belly-down on my bed in Brooklyn, clicking through dinner options online, I kept interrupting myself with thoughts of that night back at boarding school with Sydney. It had felt so fun and so icky, but more than anything it had felt necessary. It bonded us together as a team and bound us to the diet we'd start in the morning. Our shared complicity in such a disgusting event guaranteed our penance for the next day, at least. And of course there was no greater taste than the food we'd soon be quitting. I don't believe, as some do, that disordered eating and alcoholism are equivalent afflictions, but the binge is one crossover that cannot be denied: the Final Pig-Out or the last bender. What is more relished and regretful?

I called DuMont, a bistro-ish joint in Williamsburg, and ordered my favorite burger with American cheese, sautéed onions, mushrooms, and a side of fries. And onion rings. I didn't really feel like a glass of wine but I poured myself one anyway. I was going to do it one last time, even if it was on this small scale. A cheeseburger wasn't an entire Chinese restaurant, but it was big and heavy with the same secrecy and meaning of that night in high school. When my takeout arrived, I turned on Netflix, which suggested I might enjoy watching *Fanny and Alexander*. (Of course, I never would. I just couldn't delete it from my queue, for the same inscrutable reason I couldn't unsubscribe from *The Economist*.) I scrolled past TED Talks and '90s Disney cartoons, finally settling on a *30 Rock* rerun because the show felt like the right mix of silly and grown-up—and probably also because it stars a binge-eating woman. She's a binge-eating woman who's, like, a size 4, but Tina Fey can have that one.

My food was there and then it was gone. I'd eaten every bite right down to the lettuce and flavorless tomato slice. I was stuffed in a familiar way, but the usual anxiety didn't rise to meet it, because I knew that tomorrow something would change. Something had already changed, and this dinner was the dying breath of something else. It was nostalgia on a deep, dark level, and the child and teenager and young adult who'd gotten so used to this routine whispered, "Please, please don't give up. Let's eat more cheeseburgers and watch television and Google 'Nutrisystem' until we fall asleep." But I didn't have it in me anymore, and the discomfort in my gut reminded me why. I didn't want my life to be a series of nauseated spells or hunger pains. I wanted to turn off the television, or at least be able to turn off the television without worrying what might happen in all that silence. I finally had a real life in my hands and I wanted to hold onto it. That meant letting go of food. It wasn't a new beginning. But it was a beginning nonetheless.

It's not that I wish I hadn't done this, but like the desire for the Final Pig-Out, the shame of it is still there, too. There are many moments I wish I hadn't *had* to go through in this last year, because they're not all triumphant. I want my story to go up and up and up. But from the moment I hauled myself up off the ground in the woods, things were never quite so perfect and crystalline—so East Hampton—again.

Life on a diet is linear: You begin, you lose weight, and you're done. Then it's on to the mythical "maintenance" mode (which is also dieting, but for eternity. Congratulations?). From the moment you quit, you feel like a train that's jumped its track. You careen up and down over unfamiliar hills, you turn back toward valleys you've seen from only one perspective, and you pause for the first time, nervous and thrilled to realize that, in fact, you are not a train but a human being. Human life is, unfortunately, a lot more difficult than train life, but at least it's real. Forget "happy" and "whole" and all those other simple things we're supposed to aim for every day when we wake up. Those things are truly wonderful, but if you're not careful, they can become another way of saying "perfect." And I hope we can all agree that aiming for "perfect" is nothing short of bananapants. "Real" is the best you can shoot for.

That dinner was my final Final Pig-Out, though even I didn't quite believe that yet. When I curled up in bed that night, thrilled for what lay ahead, I still hated my body and feared food. I was still the woman who avoided whole city blocks so as not to walk past reflective glass, and who thought that eating after 7 p.m. was a crime on par with infanticide. I was still hanging around in my bottom, and that was okay. I'd been hiding my whole life—what was one more deep, dark hole? I knew I wouldn't be in there for long, and anyway, at least I didn't have to figure out just how I would start climbing out of it yet. Not that night.

All of a sudden, it was morning.

Chapter 3

Embracing the Plate

There's a well-earned stereotype about how much New Yorkers love to talk about public transportation. The first half hour of most social occasions consists of everyone taking turns to talk about how they arrived, which lines are delayed this weekend, and a brief, uncertain silence in response to the guy who biked there. The same is true for dieters and ordering food: if you ask me what I did for lunch, you better not have anywhere to be for the rest of the day.

That Monday, back at work, I felt suspended in a kind of limbo. I'd had my Final Pig-Out, but I didn't have a diet to start. All I had was a grand declaration to not start one again, and while I'm at it, somehow turn that into a compelling column. Now, I had to actually do the work of figuring out how to execute both those things. And since actually doing the work is the worst, I made the completely healthy and nonavoidant decision to order lunch instead. I pulled up Seamless.com, the online food-delivery service much beloved by those of us too ~~lazy~~ busy to pack lunch. All you have to do is enter your address and an endless list of restaurants appears, letting you click through every menu in the area without actually getting off your ass. On the one hand, it's a helpful service. On the other, it's a deeply codependent relationship unlike anything I've experienced with another human being. As I scrolled through the list of options, the usual routine began in my head:

> *Seamless:* Okay, Kelsey, what do you want for lunch today?
>
> *Kelsey:* Fuck.
>
> *Seamless:* Oh my. A spinach salad, perhaps?
>
> *Kelsey:* What's that supposed to mean?
>
> *Seamless:* I just remembered that you liked the spinach salad from Fresh & Co. last week. Remember? With the lemon vinaigrette?
>
> *Kelsey:* No, I didn't. It tasted like weed.
>
> *Seamless:* Hmm, how about a turkey burger with mushrooms and onions?
>
> *Kelsey:* Maybe. Mushrooms and onions are vegetables.
>
> *Seamless:* That's true.
>
> *Kelsey:* And a turkey burger isn't as heavy as a beef burger. Maybe I should have it.
>
> *Seamless:* With fries?
>
> *Kelsey:* Jesus, back off!
>
> *Seamless:* Okay, no fries! Greens on the side?
>
> *Kelsey:* Oh, so I can't have the fries now? What if I want both?
>
> *Seamless:* You can! It'll just be a few bucks extra.
>
> *Kelsey:* God, I'm sorry, Seamless. This is just really hard.
>
> *Seamless:* I know.

Kelsey: I'm having my picture taken tomorrow for this new column.

Seamless: Honey, I know.

Kelsey: And I'm not supposed to be on a diet, but I want to look good in the picture.

Seamless: Right.

Kelsey: I know how crazy that sounds.

Seamless: ...

Kelsey: Seamless?

Seamless: What? Oh, sorry. I think your Internet went out for a second or something. Listen, there are millions of different lunches out there—some of them are 15 percent off. We'll find one that's right for you. I promise.

Kelsey: Thank you. Man, you're the best. Aaah, I can't believe I'm crying!

Seamless: Hey, you know what I think?

Kelsey: Tell me.

Seamless: Sushi.

Kelsey: Yes.

Seamless: Here, let's get you that lunch special you like: One spicy tuna roll, one tuna-avocado roll. It comes with a side salad that you'll probably throw away.

Kelsey: Sushi's such a clean food, right? It just feels so clean and fresh and healthy!

Seamless: Yeah, you usually get it on Mondays after a big weekend.

Kelsey: Are you trying to say something?

Seamless: Confirmed! Thanks for ordering from Hamachi Sushi!

Hold the referrals. I already have a therapist.

Once I'd recovered from the ordeal of eating a lunch that would satisfy my hunger and, far more important, satisfy my need not to be dieting but also not to be eating a burger the day before a photo shoot, there was really nothing left to do but start changing my life. *Fine.*

The not-so-fresh start began just like all journeys of self-discovery and transformation: with Google. Entering "intuitive eating nyc" got me the usual billion results and one ad for a weird flat-belly trick. As expected, there were dozens of nutritionists, dietitians, and eating-disorder counselors who specialized in intuitive eating. "Let me help you make peace with food—and your wonderful self!" one nutritionist's website proclaimed in enormous italics. "Embrace the plate and learn to live again!" high-fived another. With its dreamy colors and loopy fonts, this site was faintly reminiscent of the one I created in seventh grade to curate Leonardo DiCaprio fan fiction.

It is both helpful and unfortunate that we live in an age where one cannot exist as a functional human without a web presence. In all likelihood, these were perfectly capable professionals, but thanks to overzealous website templates, they came off like My Little Ponies. And if I'm honest, I had to get off my extremely high horse. Step one to any get-your-shit-together process is a good old-fashioned ego check. When you need help, you can't ask for it with your nose in the air . . . is what I told myself while clicking through website after earnest, pastel website. After all, I did want to "embrace the plate." I just didn't want to talk about it.

I found Theresa Kinsella's site about ten minutes into my search. It had its share of gentle colors and positive affirmations, but there was a marked lack of cheese-ball sentiment, making her stand out like a rose among fake roses. I didn't choose Theresa for her website, however. I chose her because, out of everyone I reached out to, she was the first to write me back. Thank you, Google.

Hi Ms. Kinsella,

My name is Kelsey Miller, and I'm a writer at a women's life-style website, Refinery29. I'm hoping to start a first-person series about intuitive eating and healthy fitness. I've been a lifelong yo-yo dieter, and finally hit a breaking point recently. I know a little about the theory, but was hoping to work with a professional. I would, of course, link to your website and reference you as my guide throughout the series. Would you be interested in discussing further?

Best,

Kelsey

At twenty-nine, I wasn't as broke as I'd often been. Ordering lunch, for example, was a relatively recent luxury. But I wasn't so not-broke that I could foot the bill for my own lifestyle transformation.

A word on free stuff: This is a perk most web and magazine writers enjoyed. But, in general lifestyle journalism, it was also a necessity. If your job requires writing about things and experiences, you have to actually check out the things and experience the experiences. There-fore, a lot of individuals and companies are willing to offer you things and experiences, hoping for press. It may sound ugly and parasitic, and I suppose it sometimes is. But personally, I'd never had my arm twisted as a journalist. Most of the time, people sent me unsolicited stuff like lentil chips or flavored booze along with a breezy press re-lease about how much my readers were going to love it. If I actually liked the free thing, I might use it in a story at some point. If not, I left it in the office kitchen in case one of my colleagues enjoyed pancake-flavored liqueur (it's real, it's gross, don't bother).

For all the free snacks sitting under my desk, I'd rarely actually *asked* for something—let alone something so big. Then again, I had a feeling the column I was about to write would be bigger than anything I'd ever written. Still, Theresa was a nutritional therapist, not a bag of lentil chips. She had all that intimidating "MS, RD, CDN" stuff after her name, so I didn't want to be less than straightforward when it came to asking for freebies.

"I can't, like, pay you, though."

We'd met at a Midtown Starbucks where I'd given her the highlights: Disordered eating! Wretched body image! Let's kick this thing once and for all so I can get started with my life, and also not be fat anymore!

She got it. Since she'd been working in the world of disordered eating for years, my story was even older to her than it was to me. Furthermore, she was as pissed off at the diet industry as I was, and just as eager to get the message out there. Theresa had degrees and experience, as well as a superchipper vibe that remained entirely free of bullshit. She was nice and optimistic and no-nonsense, a tart slice of Midwestern cherry pie.

Theresa explained a little bit about her process, which sounded a lot more like therapy than the many rounds of nutritional counseling I'd been through over the years. She'd walk me through the phases of becoming an intuitive eater, specifically related to my needs and history with eating. I'd gone through all of my Food Issues with regular therapists before—along with all the other capital-I Issues—but Theresa's work kept a tight focus.

"I don't need to hear about your sex life, for example. Unless that relates to food somehow." It kind of did, but maybe Starbucks wasn't the place to get into it.

Our first official session took place just two days later. In the past, most of my consultations with nutritionists had taken place across big, scary glass tables, often decorated with correctly portioned food models, but Theresa's Midtown Manhattan office was comfortable and prop free. The two-chair setup was familiarly shrink-y, and with the gusto of a well-seasoned couch crier, I plunged headlong into the dirty details of my dieting past. And, well, present.

"Except now, I'm just doing Weight Watchers."

"Right," she nodded. "Weight Watchers is a diet."

"Yeah, but I guess I always thought of it as more reasonable than, like, Atkins or Eat Right for Your Type and all that."

I thought of a Sunday the month before when I'd woken up already ravenous with sweet-salty-everything PMS cravings. I decided to blow all my Points on an 11 a.m. bowl of ice cream, then subsist on Points-free apples for the rest of the day.

Theresa shrugged. "That's just marketing. It's a diet."

My world rocked ever so slightly off its axis but I nodded. "Right!"

We forged ahead, Theresa asking about how I decided when and what to eat, how much I thought about food, and what my goals were for this process.

"I don't want to obsess over food anymore. I want to learn to eat like a normal person."

Saying this, I felt my own pastel colors bleeding through. I was supposed to be the new me—no longer a scared little fat girl hiding in the pantry with a handful of chocolate, but a confident plus-size woman taking control of her life and hiking. Five minutes in that chair and the baby-blue truth came out. I dropped my precious ego and kicked it under the chair.

"I realize this isn't working and it's never really worked. I just want to eat normally, and I don't think normal people need an app to tell them how to eat. I want to be healthy. I don't know if I'm meant to be skinny and I don't *need* to be skinny, but this"—I threw my hands up at myself, uncomfortable in too-small clothes, shifting around in my chair to try to find a position that would somehow hide my stomach and my upper arms—"this doesn't feel like my normal. I want to find that place."

Theresa nodded, and I realized my eyes had filled with hot, stinging tears. And that there was a box of tissues on either side of my chair. This woman knew what she was doing.

"I just don't want to do it anymore. I want to eat when I'm hungry and stop when I'm full. And to not be fat."

She wrote something down, and I worried I'd misspoken. First session or not, I prefer to be an A-plus client.

"I mean, find my normal weight range."

She looked up from her pad. "And what if this is your normal weight?"

I side-eyed the tissue box. *Is she for real?*

"I don't think it is."

"How do you know?"

"I guess I don't have any proof except that I didn't get here by 'normal' eating."

"Okay."

She waited. Theresa was a waiter, not a give-you-the-answer-er.

"So, I imagine that when I eat normally, I'll lose a lot of weight. Some weight."

She nodded and wrote a brief note. I eyeballed my old friend Tissue Box again, looking for answers. Was it too soon to quit this whole thing? Too late? Theresa looked up.

"What would happen if you didn't?"

"I would be surprised?"

Screw this. Weight Watchers was fine. I'd start again tomorrow. Jennifer Hudson did it and now she has an Oscar. Or vice versa, but hey!

"Okay. I'm not saying this is your normal weight range, but I'm just posing this hypothetical: Say you went through this whole process and you"—she paused to consult the pad—"no longer obsessed over food, maintained health, ate when you wanted to, and stopped when you were full and everything else. What if you achieved all that and didn't lose a single pound?"

My initial thought was that it would be a complete and total waste of time and *good-bye*. But I sat on my ego for five more minutes, promising it a trip to Sephora later, and tried to really imagine Theresa's scenario. If I had all that—freedom from food obsession, no need to diet, a natural instinct toward healthy, satisfying eating—could I *hypothetically* be okay at this current weight?

"Maybe."

"Okay," said Theresa. "That's fair."

And she smiled. And she didn't kick me out. It was a little miracle, to suddenly feel good enough.

I wanted my answer to be yes, but it wasn't. This was my new chapter, and I didn't want to fill it with my filthy old habits. I'd been a liar of convenience all my life, relying on the kind of falsehoods that grease the wheels and open escape hatches, letting me slip out of any uncomfortable truth. "I'm not interested in a serious relationship, either," "Oh no! I didn't get your e-mail," "The leftover birthday cake is gone? The cleaning guys must have tossed it. That sucks!" I was the kind of liar who was begging to be caught.

"Yes," I wanted to tell Theresa. "All I want is health and happiness. That other nonsense is behind me." That's what the confident plus-size woman would say right before she went hiking. That was who I wanted to be, but I just wasn't yet. I left Theresa's office hand in hand with the weepy, little fat girl, knowing we weren't done. She was the lifelong liar in me, and she didn't know any better. I'd have to tell the truth for both of us.

Chapter 4

The Part Where I Blame My Parents

I was eight years old the first time I got caught, and the crime was a handful of chocolate chips. I was on the phone with my dad, a nightly ritual.

"Adam's on the phone," my mother would call, and I'd take the receiver with its endless spiral cord and step inside the pantry, turn on the light, and close the door.

"Can't she say, 'Your father's on the phone'?" he'd ask, and I'd lean against the shelves, assessing the goods. Our house was small, my siblings young and loud, and the pantry was the only place a person could close a door that wouldn't immediately be opened.

"How did the quiz go?"

"Fine."

"Did you have a sense of how well you did?"

"Fine."

"Do you know how much I love you?"

"Yeah."

This conversation was our well-practiced routine. I knew other kids of divorce who treated their long-distance fathers more like relatives than parents. But, though he lived far away, my dad called often enough that I had the luxury of getting bored with him.

I spent most of these calls preoccupied with the shelves. My mother had a small catering business, and the closet was perennially jammed with large-batch boxes of baking ingredients and other dry goods. With the door shut, I shook stale sprinkles into my mouth and sucked on cinnamon buttons intended to be noses of gingerbread men.

"Is there something in your mouth?" Dad asked. "What's that sound?"

"Raisins."

Raisins were my cover, every time. Though I knew grapes were off-limits ("pure sugar," my mom said), raisins were smaller, harder, and I didn't like them as much. Their mild grossness made them Good.

But on the back shelf of the pantry, tucked among dusty plastic bottles of cake decoration and boxes of Grape-Nuts that nobody ate, was a plastic tub, the size of a fish tank, of Nestlé Toll House Chocolate Chips. This container was the first thing you saw when you opened the door: its giant red top, big yellow label, and enough chocolate chips to bake a batch of five thousand cookies.

We rarely had sweets in the house, and if we did, they were my mom's pints of Häagen-Dazs coffee ice cream, which were not easy to sneak without making a visible dent. Sometimes I'd find bags of Fun Size candies on top of the fridge, which my stepfather had impulse-bought on a supermarket run. Our nanny, Karen, kept a bucket of leftover Halloween candy next to her bed for months after the holiday. But again, these indulgences were hard to pull off without being detected. Someone might walk into the kitchen before I could get the step stool back in place, or Karen would note the disappearance of all her Reese's cups. I was good, just not good enough for those illicit treats. James Bond wasn't good enough.

The Toll House chips were for large-batch baking projects Mom often did as a caterer. They were an ingredient, not a treat, and therefore kept right out in the open. It was like a chocolate loophole. I could lean into the pantry, pretend to grab a can of tuna, and come out with a heaping gob of chocolate in my mouth before anyone would notice. During my nightly dad-calls, I didn't even need an excuse to be in there. And so I'd take the opportunity to slowly siphon off the contraband from that tub, my desire and terror multiplying as I watched the level go down. I was careful, telling myself I'd take just one handful, and then suck each chip into sweet nothingness on my tongue. But when my palm was empty, warm and chocolate swiped, I knew I'd have to have another. I would hang on, putting it off for five minutes, "fine"-ing my dad on the other end of the phone. And then, my pulse leaping to attention, I'd reach back, silently unscrew the top, plunge my hand into the tub, and pull out another round. It was a moment of extreme daring, a compulsive instinct I had to obey, not only for the pleasure that followed, but the fear of knowing any moment my mother could open the door.

This was the peak of our Food Police phase. Later, that's how Mom and I would both refer to the years leading up to my first real diet. This was the era of tense, well-supervised meals: her hard gaze on my plate at the dinner table, the raised eyebrow as I reached for another helping of mashed potatoes. Mom wanted to help set me straight and I sorely needed it, budding criminal that I was.

I don't remember exactly when or how it began, but I know there was a time when I could eat or ask for food without considering the consequences. In one of my grandfather's photo albums there's a shot of me somewhere around age four, glancing casually at the camera, tuna sandwich in hand like it was no big deal. Each time I see it, I'm stunned by the moxie on that kid, eating tuna on white bread, and probably with full-fat mayo.

But as long as I'd been conscious of having a body, I had known there was something wrong with it. There was just too much of me, and no one found this more offensive than my mother. It was as if my body was a drunk, vulgar guest I'd brought to the party and couldn't keep under control.

Her own body fell into the general category of thin. It seemed to me that there were really only two ways to be: thin, pretty, and long hair, or fat, ugly, and who cares what the hair looks like? Mom had swingy blonde hair and long legs made lean with yoga. She always had a pint of coffee ice cream in the freezer, and ate it right out in the open. Even after giving birth to my two siblings, just eighteen months apart, she never crossed over into the realm of fat and loathsome. Baby weight or not, she always had the carriage of a thin woman.

A kid wants her mother to like her, and I was failing. True, I was smart, well-behaved, and sweet, but none of that trumped my round little tummy. All that just made me a fat goody-goody. But when Mom declared a Food Police state, I knew it was my chance to get in with the popular crowd. I just had to impress the leader.

✳

"What's up?" my mom had asked one day as we drove back from school.

At eight years old, I was just beginning the journey into chubby pubescence. Normally, I loved the times when she picked me up instead of Karen. Conversations that would have been brief or edgy at home were made breezy when she drove, the activity uncorking her. But that day I sat curled up quietly, arms crossed and fingertips poking into the doughy flesh of my sides.

"Nothing."

"Are you sure?"

I nodded, leaned my head against the window. I could smell my own hair.

"Well, if you don't want to talk about it, then maybe you should try and snap out of it."

My eyes spilled over and soon I was sobbing. It was the stupidest thing. I'd gone on a weekend trip with my best friend Amy and her mom to Rocking Horse Ranch, a Catskills resort where kids rode horseback through trails so flat and unscenic that only a horse-crazed third grader could possibly have any fun. I came back to school with the hilarious anecdote about the horse I'd ridden all weekend.

"His name was Double-Dutch Bubble Butt!"

Approximately four seconds later, it had become my nickname for life.

I wept the story out to my mother as we drove through the pebbled driveways and carefully unmown meadows of Bedford Hills, heading home to Croton and our little house by the river.

"Oh, baby." She sighed. "I'm sorry. That really stinks."

"It sucks!" I moaned, further testing the waters with an almost-curse-word.

"It does suck," she nodded. "Those kids...Honey, I'm just sorry."

"I hate it, I hate this!" I said, grabbing at my belly. She was in, this time. I had her on my side. Letting the tears out was always risky, since waterworks could just as easily be met with an eye roll. But the gamble had paid off this afternoon, and good thing, too. Crying was inevitable, but had I caught her in an eye-rolling mood the forty-minute drive would only serve to irritate her further with every silent tear.

"I just want to be someone else!" I was in full-blown melodrama mode now, swooning against the headrest.

"Well, Kels." Mom rested her forearms on the wheel as she eased to a stop at a red light. Her tone shifted just so. Sympathy time was up. Now it was all about bootstraps. "You know, you don't have to put butter on everything."

I hiccupped, stared up at the passenger-side visor mirror, eye to red eye with myself.

"Right? It's not like you can't do something about this." She pointed an elbow at my middle.

"I know."

"I know you know. Listen, you can do this. You just need to stop snacking so much, right? You've got to stop with the junk. I know

Amy can eat chocolate ice cream for breakfast and still look like a twig, but most girls can't."

I thought of Amy's house. Her mom kept a candy drawer in the kitchen, no rules or anything. Both mother and daughter were tall and reed-thin and ate take-out every night in front of *Jeopardy!* I'd just about lost my mind when I first saw the inside of their freezer: There was half a goddamn Carvel cake in there that they'd *forgotten* to finish after Amy's birthday.

"I don't eat chocolate ice cream for breakfast."

"I didn't mean literally, come on."

"I'm sorry!" The sobs began a second wind and Mom reached over, grabbing my hand with a little shake.

"Hey, enough. This is not the end of the world. You just need to shape up."

I turned my hand around inside her palm, holding her hand back with a squeeze. The light changed and she let go, eyes back on the road.

"Y'know what I mean, jelly bean?"

That was when the head-shaking and lip-pursing at the dinner table began. Every time I extended a hand toward the bread basket or the gravy boat, Mom's eyes would snag it like a fishhook. I'd look up at the "no" on her face and sit back before anyone else could see that I'd been reaching in the first place.

At restaurants, I'd order a side of fries and she'd raise an eyebrow.

"You sure about that?"

The waitress would look between us for a moment, unsure of her role in this stalemate.

"I meant salad."

We went on for years like this, the fridge filling up with carrot sticks and the ice cream stashed behind the ice dispenser, out of sight but always on my mind. A fat kid always knows where the ice cream is.

Even if I was just a not-so-skinny kid, I knew that was as good as obese. *You are obese*, I reminded myself daily, standing naked before the small mirror in my room on the basement level of the house. I'd initially hung it on the wall to be part of a vanity table, hoping to get a cushy stool to place in front of it, so I could sit and brush my hair a hundred times before bed, probably something I saw in a movie about pretty girls with flat stomachs and zero armpit hair. But I never got the stool, and was now stuck with a mirror placed exactly high enough to see my midsection each time I walked by. Instead of brushing my hair each night, I jumped up and down in front of it, gaping with mesmerized horror at the jiggly roll below my navel and the floppy blobs that would be breasts on any other girl.

It was a mean little ritual, this routine assessment of my disgustingness. Some nights it overwhelmed me and I dropped to the ground, first doing crunches, then leg lifts, then push-ups, until my vision went fuzzy and I crashed to the floor, banging my knees. My room's cement flooring was covered in white linoleum, with plenty of throw rugs for warmth. But as the exercises became part of my nightly routine, I sought out the hard, cold spots on the floor, positioning my legs over them so that I could bang my knees for the grand finale. The ritual grew in time and detail as I grew more hateful and afraid of what I saw in that mirror. I exercised and prayed and whacked my wristbones on the bedframe at just the right angle, three times; always, I concluded by banging my knees against the floor, one, two, three. It was the only thing that hurt enough so I could finally stop and go to sleep.

Despite these nights of painful discipline, each day I woke anew a criminal. Before I discovered the hopeful thrill of dieting, I was desperate for someone to keep me in line and grateful to my mother for taking on this thankless task. I needed those eyes on my grabby little hands or else the jiggly bit would take over the rest of me. I knew it, because every time I left the house my mind went on high alert. I didn't just know where our ice cream hiding spot was; I knew where *all* the hiding spots were. I knew the vice principal kept a silver dish of Hershey Hugs on his coffee table, and that his door was left open even after he'd left for the day. I'd leave after-school play rehearsal or reading club and walk up and down the hallway, swinging my arms in a farce of nonchalance, then dart into his open door and snatch two-thirds of whatever was in the bowl.

I knew that Amy's mom kept chocolate-covered Oreos in the door of the refrigerator.

"Did you eat all my mom's cookies?" Amy asked me on the phone one night.

"Oh. Those Oreos? No, I had like one."

"Because they're all gone now. It's just the empty wrapper."

"Oh geez, no. I don't know what happened, but I only had a couple."

"It's fine if you ate them."

"No, I know! But I seriously just had a few of them. There were like three left."

"Okay. They're good, right?"

"Yeah, they're okay."

I was good, but not perfect. And each time I got caught the shame was so great, my blush so quick and searing that I thought I might physically burn. Being busted by a friend was one thing—I could just avoid Amy for a few days, fantasize about transferring to a new school, perhaps in Eastern Europe. But with Mom, each infraction was a mark, indelible and damning. Take too big a slice of my little brother's birthday cake, and she would turn her face from me, her words clipped and brief for the rest of the meal. Later, I might jump to help clear the table without being asked; it wouldn't make up for my mistake, but it would give me an excuse to go into the kitchen where she angrily scraped plates into the trash.

"I'm really sorry." I went quiet as an orphan, Oliver Twist with his hands out. But it was the wrong play. She dropped a plate into the sink.

"I just don't understand. I am doing my damnedest to help you here, and you just want to eat cake all night."

I had become a seasoned sneak, a spy in a school uniform. There were napkin-wrapped cookies slipped into the inner pockets of my winter coat and Halloween candy folded up inside my sweaters at the top of my closet. In front of others I ate properly portioned, unbuttered vegetables and asked for seconds only on salad. Alone, I honed my skills at soundlessly opening wrappers and letting a potato chip dissolve on my tongue without any visible chewing.

In all my months of secret pantry snacking, I'd never once been caught. So, that evening when my mother swung open the door just as my fingers had plunged into the Toll House container, we were both stunned into silence. We held the tableau for an endless moment, such a brazen violation: my hand was caught in the cookie jar. My dad's tin-can voice called through the receiver ("Hello?! Did you drop the phone?!"). Mom looked from my hand to my pale, ever-rounding face.

"I'm done."

The door flew shut. And I ate the chips.

To be clear: I know I'm not Oliver Twist. I don't have nearly enough fucked-upness for a Fucked-Up Family memoir—at least not one I haven't already read five times. My mom wasn't Joan Crawford, my dad wasn't a deadbeat, and my grandmother didn't keep us hidden in the attic for three years in a secret incest plot. I didn't have it *that* bad. I just didn't have it great.

My parents split up when I was two years old. Having no actual memories of their marriage, I didn't feel so much like a "child of divorce" than a child who'd been erroneously assigned to two people who couldn't stand to be in the same room. I was fascinated to hear stories from the time they'd been a couple and marveled at their engagement photos in the albums on my grandparents' shelves. But when I daydreamed about my young, happy parents, it wasn't with the secret yearning for Mommy and Daddy to get back together. I just wondered how the hell they'd even been a couple in the first place.

My version of their story is one pasted together from other peoples' anecdotes, filtered through the lens of nostalgia and New York City lore. I could take a walking tour of my parents' romance, starting with a brownstone basement on East Thirty-Seventh Street, where they met. Next would be Grace Church, the Gothic revival landmark on Broadway, where they married a few years later. From there it's just a five-minute walk over to East Seventeenth Street, where they lived in a fifth-floor walk-up next to Stuyvesant Square. They'd both been the renegade kids from nice families. Mom had grown up in Gramercy Park, calling herself "the blonde sheep." Dad was a musician from Washington, DC, and had defected to New York in the late '60s from a childhood of white gloves and English boarding schools. She was younger, he was older, and together they set out to build a family and get it right. They moved to the suburbs and had me, and shortly thereafter it all went wrong.

No one ever told me just how or why, and I suppose that's the decent thing to do. There were a lot of things no one ever told me about: the wild ups and downs my mother had been cycling through since childhood. All I knew was when she was fun, she was the *most* fun, telling colorful stories and showering me in adoration. Sometimes it would last for months and I relished every moment, filling up on her love. Because when she got quiet and tired and angry, it was as if her darkness would swallow us both. There were clinical names and diagnoses for this cycle, but no one told me that back then. Why would they? What would a toddler do with words like *borderline* and *bipolar*?

There was another word I didn't know until much later. That
brownstone basement where my parents met was the site of a local
AA meeting. My dad's sobriety would remain intact, but my mother
had two demons to contend with. Mental illness and alcoholism mix
all too well. As a child, I didn't know when she was sober or off the
wagon, stable or symptomatic. She was just my mom.

My mother was twenty-five when they divorced, and we moved
into a rented duplex on the grounds of a country club in Sleepy
Hollow. (See: aforementioned not-that-badness. Even when we
were broke we were broke at a country club.) She had just finished
a degree at the Culinary Institute of America and worked as an editor and food stylist at *Gourmet* while I attended the local preschool.
I'd bop around the magazine offices a few times a month, the editorial department keeping half an eye on me as I colored with their
marker sets and smushed my face onto the Xerox machine, making
color copies for everyone.

Mom began dating an investment banker named Steve, and soon
our group of Sleepy Hollow friends grew. They always seemed to
be throwing casual dinner parties at one another's houses, each
night ending in a cozy cloud of cigar smoke and the Grateful Dead.
Sometimes there were other kids around, but I didn't mind it when
I was the only one. Some nights, I'd be allowed to stay up late and
play with the warm and tipsy guests who put their lipstick on me
or braided my hair, goofing around until I fell asleep somewhere
that wasn't my bed.

When I think about those boisterous evenings now, I blame everyone for what happened. Yes, my mother should have seen it first,
but I could burst with molten outrage at each of the adults in that
house who cooed over how precocious I was and then turned away,
bored. I want to shake them by their selfish shoulders and shout
over the stereo, "I can see you're just trying to enjoy your twenties, but isn't it a school night?" Surely, I would have sulked and
screamed at being treated like a child. After all, I was a member of

the gang and they were *my* friends, too. And so, a few years later, when one of them began to put his hands on me, it never occurred to me to tell my mother or anyone else. None of them seemed to notice it that first time or the second or the third. No matter how my skin went hot with fear and revulsion at his touch, I knew that nothing could be really wrong here. He was just being friendly.

It would be years before I said anything and many years before I said it using the right words. I didn't want that to be part of my story. Instead, I told the funny bits of my childhood: the time I pushed aside my plate at Indochine and conked out at the table, and other quirky anecdotes starring Mom as the WASP-y bohemian and me as her little smart-mouthed sidekick.

With Dad, I was back in the stroller. He'd moved back to the city after the divorce, and most weekends, we tooled around Manhattan, frequenting our favorite playgrounds in Central Park and strolling past the other, far inferior ones that didn't have swings or monkey bars. Every morning, we got poppy seed bagels and cartons of orange juice, discussing what movie we might catch that afternoon. At night, we ate heaps of Daddy's Famous Spaghetti before I'd play with his cassette recorder, singing commercial jingles into one end and delighting to hear my own voice come out the other.

Dad was a singer-songwriter, and having been on the front lines of the music scene in the '60s and '70s, he'd already lived the kind of life most of us will only hear about in Bob Dylan lyrics. He'd lived on Saint Mark's Place when the rent was fifty dollars, and seen the Beatles play club gigs in Paris before they hit the US. I might have fallen asleep at Indochine, but he bussed tables at Max's Kansas City. No matter how many restaurants I pass out in, I'll never story-top my dad.

But that had happened twenty years and twelve steps before I was born. He'd been sober for years when he met my mom, and all those juicy tales were part of a history he was trying to leave behind. By now, Dad was burned out on New York and the music business, visibly gutted by the breakup of his marriage, and always so desperately sad when I waved good-bye to him. Even as a toddler, I just wanted so badly to make him feel better. I think I succeeded, sometimes.

Dad left New York and moved to Paris when I was five, taking an apartment not far from where his sister lived with her French husband and children. Knowing him, he must have explained it to me over and over again, but I don't remember the details. I was sad and scared to see him go, but I believed him when he said he *had* to. In my mind, it wasn't a decision. How could it be when I was the most important thing in the world to him? He didn't have a choice; he simply could not live in New York anymore, and the only place he had to go was three thousand miles away. I took it as a given, just as I had always understood my parents' divorce was just a thing that happened. Shortly after his move, I flew over for a lengthy summer stay. It was wonderful, having months of unbroken time together, but every night I dreamt of my mom and woke up in tears.

"You were always very attached to your mother," Dad now likes to say, recalling my childhood and his ever-present distance in it. Perhaps because I dearly love my father, I hear this not so much as an excuse as a lament. If only I hadn't been so anxious and sorrowful without my mother. Then what, I don't know. There's only the "if only."

I flew back to New York, pudgy with Nutella sandwiches and *pommes frites* from my aunt's kitchen. Mom was engaged to the guy she'd been dating, and shortly thereafter, pregnant, too.

Dad came back to the States a couple years later—not to New York, but to Washington, DC, where he'd grown up. Now we were back to long-weekend visits, or even just day trips, when he'd drive up early in the morning to take me to lunch and a movie, and then head back down I-95 before dark.

My mom and I had left the country club and moved in with my new stepfather, Steve, into his little riverside house in Croton-on-Hudson. He'd lived there since his college days, and the place remained littered with relics of the party-cum-crash-pad it had been.

"Is this for closing potato chip bags?" I once asked, fishing the roach clip out of a drawer.

Mom smirked and laughed, taking it from me and shouting to Steve, "Honey, guess what Kelsey just said!" Another little story I like to tell.

The days of *Gourmet* were over, but our house was still full of people—two more than before, with the arrival of my new baby brother and sister, born eighteen months apart.

My dad's place, by contrast, was sparse and unlived in. When I came down to DC for visits, he'd pull out the convertible loveseat he'd tucked away behind a bookshelf with a little bedside table to give some sense of a bedroom. Our visits were regular and comfortably routine. I'd fly down from Westchester Airport, rocking an Unaccompanied Minor pin on my jacket. It was usually just me and four to seven extremely suited businessmen on the otherwise empty shuttle. I was the only one on those flights who didn't look like I was heading down to Washington to give the president a piece of my mind. Dad met me on the other end, waiting at the gate. He'd always have downed a giant coffee while waiting for me, so he'd park me at a bench near the men's room and instruct me to scream if anyone came near me.

Our weekends consisted of spaghetti dinners, Blockbuster rentals, and me whining through a trip to the National Gallery as Dad swore up and down how much I'd appreciate thirteenth-century religious art one day. (Still waiting. Any minute now.)

"You sure you're not too B & L?" he'd ask five hundred times each weekend.

"I *promise*," I'd reply, well versed in our call-and-response.

"B & L" was our code for "bored and lonely." Aside from how much sleep I'd gotten and whether or not I knew how much he loved me, Dad's main concern was my potential boredom-and-loneliness when we were together. After all, I had no friends in Washington, and we never saw anyone except each other. Dad rarely dated; only twice had he cautiously introduced me to a woman he was seeing. Not until I was in college did he settle into a long-term relationship; until then, our world was tiny: two seats at the table and two glasses in the cabinet. I knew that when I left he only used the one, and the thought of his own loneliness tore at me each time I poured a glass of water.

But though I worried about his own boredom and loneliness, I wasn't B or L during our visits. It was great. It was normal. Parents were supposed to drag their kids through museums, and kids were supposed to roll their eyes and whine about it. Having a dad in another city was the most ordinary thing about my family, and I felt the most like an ordinary kid when I was with him. I got to be irritated with him when he nagged me to floss. I got to gush about my latest book or musical obsession, demanding that we listen to "On My Own" on repeat for the entire car ride, and then moan and drop my head back in despair when he demanded that we listen to the first three seconds of "Just Like a Woman" over and over and over again all the way back home. "Just the first three seconds—do you hear that snare?!"

Then I would have to leave. That part was awful, each airport drop-off so raw and poignant that I stung with the memory of my father's tearful waving. First came our drive to the airport with a stop by the supermarket where he'd buy me a bag of chocolate-covered raisins from the bulk candy section. This was as much a ritual as the gallery trips, my little treat to sweeten the flight home. In the car, I'd fiddle with the plastic bag in my coat pocket, handling the candies but not yet eating them. Though we never discussed it, it was an unspoken rule that I wouldn't eat them until after takeoff. I think Dad liked to imagine me, alone in a window seat, gliding along the eastern coastline, savoring this little souvenir of his love.

At the gate he'd pull me in for tight hugs, more and more as boarding time approached.

"Do you know how much your papa loves you?"

"Yes, Dad."

"Do you really, Kels?"

"Yeah, of course. I love you, too."

"Do you know I'm always thinking about you?"

"I know. I promise."

Finally, it would be time. Then it would be me rushing into his arms for one last squeeze, knowing it would be the one to break his heart but unable to help it. Discreetly, I'd press my face into his sweatered shoulder, taking in my papa's smell—Irish Spring bar soap, shaving cream, and Gain detergent, clean and identifiable, every time. I held the scent, consciously making the memory. Then we'd press hard kisses into each other's cheeks and I'd look away from his tears, the worst, worst part of every weekend. It was a terrible power, to be able to make my father cry.

"I'll be back for Thanksgiving in five weeks!"

"I know. I just miss you when you're gone. Remember I love you, always."

I'd kiss his cheek again, then one last one and then the real last one. Heading for the Jetway, I'd turn to see him waving, blowing a quick kiss. A few more steps, turn back, and there was his hand still in the air, reaching over heads and past backpacks to find me, let me know he was still there. Just before I turned the corner, one last look: my father's face, now craning to hold me in his gaze. He waved and I waved back, smiling big until the crowd pushed me forward, out of his sight.

At last, takeoff. Chocolate-covered raisins downed in big, tasteless handfuls. Headphones and a paperback to wipe Dad's tearful smile from my mind. Sitting on the curb at Westchester Airport waiting for someone to pick me up.

More often than not it was Karen who pulled up in the Subaru, with Z100 blasting on the radio, loud enough so we could sing along without hearing our own voices. Karen had been with us since the Sleepy Hollow days, a college student who babysat me frequently. When we moved into Steve's place, she came with us to look after me and then my siblings. Karen's room was in the attic, a small nest on top of the house, only accessible by a set of foldout stairs. The little kids couldn't get there without help, but I climbed up the stairs most nights to watch TV with Karen, hoping she'd let me sleep on the floor next to her bed. She usually said yes if I scratched her back for a while.

My own room, all the way downstairs, felt so remote and segregated. During the daytime, I relished the isolation, sealed inside this cozy, windowless womb of books and music and computer games. I checked out books on tape from the local library and spent whole days cocooned in other peoples' stories while the racket carried on at a comforting distance upstairs. I played computer solitaire while Benny Hogan fell for Jack in 1950s Dublin. I painted my toenails on an unmade bed while Idgie and Ruth served fried green tomatoes at the Whistle Stop Café, wondering, *Am I supposed to think they're lesbians? Or does that mean* I'm *a lesbian?*

But after dark I lost the ability to escape into a fantasy. Each night was a bottomless stretch of silence, a terribly blank canvas upon which any number of horrors could be written. Carbon monoxide could gently smother us to death; my baby sister could roll over and suffocate in her sleep; Indian Point, looming less than three miles down the road, could melt down at any moment, killing everyone from here to Manhattan in a mushroom cloud of radiation, but me and my family first. They tested the sirens every Saturday afternoon, one long, harmonic bellow, hitting pause on all conversations within a five-mile radius. Each night, I lay awake and at attention, conjuring the sound into reality and knowing that any such warning was futile, and that instant, white-hot death was screaming through the sky, faster than the speed of sound.

Sometimes I managed to stay in bed, begging prayers of protection against each possible natural disaster, and dropping into shallow puddles of sleep. But most nights, I crept upstairs, checking the stove burners, locking our unlocked doors, then unlocking and relocking them, and then just once more. I listened for breathing at bedroom doors, curling up outside my mom and stepdad's room on a nest of couch cushions and blanket throws until the sky turned gray with dawn and I let go, careening into slumber.

"*Et voilà!*" Karen announced, placing a large soup bowl on the carpet in front of me. It was allegedly filled with ice cream, but the actual substance was buried so deep in whipped cream and chocolate and what must have been a whole jar of sprinkles.

"What's this?"

"A banana split! It's a special occasion." She sat down next to me and turned up the volume on the television. The special occasion was the Gulf War.

It was clear that I was more than just Karen's charge. I was the one who helped her wrangle my siblings, and watched *Beaches* with her on Saturday nights. After she left college, I was probably the closest thing she had to a friend. And I was the one she ate with.

Like most girls of a certain temperament, I spent early adolescence reading eating-disorder fiction, like *The Best Little Girl in the World* and *Dying to Be Thin*. I could diagnose a sixth-grade bulimic a mile away, but it never once occurred to me that there was anything unusual about Karen's giant "special-occasion" meals, followed by hours of nausea or parking-lot vomiting. Who wouldn't get sick after downing five White Castle sliders and a milkshake, plus half of my milkshake? She always felt better after, so what was the problem?

For a long time, Karen was the closest thing I had to a friend, too. When she did the school pickup and found me weepy and embarrassed by some recess humiliation, there was only ever one response.

"Just tell me, smushy-face. It'll be okay. What did he say?"

On one such occasion, I slid down in the seat and wrapped my arms around my face. There was no way I could say it and actually look at her.

"He just kept singing, 'Two, four, six, eight, Kelsey likes to masturbate.'" And I howled into my arms, outraged at being forced to utter the word *masturbate*.

She paused—the worst possible silence. For God's sake, never be silent after a kid says "masturbate."

"And this was Robbie C.?"

I nodded. Robbie C. was a dickbag. He had braces and the worst BO I have ever encountered, yet somehow managed to be one of the cool kids. I suppose I have to give him some credit for coming up with that song on the spot, but like, let's be real, Robbie C. I may indeed have discovered the sneaky wonders of late-night Cinemax, but I sincerely doubt that I was outmasturbating your twelve-year-old ass.

"That kid's a little jerk. He probably just likes you, you know?"

I moaned at her laugh-out-loud ridiculous assessment of the situation. I was fat, my ponytail always had bumps, and even if I put it on straight out of the dryer, the skirt of my uniform was never *not* wrinkled. Thanks to a scholarship, I went to school with girls whose parents had housekeeping staffs and probably dry-cleaned their soccer cleats. They wore Tiffany beans strung around their necks and their dads' extra Rolexes hanging loosely around their nimble, lightly scented wrists. I was 300 percent sure this wasn't crush related.

I dropped my arms. The road outside my window wasn't the usual route home from school.

"Where are we going?" I asked, looking over to see Karen ready with a smile and a side eye.

I have a hard time getting angry at Karen for taking me to the diner that day, drilling deeper in the message that everything could be made better with an order of Belgian waffles à la mode. Because in one way it did make the bad day better. That secret treat reminded me that there was someone in the world who knew it was more important for me to feel loved and looked after than to attend the piano lesson on my schedule. I was worth making up an excuse for.

For that same reason, I can't really get mad at my dad about the chocolate-covered raisins. I don't begrudge my stepdad for taking me to IHOP before the SSATs, telling me to put down the flash cards and order whatever I wanted. I won't blame my mom for pulling into Friendly's at 10:30 in the morning for a peanut butter sundae, just after the X-ray confirmed my arm had indeed been broken.

These were moments of kindness and exception to the rule. The rule might be tough and unpredictable, and you might need to hide in the closet with a fistful of chocolate chips just to keep from screaming. But along the way there were times like these where one of my many caregivers reached for something sweet to give me, to let me know that when bad things happen, there is a simple, chocolate-covered solution, even if it's over as soon as you hit the bottom of the bowl.

Soon enough, I would discover something even better. It was more effective than running from the Food Police and more comforting than bingeing on burgers with Karen. It was my first diet and I believed it would make all my dreams come true.

I was almost right.

Chapter 5

The New Diet Buzz

I felt the Buzz for the first time in the fall of sixth grade. I'd been at the same small, private school since kindergarten, a white-washed, tree-speckled campus in Bedford, New York. If you are not familiar with this area of Westchester County, picture the prettiest town you've ever been to, then make it rain money for fifty years. Now superimpose Robert Redford's smile. Thus it is always in Bedford.

It wasn't the kind of upper-crust private school I sought out in books and movies, lusting after their little wooden half desks and rigid adherence to needless formalities. I would have been thrilled had someone corrected my curtsey or addressed me as Miss Miller. But Riverwood was a school for liberal rich kids. We wore uniforms, sure. But we also tapped for maple syrup in the woods off the lacrosse field. We were given limitless access to Cray-Pas, and we dug around the playground for arrowheads. We sat in a lot of circles.

The thing is, though, kids aren't liberals. By nature, adolescent society falls somewhere between paranoid totalitarianism and a boobs-based meritocracy. Either way, it's hard to make your way in the world as a pudgy, unibrowed, not-so-rich kid, even if you do know all the words to the Original Broadway Cast recording of *The*

Secret Garden. I'd gotten my period a month into sixth grade and, after the initial rush of Judy Blume-ing, I'd realized what a letdown the menstrual cycle really was. On top of the bulky new pads in my life, I spent mornings jamming chubby-girl breasts into a training bra that looked more like training body armor. I was already a pro at shaving my legs, but there's no coming-of-age book that covers the wondrous discovery of armpit hair. I was graceless, shiny nosed, and gross. The school was too small for me to be invisible. But at age eleven, my visibility seemed to be a constant annoyance to my classmates. I was somehow trying too hard, just by being there. *Still? Really?* And they weren't wrong. I radiated wanting.

Most days, before I left for school, I used my younger siblings to determine where I stood on any given day. At three and four years old, they were too little to consider lying and I took full advantage of their innocence, trying on different outfits and asking, "Do I look skinny or fat?" Glancing away from his cartoons, my gangly four-year-old brother would give one of the two answers I allowed. If he deemed me "skinny," I could leave the house with my head held high(ish), good enough to raise my hand in class or withstand the appraising locker-room side eyes of my classmates. If he said "fat," I slunk through the day, a bad, disgusting girl, hiding inside the lanky curtain of my hair. Having my siblings was like being a contestant on a reality show whenever I wanted. But I stopped using them as a judging panel the day I asked "skinny or fat" and saw hesitation in their eyes.

Obviously, I wanted to be an actress. There were other girls in my sixth-grade class who fancied themselves starlets, but surely I wanted it the hardest. As a four-year-old, I'd memorized entire scenes from both *Annie* and *Amadeus*, performing them nightly with my cat as the captive audience. Not much had changed since then. If I was good at nothing else, I could at least be the biggest theater geek at school, and no one would try to take that title from me.

The aforementioned OBC recording of *The Secret Garden* was a cassette I'd already repurchased twice after the original ribbons of tape finally succumbed to the incessant rewinding of my Walkman. Whether lying in bed or staring out the car window, I always had my headphones on, mouthing along with Mary's lyrics and dialogue snippets, as well as those of secondary female characters. I'd seen the musical twice with the original cast when it debuted in 1991, and with each listen I replayed the scenes in my mind, desperately clinging to fading details. Had Mandy Patinkin worn tweed or navy during the curtain call? Had Daisy Eagan cried for real during that second performance, or was she just wobbling her chin? I was openly obsessed with Daisy, who'd won a Tony at the age of eleven for originating the role of Mary—the youngest girl ever to win.

Each evening after school, I'd unplug my radio-cassette alarm clock and place it on top of the toilet, filling the bath while the overture played. Then I'd lie down in the water until everything was submerged—all but the top of my soft, round belly, which crested above the surface. Next, I'd press the soles of my feet hard against the end of the tub, straightening my back into a plank and pulling my stomach down, finally invisible. It wasn't a relaxing soak, but it was not intended as such. Like this, in the bath, my unmanageable body was gone. It wasn't the weightlessness of water—I've heard other fat folk speak of this phenomenon, an insta-happiness of floating. For me, that buoyancy just highlighted all the bouncy blubber I lived inside. No, the bath was about hiding my body from myself, revealing only the parts I wanted to see (my nice legs, my neutral forearms, end of list), and hiding the rest under water.

I'd hold the foot-pressing plank pose until my soles tingled, then I'd release and plant them hard against the floor, another belly-hiding move. Finally, I'd give up and turn over. I could tolerate my butt sticking out of the water, for it posed no threat. No matter how round my belly got, my backside stayed flat as a crew cut. The main thing was to keep my stomach underneath and out of sight. That was where I was roundest, right from the start. Tight sleeves around my upper arms could be hidden by a jacket or a loose-fitting cardigan, but the buttons of every button-down strained across my gut all day, screaming with obviousness. A polo could be even worse; the juniors-section top bound tight across my chest, loosened at my rib cage, then sat snug and restless, riding up over my little lower belly. I'd spend the whole day yanking it down and actively trying to hunch over in order to help the fabric cover me up. It was exhausting, wearing clothes.

At night, in the tub, my stomach finally out of the way, I'd soak front-down until the water turned tepid, singing along to my musical in full voice until Karen knocked on the door because she had to pee or simply could not hear that overture again, not tonight, please, please, thank you.

I wasn't Daisy Eagan for many reasons. For starters, I didn't have stage parents or even the kind of parents I could badger into stage-parenting me a little.

"If you're old enough to find these auditions, you're old enough to go on them yourself," my mom told me, writing out directions from Grand Central to the casting agent's office in Hell's Kitchen. In that moment I prayed for a kidnapper or subway car-pusher to come along and turn me into a tragic *New York Post* cover. At least they could have used my head shot. But to be fair, she did come on some auditions with me, especially the more serious ones. And every weekend and summer day she drove (or got someone to drive) me to the Yorktown Regional Theater Company or the Hudson Valley Shakespeare Festival, where I attended workshops and courses with other theater kids. At the end of the course, my dad would drive up from Washington, DC, to see one performance, and my mom would come to another. Both agreed I was great. But neither was going to give up his or her life and yank me out of school to exploit and hone my fledgling talent so as to live vicariously through me before inevitably destroying my childhood and ability to grow into a functional adult. And that was all I ever wanted. Instead I had to do my best to exploit myself.

Sam Fairchild, on the other hand, had a stage mom. "Sam" was short for Samantha, but on each first day of school when our new homeroom teacher called that name in roll, she'd give a laugh so light, so half-assed, that said teacher would blush and look around as if trying to catch on to the inside joke. "Sam," corrected Sam. And that was the whole explanation. Sam wasn't Daisy Eagan, either—she was the only thing better in my mind, because as her classmate, I could be jealous of her in the flesh. She was a daily example of what I wanted to be and have. She was the one who reminded me that I wasn't and didn't.

Like most of the kids in our class, we'd known each other since the Democratic Republic of Kindergarten, but as we'd split off into the factions of early adolescence, Sam had quickly bloomed into the angel of our grade. First of all: blonde. Not dirty blonde, or swimming-pool blonde, but a casual, who-cares kind of blonde. She'd even come back to school that September to start sixth grade with gently gilded streaks around her face, apparently being the only human on earth for whom Sun-In actually worked as advertised. The highlights suited her tomboy-empress vibe, as she was the kind of girl who captained the field hockey team, played electric guitar, and, I'm 80 percent sure, started the pastel nail-polish craze of the mid-'90s. She shopped in the city, at Cheap Jack's and Antique Boutique. (Here, I'd like to remind you that we were *eleven*. I could barely handle the technicalities of ordering a monogrammed L.L.Bean backpack over the phone.) Our school uniform was a plain, navy blue skirt, but we were allowed to swap it out for navy corduroys, and so she started turning up in vintage navy blue bell-bottom hip huggers, which could not *technically* be considered a dress-code violation. Without even mentioning it, she'd started shaving her legs months before the rest of us. When conversation inevitably turned to the pros and cons of the Gillette Sensor razor versus Schick Silk Effects, and all eyes turned to Sam for the last word, she shrugged and told us she just used a regular men's Bic.

Second: Her parents were cool. Sam's dad was some kind of music industry guy. What kind I never discovered, but it wasn't the same kind as my dad. Sam's enormous house was filled with guitars and casual snapshots of her father with Mick Jagger, in which he wasn't even bothering to look at the camera. That kind of music industry guy.

Her mom was a former model but neither outrageously young nor so obviously mismatched as to be her father's trophy wife. Officially registered as a not-cool kid, I didn't spend a lot of time at Sam's house, but her folks spent enough afternoons participating in school functions for me to become familiar and obsessed with them. Sam's parents loved each other and liked each other. And their kids liked them. Sam played music gigs with her dad, and Sam's mom, to my most ardent envy, picked her up early from school nearly every day to drive her to acting jobs. Real ones.

Sam was thin and rich, quite beautiful and funny, but it was her burgeoning acting career that absolutely paralyzed me with jealousy. She was already famous to us; the whole school, students and faculty alike, simply could not keep its shit together when it came to Sam. And now that she was popping up in commercials, it wouldn't be long before she was for-real famous.

I'd spent the summer before sixth grade in yet another youth workshop with the Yorktown Regional Theater Company. As in each previous workshop, we'd taken acting, voice, and speech classes, then learned monologues, and finally, scenes and songs to perform in a showcase (read: parent performance). Technically, it was a musical theater revue, but Charlie D. Karvil, the theater's director, had a ceaseless obsession with *Mame*, and so watching each showcase was like watching some kids perform two-thirds of

Mame, inexplicably intercut with a handful of scenes from *A Chorus Line* and *Evita*. The Actor's Studio it was not, but this was the little pond in which I'd become a medium-large fish. So when, at the end of this summer session, Charlie D. Karvil announced he'd be taking the eldest of us into Manhattan to perform our monologues and songs in a *real* showcase in front of talent agents and managers, I felt white-hot with anticipation and destiny. *Destiny*— a word I probably haven't used in a decade. It's a word so glittery and ridiculous that only an eleven-year-old can truly embrace it without irony. In that moment I was filled to the brim with it.

Weeks later, I sat in a black box theater in Midtown, waiting to perform. My whole body hummed with nerves, and yet I was absolutely sure of the future: fame. Daisy Eagan would be my best friend. Sam Fairchild and I would carpool to auditions together. Every single thing would be different, new, and better. When my name was called, I sang sixteen bars of "Hold On" from *The Secret Garden*. I performed a piece from a kids' monologue book about a girl who learns a lesson about confidence and not stuffing your bra.

Two days later, the phone rang.

Mom came with me to the offices of Rainbow Management, a small, beige-carpeted office in the East Thirties. I'd been to a few casting sessions before and wasn't put off by the unimpressive waiting area, the shabby sofa, and the dusty water cooler in the corner. On TV shows, talent agencies looked palatial and overly air-conditioned, but in reality (New York reality, at least) someone makes your dreams come true in a cramped converted apartment. But they had head shots on the wall, and I recognized some of those heads, which was all that mattered.

"We think she's just a breath of fresh air."

Maureen spoke to my mother first. We were seated across a large, circular table in what would have been a dining nook. Maureen and her partner, Dave, constituted the bulk of this small management company, handling around fifty child and teenage performers ("Mainly film and television but a few on Broadway, too. And we heard that voice, Kelsey, don't worry!" Dave said with a wink, becoming my favorite person ever, in the world). Mom smiled at Maureen then at me, suddenly put in the hot seat.

"Well. Yes! She's always been a performer."

"I bet she has." Maureen gave me a small smile and looked back to Mom.

"When she was little and couldn't sleep, she'd stand on top of her bed and sing *Annie*. In the middle of the night, I mean."

Dave guffawed with laughter, and I swore further allegiance to him. Maureen held the same smile-nod, trained on my mother, and held her silence for a moment as if waiting for Mom to deliver some stage-parent code word. Or, maybe she just hated me. Did she hate me? Was there any way I could try to die, right that second?

At last, the staring contest ended.

"Look, we'd like to consider representing Kelsey. Ideally, we'd put her under contract for a year and see how it goes," Maureen explained. "But she could be a girlfriend type or a best-friend type, and that's a nice flexibility."

"A girlfriend type?" Mom asked. "She's eleven, you know."

Maureen leaned in just a hair. "But she's developing. She's at least a B cup, right? Obviously, she can still be cast as a daughter, but we're past the point of 'cute' here." She looked at me at last. A smile. "You don't want to be the daughter, anyway."

Dave jumped in: "We think she's just great, super funny and talented. Lovely face, of course." He turned to Mom. "But obviously, in this business, there are certain unavoidable realities."

Mom tilted her head and drew in her breath just slightly. I nodded hard, businesslike.

"No one's saying there's anything wrong with her, but it would make things so much easier if we lost a little weight." Maureen folded her hands and sat back, news delivered.

"Not a lot. Maybe ten pounds would make all the difference," Dave concluded. He raised an eyebrow at me. "I mean, you want the leads here, right?"

At this point I realized I was nodding along with their every word and made a conscious effort to stop bobbing my head. But I couldn't. I wanted them to know that I got it. If I hadn't seen this coming now, I'd known it would eventually happen, for in my fantasies I was thin like Daisy and Sam. That was part of the deal with being a famous actress, and I was thrilled to have someone tell me so directly just to do it—just be skinny and everything will be fine. At the same time, I was awash with an unspeakable shame. Maureen and Dave had called me out as a fat girl, unsightly and unlikable, and they'd done so in front of the person I most desperately wanted to like me: my mother. But maybe I needed that. Maybe this was the eleven-year-old, chubby-girl version of hitting bottom. And they'd given me the greatest incentive to get up and do the work. Lose ten pounds and I'd get a professional acting career? I'd be "the girlfriend"? Sold.

"No problem!" I jumped in. "I can do that."

My mom looked over at me, a tight smile I couldn't read. But Maureen turned to me at last.

"Great. So, come back and see us in two weeks."

Ten pounds in two weeks. No problem at all.

When I look back at photos of myself from that period, I realize that losing ten pounds would have taken me from plump to flat. I didn't have a weight problem; I was just this side of pudgy—the kind of adolescent who went soft and round versus tall and gangly. Losing that weight would have simply deflated me slightly. In my mind, of course, I was sincerely obese, a jiggling mass, unworthy of being anyone's girlfriend, best friend, or daughter. I'd known it in my heart for years; Rainbow Management had made it official. Then they'd given me the solution.

The diet was simple. I already had a well-honed sense of Good and Bad foods by this point, so I simply eliminated all but the Goodest of the Good. For two weeks I ate nothing but raw green beans, cucumber wedges, skinless chicken breasts, and low-fat lemon yogurt. Mom and I were in on it together, finally on the same team. Every day, I came home from school to find the fridge stocked with Tupperware containers of my fresh green snacks. I poured huge, pink glasses of Crystal Light and chomped away at whole pounds of raw green beans until my stomach bloated with a bubbly kind of fullness. At night, my chicken breasts were shoveled down in minutes. Dinner was now a perfunctory task just to get me to bed so I could get to tomorrow, which was another day closer to the next meeting with Rainbow.

Despite now recognizing this as an undeniable crash diet (and such a '90s one, with the yogurt and the cucumber) I was never hungry during this time. If I was, it was entirely muted by the New Diet Buzz. Others might describe this feeling as being in the zone. But "the zone" implies something you can get back into, and, in my experience, you get only one shot with a diet. During those early days of that first diet—and every diet after it—I was high on the easy initial weight loss and the newness of it all. My system shocked, I dropped five pounds almost overnight, and the morning weigh-in became a delight I daydreamed about in school. I was dead set on a goal that was both magical and within my grasp, and every day that I adhered to the meal plan I woke up closer to it: clothes looser, cheekbones sharper, belly sinking lower in the tub. It wasn't an illusion, either. I was doing it. I was eleven years old and eating *nothing*—of course I was doing it.

I suddenly had a laserlike focus unlike any I'd ever experienced. I willfully kept blinders on, knowing on some primal level that there was no room for distraction or temptation. Other people's food didn't interest me at all, but why risk it by being around other people? Amy and my other few close friends knew about the possible contract, a secret I'd been able to sit on for all of twenty minutes. But I didn't tell them about the weight I'd been asked to lose, nor the diet that occupied my every waking thought. Why bother? I'd soon be thin, famous, and an entirely new person.

Instead of ten pounds, I lost thirty. Such a dramatic loss can only be chalked up to the fact that I was a child, and the carrot on the end of my stick was stardom. My body was more pliable than it would ever be again, and my mind, I'd soon discover, was hardwired for obsession. But this is the assessment of the adult looking back on the kid, five billion therapy sessions later. Back then? Honest to God, there are no good enough words for the kind of joy I felt.

Felt isn't even the right word. I was composed from head to toe of sheer, maniacal success and happiness. I had done it, times three, A+++. I was sincerely skinny for the first time in conscious memory. In the bathtub, I gawked at my previously slender legs, which were now even thinner and gapped at the thigh. Lying in bed, I ran my hand back and forth in the new well between my hipbones and the even deeper one between my rib cage. I didn't have to pray or bang my knees against the floor. Instead, I pressed my inner wrists against these thrilling bones until it hurt, a new nightly ritual that lasted for hours, the excitement too great for me to sleep.

None of my clothes fit. Mom took me to the Jefferson Valley Mall for a few new outfits, plus a special one to wear to my next meeting with Maureen and Dave. Handing me Small after Small, she grinned with real pride, unable to take her eyes off me.

"You did it."

But I'd needed her help to do it. And though I wanted that contract more than anything, nothing could have felt better than her smiling eyes on me. After the food policing and the failure, we'd finally done it, together. She'd washed and chopped my cucumbers into wedges, and I'd eaten them and only them each afternoon. I'd been good and now I was Good, just like those cucumbers. So, here we were shopping like a real mother and daughter. Like Sam and her mom. I was crystallized with joy, Buzzing like I never would again in my life.

There was a slightly delayed reaction at school. My classmates had looked past me every day for years, but once I turned up in my newly cinched uniform and belly-grazing tops, rumblings began as to whether my status as Officially Gross should be reconsidered. With just days approaching my next appointment with Rainbow, I began to let the news leak to a wider audience (for example: everyone I spoke to over the course of a day). This, combined with my new not-fatness, meant that I was someone to talk to, someone to pick for your dodgeball team. Overnight, I'd become a girl instead of a sexless beach ball in a skirt. Literally, every single thing was better now that I was thin.

"So, I'm actually going to sign with a manager," I told Sam one day in Science. I spoke *to* Sam Fairchild; that's how high I was on skinny.

"Cool. Which?"

"Rainbow Management?" She looked up into the middle distance for a second, then back down at her Trapper Keeper.

"Huh. I don't know them. That's great, though."

"Yeah. They do mostly TV and film stuff, but also Broadway."

She shifted an inch in her seat to half-face me, because I'd insisted on making this a conversation. "I'd like to do Broadway, I think. But movies too, of course," I added.

She shrugged. "Broadway's not my thing."

"Are you doing anything now? I mean, what are you doing right now?"

"Um, just some callbacks. And I have this Noxzema campaign coming up."

She talked as if booking a national skin-care campaign at the age of eleven wasn't a particularly thrilling achievement. This Noxzema thing, it was a B+.

"Is that Frigid?" She pointed her chin at my hand where I'd painted my fingernails in silvery blue the night before.

"Yeah, I just got it."

Frigid was the unrivaled star of my Hard Candy nail polish collection. The pastel polish trend was so universally identified with Sam that anyone with baby blue nails would immediately be pegged as a follower. Still desperately covetous of the look, I had opted to buy a set of Hard Candy pastel *metallic* shades, dropping all my remaining Christmas cash on six twelve-dollar bottles. The outrageous price was partially justified by the gummy rubber ring that came wrapped around every bottle cap. My fingers had always been too pudgy to comfortably wear them, and though every other part of me was now whittled down to an acceptable size, they remained the last bastion of my chubby past. Nevertheless, I jammed the rubber bauble down my right ring finger daily, and now stared in tingly awe at our nearly matching hands: Sam's painted in neat, matte Sky, and mine in three sloppy coats of shiny, light blue Frigid. She reached over and grabbed my fingers for examination.

"God, you get right up there to the cuticle edge."

To this day, I don't know if this was a compliment or a dig, but I think of it every time I paint my nails.

At recess that day, as I regaled another group of sudden friends with the details of my upcoming Broadway career, Sam bopped over and yanked me up by the wrist.

"We need another player."

The game was something to do with bouncing a ball in the right chalk square, and though I'd seen kids play it hundreds of times while I sat folding origami cranes or reading on the grass, I had no idea how. I never ended up learning, either. This was the only time I'd play, and I was too distracted by the rest of the group looking at me with uncertainty as Sam walked me through each step. Still, I laughed with nerves and real happiness, even as I lost. Emboldened by attention, I pulled out the retro novelty camera I'd gotten for Christmas and asked one of Sam's inner-circle friends to take a picture of us. Sam instinctively put herself back-to-back with me and elbowed me in the side.

"Show him your nails."

We put our arms out, tilted our chins down, and I looked right into the camera. The kid snapped four photos in a row, and halfway through the second a fifth-grade girl ran through the shot, drawing Sam's gaze up and away in irritation. But my head never moved and my smile never wavered. Those were the only pictures ever taken with that camera. I just never felt like using it again. I keep the photos pressed inside my sixth-grade yearbook, the only pictures in the whole book that document my brief time as small, pretty, and a member of the team.

"*Much* better."

I was twirling. When Mom and I arrived at the Rainbow Management office days later, I'd wondered how the big reveal would go. The entire point of this meeting was my physical inspection, and so why bother sitting down and hiding my legs under a table? They buzzed us in, said hello, and I just stuck my arms out and started to twirl.

"*So* much better!" Dave echoed. "High five, girl!"

After sufficient staring ("sufficient" being relative; I could have let them stare all day), we settled at the big, round table, littered with head shots and overcopied contracts.

"So, she looks great," Maureen told my mother. "You did a great job, honey. No question."

The conversation continued like this for whole minutes, Maureen and Dave commending my slender face and athletic legs and "that tiny little tummy." My heart thudded with each compliment, pushing bright pulses of panic out through every vein. Had I been more clear-headed, I might have realized that no one had handed me a paper to sign. Only when they finally ran out of niceties did I recognize the silence in the room as awkward.

"So, here's the thing," Dave opened. "We've got a girl—I can't think why this didn't come up earlier..."

Maureen took over. "We have a girl on our roster who looks quite similar to you, and she's booking a number of roles at the moment."

"What does that mean?" Mom knew what it meant. I knew what it meant at this point, but there was only one way out of this meeting.

"It just complicates things slightly. It means we need to think about whether Kelsey's a good fit for us right now."

"And if we're the right fit for Kelsey." I suddenly recognized the slick rhythm of their spiel; how often Dave and Maureen must have sung this medley of harsh truths and high fives to get kids like me out of their office without tears. I wanted them to spell it out.

"Do I still get the contract?"

All three looked at me: a child.

"You know what? Sure, you guys take this home." Dave fished out one of the overcopied documents from a file in a heap of files. "You can have time to look it over and think about it. And we'll do the same here, right?" He caught Maureen's gaze. She nodded. No one bought it except me.

If I'd become a famous (or even failed) child actress, you'd already know because it would be the first thing I'd tell everyone I'd ever met. Rainbow Management never called to follow up. The contract sat in a drawer next to our home computer for ten years. Occasionally, I'd stumble over it while searching for a copy of my birth certificate or passport, and it was like finding a relic of an old heart-break. Each time, I'd return it carefully to the back of some folder, until the summer after my junior year of college, when I finally threw it out. I was in the midst of another New Diet Buzz, this time with Jenny Craig. Having already lost four pounds, I'd hit that stage where I was sure this one was *the* one. Finding the old, unsigned contract felt like a jinx.

After that last meeting at Rainbow, it took only days for me to quit the green-beans-and-yogurt routine. By the end of the month, I'd gone back to my old version of normal eating—one that wasn't actually all that "normal," and would only become more extreme in the months and years to come. I'd failed and been failed, and now I had to face the consequences: un-tell everyone at school about my big-shot manager, hang my new size S and XS clothes in the far left of my closet, and find a way to fit into them again. Until I did, I would be irrefutably less than the Sam Fairchilds and Daisy Eagans and all the other thin, pretty, chosen girls.

After the Buzz comes only the fizzle and then the flattening. It's inevitable, because the Buzz is about anticipation of a brighter, skinnier tomorrow where everything will be new, different, and better—because you will be new, different, and better. And when that first disappointment hits, the New Diet Buzz is over and there is no getting the magic back. From there on out, it's like trying to get back into a bubble you've already popped.

After that first real diet, I gained all the weight back and more. But I'd tasted the manic power of skinny. That first, pure Buzz became the dragon I'd chase for almost twenty years.

I didn't really stop until the day I walked out of Theresa's office after my first intuitive eating session. Not until then did I look around and realize what a tangled forest I had wound up in, and how clear the path out was. I strode down the street, thinking, *I want some peanut butter toast, so I'm going to have it! What a world!*

It was the New Diet Buzz. Even if this time was really different, that initial rush came on like clockwork, as potent and delicious as it had ever been. I didn't want this to feel like a diet. I didn't want to feel this good, because that meant that failure wasn't far behind. I kept saying that it wasn't about winning and failing, but did I actually believe that? Was this just a bigger, showier attempt to get the other kids to like me, or did I really want to get my shit together, for real, for me?

Maybe. That was still the best answer I had.

I did know that I wanted some peanut butter toast, though. That evening, I went home and spread Skippy onto two slices of hearty sourdough, the first bread I'd bought in years without doing nutrition-label math. I drizzled on a spoonful of raw honey, added some banana slices and a pinch of sea salt. I pushed a pile of mail to the side of the wobbly IKEA table in our narrow living room, and sat down to eat. No TV, no phone, no e-mail in front of me. Mindful eating would become a challenge in the weeks to come, but for now it was a novel experience, made all the more vivid by the Buzz.

The first bite was like seeing sunlight through your window in the morning just after you've been dreaming of it. After all that prelude, the sensory experience was so overwhelming that I felt my glands clutch for a moment as if I'd bitten into a lemon, but a lemon I *really* wanted to taste. I ate, savored, swallowed, and was filled in a way that felt so absolutely good that I was almost embarrassed. In short, I had a pretty good dinner. Maybe my first.

I went to bed still marveling over the thrill of eating toast. I'd only just started, and already this thing had helped me untangle an old and painful knot from the past. *Maybe that's it?* I thought. *Childhood solved.*

Right.

Chapter 6

A Brief History of Things I Haven't Eaten

S o, what kind of diet is this?"
     The week I publicly quit dieting, I answered this question approximately eleven billion times. Everyone from my long-lost middle-school friends to my gynecologist to my dad's third cousin who hadn't seen me since I was eighteen months old wanted to know exactly what I was putting in my mouth. And when would it make me skinny? Thank you, Facebook.

Thank you, me, in fact. I'd written the first installment of my new column, the Anti-Diet Project, just days after meeting with Theresa for the first time. I watched with a tearful hybrid feeling of excitement-horror-glee-nausea as click after click drove my little post to our top story of the day. It was essentially a longer version of the missive I'd thumbed out on the bus when pitching the column to my boss: *No more diets! Who's with me?!* A lot of our readers were. I wasn't the only one who was sick of feeling fat and disgusting and also completely incapable of getting it up for yet another bullshit eating plan. Though I wasn't surprised, I still didn't expect all the feelings that slammed into me when I saw the hundreds of people sharing the story and saying, "I get you!"

And I didn't expect just how many people really, really *didn't* get me.

"I read your post and decided to have low-fat tomato soup for lunch instead of a big, fatty sandwich! I had a cookie after (bad Mrs. G!) but I'll try again tomorrow. Look at that—you helped me already!"

This Facebook message popped up within hours, from an old middle-school teacher with whom I already had an uncomfortable social-media relationship. She'd once commented on a photo of me in a cocktail dress, saying "Sexxxxay!" This, from the woman who once scolded me for getting "too flowery" in an essay about the American Revolution.

I didn't need to know about your lunch, Mrs. G. And, no, I didn't help you. If you wanted a "big, fatty" sandwich I would have told you to get it, and instead you got the opposite. While it's true that I used words like *fat* and *weight* in my post, I also used about two thousand more, none of which told readers *not* to eat anything. So don't lay that tomato soup on me, because (hang on, I need another soap box. Okay, I'm ready:) intuitive eating is not a diet.

Intuitive eating sounds like something one might say with air quotes. No matter how commonsense it really is, each time I tried to describe it, I came across as a new age zealot, or someone at high risk for cult recruitment.

"It's about learning to eat the way you did as a small child. You didn't worry about carbs when you were three. You just ate what you wanted when you were hungry."

"And that's a good thing?" Debbie asked. We'd met up for dinner after work. It was one of many conversations I'd been having with close friends, disclosing my new lifestyle. Some were instantly supportive and others vaguely concerned. Debbie, my good friend since high school, was a psychologist in training, so her first response was a question.

I had my answer locked and loaded.

"Absolutely!"

She eyed the basket of oily corn chips between us at the table.

"Think about it. It's really the worry and the restriction that makes you eat an entire basket of chips."

"Interesting."

Not good enough. I launched in, determined to win her over.

"Okay, imagine if I said, 'Have all the chips you want, there will always be more chips, no one will ever take chips away from you, *and* eating chips is completely okay.' If you really believed that, you'd probably just have a few and be satisfied, knowing you could have more whenever you wanted."

She tilted her head thoughtfully, considering the chips. For a moment, I wondered if I wasn't just wrong but crazy.

Finally, she nodded.

"Yeah, okay. I get it."

Despite the fact that even I couldn't quite believe it yet, the validity of intuitive eating still speaks for itself. Before authors Evelyn Tribole and Elyse Resch (both nutritionists and dietitians) named it as such, the concept of the un-diet had been brewing for decades. Ever since dieting became a pervasive, insidious theme entrenched in our cultural consciousness, there have been those who realized that it didn't work—and, in fact, it did more harm than good. Most rational people, if they really think about it, know that dieting is unsustainable and unhealthy. "Intuitive eating" is simply the formal name of the philosophy that teaches people with food issues how to eat normally again. Anyone with basic intelligence can see that our bodies are born with the full capacity to feed themselves properly, and that all the information we need to maintain a healthy diet comes from common sense and our own internal signals.

The tricky part is actually hearing those internal signals and following them. Even those rational, intelligent people live in a world full of loud, constant messages screaming, "Food: You're doing it wrong." And, why wouldn't we believe it? It's not as if everyone on earth is healthy, fit, and perfectly happy with the way they look. It *must* be our fault; our brains and bodies are the problem, not the solution. Someone else must have the answers. So, when some hustler comes along with a glossy spokeswoman and a high-shine book cover, we want to believe their promises. I know I did, every time.

WEIGHT WATCHERS

I joined Weight Watchers for the first time a month before starting eighth grade, along with my mom. She wasn't overweight, at least not like I was, "but I could always stand to drop a few," she said.

Earlier that same year she'd sat me down to tell me about the nightly meetings she'd been going to for the last few months. We'd never had one of those formal parent-child talks I'd read about in books, and for a moment I expected her to tell me she was dying. But no, she was an alcoholic. And going to those meetings was how she would get better. Up until that moment, I'd never suspected she was an alcoholic, let alone one who'd fallen off the wagon. The concept of alcoholism existed only in the realm of fiction and re-demptive movie endings. The drinking that went on in our house was just what grown-ups did. Finding out my mother and my fa-ther, who confirmed his own long-term sobriety that night on the phone, were both in Alcoholics Anonymous filled me with shaky relief. In the months to come, Mom would take up Pilates and evolve into the thinnest, blondest version of herself; the kind of mom who picked you up on time in a tidy car, looking lean and casually cool in yoga pants and lipstick.

Together, we attended weekly Weight Watchers meetings in a conference room at our local athletic club where Janis, a snazzy, short-haired, fifty-something ballbuster led us through weekly weigh-ins followed by thirty-minute lectures she'd written out with multicolored highlighters on giant white easels. *Beating the Holiday Weight Gain* or *Things to Do Besides Snacking* were typical challenges we all worried over, and once Janis had gone through her plan of attack she opened the floor to suggestions.

"Pack a low-Points snack you can bring to the office, like celery sticks," one woman offered.

"Sure, I mean it's still snacking," Janis replied. "But it's better than hitting the vending machine." She listed our ideas under hers in another bright marker.

"Get a manicure!"

"Love it. Get a manicure. Keep those hands occupied."

I raised my hand for the first time. As the only non-mom in the room, I generally kept my hand down during meetings, but for once I had a suggestion that wasn't already on the list.

"Sometimes I try reading."

"Okay," Janis said with a smirk. "Anyone else think, 'Oh, I'll just read a *book*?' when they get hungry?" The group chuckled, but she shrugged and added it to the list anyway. (Sor-ry, Janis. Seemed a lot more reasonable than running out for a manicure every time a cookie craving hit.)

At thirteen, I was officially chubby, but looking back, I was by no means grotesque. I was pretty cute, in fact. And, having just transferred to a new public school where I quickly made new friends, I was cute *and* noticed for the first time. It was great and new and weird. I had crushes on people and other people had crushes on me! The latter experience was so bizarre and alarming that I ended up taking one poor, confused boy to the student counselor's office after he passed me a sweaty note professing his love.

I had responded to this culture shock (and the thrilling new phenomenon of cafeteria French fries) by promptly gaining eight pounds. Weight Watchers seemed like an ideal solution. It turned every food into Points that I could easily plan my day around, and gave me a scoring system for how well each of those days had gone. No matter how badly I had flunked the science quiz or how not in love with me Sean Damico was, if I stayed within my points by the end of the day, it had been a great one.

I lost thirty-six pounds that first year on Weight Watchers. Back then, the Points system was calorie based. (This was a simpler time, before low-carb and Paleo and the armies of antigluteneers.) Therefore, I achieved this weight loss mainly with breakfasts of Carnation Instant Breakfast (2 packets of mix + 1 cup skim milk), and lunches of prepopped fat-free popcorn, fresh grapefruit, and a bottled Starbucks Frappuccino—the skinny girl's greatest indulgence in 1998.

My mom had invented a handful of chickpea-and-tofu-based dishes when it became clear that I wasn't just being dramatic about being a vegetarian. Therefore, dinner became my main source of actual nutrition, though my preferred evening meal was two Boca Burger patties and a huge pile of ketchup.

Just as it had in sixth grade, the magic of skinny proved real and verifiable. This slightly thinner version of me was allowed to be a real girl. I ordered pastel slip dresses from the Delia*s catalog and learned to match my shimmery lipstick to my shimmery eye shadow. I took my first and last Home Economics class (they called it "Life Skills," but no one's buying that when you're being taught to iron) and sewed my own Halloween costume—a replica of Claire Danes's angel dress from *Romeo + Juliet*.

"You look hot," Sean Damico, my one true crush, said, pressing me against the soda table at Allie Janecki's Halloween party. He reached behind my back and pulled the fabric of my angel dress taut against my body, then gave my torso a long, hard appraisal. He traced an hourglass in the air and shrugged. "Borderline sexy."

For years to follow, I played this scene over in my head, imagining the thousands of different things I might have said or done next. I'd never been pressed against anything, or looked at with even casual lust by someone I actually wanted. All at once, I was speechless and thrumming with adrenaline, staring at his half-mast eyes while he waited for my reply.

I rolled my eyes. "You don't have to be nice to me."

"What?"

"You don't have to say stuff like that."

"Okay."

"I know Allie told you to talk to me."

"What are you talking about?"

"Nothing."

He picked up his soda cup and leaned in close to my ear, shouting louder than the music required.

"Jesus. Next time you can just say 'THANK YOU.'"

I made it through the school year counting Points before the magic of Weight Watchers fizzled and the weight slowly crept back. Sean started dating another girl who liked him so much she'd scraped his initials into the back of her hand with a paper clip. By the middle of ninth grade, I was up to my old weight plus twenty pounds. The Juliet dress hung in my closet next to my eleven-year-old skinny clothes. The soda-table incident remained the highlight of my romantic life.

EAT RIGHT FOR YOUR TYPE

In the summer of 1999, I was accepted as a last-minute entrant into the Walnut Hill School for the Arts, a small boarding school in Natick, Massachusetts, where I'd spend the next three years learning Meisner technique and waiting to be old enough to play Harper in *Angels in America*.

I was spending the summer as an apprentice at the Hudson Valley

Shakespeare Festival and decided to take on a new regime in advance of my upcoming career as a glamorous boarding school celebrity. The program was somewhat physical, so I figured I could skip the workout plan thanks to tumbling class and afternoons spent hauling props back and forth across the bucolic estate where the festival was held. All I'd need now was someone to tell me what to eat.

Eat Right for Your Type, a popular program devised by Dr. Peter J. D'Adamo, posits that the foods we eat react chemically with our blood, and therefore blood type is the most important factor when it comes to metabolism and maintaining a healthy weight. In nearby Chappaqua, I met with a nutritionist named Francesca, who pricked my finger and pressed the bloody tip to a piece of paper that would reveal my blood type. As we waited for the result, she served me a glass of lemon water and explained the science behind Eat Right for Your Type. There were lectins and antigens and alleles and all those other things that flew over my head in biology— all of which turned out to be the reasons I was fat! (This time *fat* meant a size 12/14.) As it turned out, another reason I was fat was that I was a vegetarian when I should have been eating meat. So, so much meat.

"See, you're a Type O. You're a huntress!"

Francesca took out a pad and scribbled out my meal plan for the week, plus a list of supergood foods, neutral foods, and foods that were "basically poison." My supergood foods were things like beef, lamb, spinach, mozzarella cheese, figs, and mutton.

"Mutton? Like Henry VIII?"

"Exactly! Like a king!"

My neutral foods were pretty Tudor friendly as well: quail, rabbit, barley, and so on. Just no goose—absolutely not. Goose was poison. Other poisons included cabbage, cauliflower, kidney beans, mushrooms, peanuts, and skim milk.

"What about whole milk?" I didn't even like milk, but I could not contain my curiosity at this point. She closed her mouth and sighed through her nose, consulting a chart on her desktop computer.

"Let's see . . . Whole milk is 'unknown.'"

"Unknown."

"Right, we don't have enough data about whole milk and your blood type. But, just to be safe, I'd avoid it. Ice cream and yogurt are on the poison list, so, what do you think, kiddo?"

I THINK YOU SOUND LIKE A FUCKING MANIAC, FRANCESCA. I THINK YOGURT IS YOGURT AND PETER J. D'ADAMO IS BANANAPANTS AND HENRY VIII IS NOT AN IDEAL ROLE MODEL FOR A TEENAGED GIRL IS WHAT I THINK.

Excuse the outburst—that's just my rational grown-up self, feeling more than a little outraged on behalf of the fifteen-year-old sitting there with a bloody finger and wondering if the A&P carried mutton.

Back then what I thought was, *Wow, if only I'd learned my blood type earlier. All this could have been avoided! Life will be infinitely easier and skinnier from here on out, as long as I can figure out how to eat meat again without crying.*

The Type O Diet, as you can see, is a slightly wackier version of Atkins. I purchased D'Adamo's book and enlisted my Hudson Valley Shakespeare pal, Melissa, as my diet buddy. Though she was already skinny and ate whatever she wanted, she signed on with gusto. Turns out that she was skinny and ate whatever she wanted because she was a Type AB. The chapter on this blood type seemed oddly vague and mystical in comparison to the others. Perhaps because it was a newer blood type, "science" was still not totally sure what one should and shouldn't eat as an AB. There were some beneficial foods and no-no foods, but D'Adamo seemed to think AB's could *probably* eat whatever they wanted as long as they didn't eat too much of it (unlike us ancient O's who would simply burst at the sight of a mushroom). For no good reason, he added that AB types are often incredibly charismatic and fascinating individuals, noting that John F. Kennedy and Marilyn Monroe were both Type AB's. So, medically speaking, Melissa was the greatest sex symbol of the twentieth century, and I was Henry VIII.

I crept back into meat eating over the course of three months, and by the end of the summer was still following Francesca's plan to the letter. I was allowed up to five eggs a day, so I typically had an enormous omelet plus five strips of neutral turkey bacon for breakfast. For lunch, I'd ride into town with my fellow apprentices (though we were the kind of teens who preferred the term *apprenti*) Cat, Henry, Derrick, and Melissa. Each day, I bought a quarter pound of lean turkey breast from the deli counter of the local supermarket and four or five plums from the produce aisle. Standing in the checkout aisle, I'd ogle the forbidden, poisonous strawberries with the lust of a barely dry drunk. Outside, I'd sit on a bench with the rest of the group, eating slices of turkey meat with my fingers.

We'd become a tight circle of friends in that inevitable way of summer theater programs, but Melissa was my closest friend— meaning I believed her to be a much better person than I was. When her blood type confirmed this as a fact of science, I felt justified in putting her on my pedestal.

She was a year older than me, went to a slightly better school, and bought all her clothes at the Westchester—a mall so fancy it didn't have *mall* in the name. Even though she didn't need to be, she was somehow better at my diet than I was. Above all, she didn't give a shit. (Not giving a shit seems to be the through line of all cool girls since the dawn of man, and none of us shit givers will ever achieve it, for wanting not to give a shit is, in fact, giving one, and therein lies the paradox. We're doomed to care.) I watched as Derrick and Henry fell goonily in love with Melissa, and then as older cast members developed irresistible, morals-challenging crushes on her sixteen-year-old self, none of which fazed her remotely. *Damn*, I'd think. *You and your sexy blood.*

After each performance of *Titus Andronicus* we'd get in her Jeep and drive to the twenty-four-hour deli for pints of Häagen-Dazs fruit sorbet, eating two at a time, sitting on the curb.

"I don't think this is what Peter J. D'Adamo had in mind," Melissa once remarked.

"It's dairy free!" I'd shriek like the mad tyrant I was, then jam the plastic spoon back into my pint, chipping away at the raspberry ice until my belly burned with sugar and my mouth was fully numbed.

I lost twenty pounds that summer. It wasn't enough, but it was something, and I was still high enough on the New Diet Buzz that surely it would carry over when I started boarding school. Right?

"I'm fairly certain they have turkey slices in Massachusetts," Melissa assured me. She'd lost eight pounds from her small frame, but it somehow didn't register as gaunt or bony. Really, she just looked like she'd gotten a good tan. We hugged and swapped e-mail addresses, making tentative plans to hang out over Thanksgiving break.

By then, I'd have dropped the remaining forty pounds I wanted to lose, found a boyfriend, and been cast in a show. By then, I could join her up on the pedestal with the rest of the ABs, having it all (but not caring about any of it).

THE DIET-EVERYTHING DIET

Exactly the opposite of all those things happened, immediately. There's a certain kind of kid who's ready to fly the nest at age fifteen and is unruffled by the daily rigors of acting and singing critiques in front of their peers. Then there are those of us who shatter at the mere suggestion you might want to try those last three bars again. My first semester at Walnut Hill was a lesson in panic and humiliation.

It wasn't the school's fault: Walnut Hill was and is an exceptional type of prep school. There were only two others with a

similar model in the country: Interlochen in Michigan and Idyll-
wild in California. Students not only need to pass muster academi-
cally, they must audition for a particular major.

Prep school wasn't mandatory in my family, but it was the usual
route. Despite both my parents' disregard for their WASPish her-
itage, and their lack of wealth, education was education. I didn't
have to go, but I had to give it a shot. In the midst of applying
to a dozen other traditional prep schools, I had auditioned to be a
theater major at Walnut Hill, with a monologue from *The Diary of
Anne Frank* and a song from *The Secret Garden*. My middling SSAT
scores had landed me on a waiting list, and I'd resigned myself to
another perfectly content year at my public school when the acceptance letter arrived along with a package of student information.
Academic classes ran morning through early afternoon, I was told,
followed by late afternoon and evening study within our majors.
For theater students that meant acting technique, vocal coaching,
voice lessons, dance, dramaturgy, and occasional special subjects like
makeup and set design. After that, we'd be in either rehearsal or tech
for one of the five productions mounted over the course of the school
year. I mention this rigorous schedule mainly to brag about what a
hardcore high schooler I was, but also to highlight the particularly
unique bubble I lived in for three years. Mostly bragging, though.

Change has never been my strong suit. I struggle to adjust to a
new software update on my phone. So, moving from my childhood
home into a chilly dorm room with an even chillier roommate—a
Japanese violinist who didn't speak English but was fully capable of
communicating how disgusting I was for not emptying the waste-
paper basket every day—felt like a catastrophe. And I'd chosen it.

Food was standard boarding-school fare: Tater Tots, beef stews,
pizza-bagel treats on the weekends. There was always a fruit bowl
sitting on the sidelines and a meager salad bar, frequented mainly
by dance majors. But given the choice between pizza-bagels and an
orange, I think any respectable teenager would ignore the fruit.

The quality of the cafeteria aside, my brain clicked into Away Mode. Eat Right for Your Type went out the door for logistical reasons (high school dining halls don't generally cater to Henry VIII) but mainly because Away Mode meant time to eat. Growing up, it had been my habit to stock up on treats and indulgent second helpings whenever I was out of the house, or simply out of sight of anyone I knew. At Walnut Hill, I was away from home for months at a time and felt—or truly wished to be—invisible to everyone.

Despite myself, I managed to make a few friends, Debbie being one of the first. She was an art major and a day student with her own car. We'd sometimes drive into town for lunches at the bagel shop, or anywhere she felt like—any off-campus food was my greatest delight. Chrissy was also an artist and one of my only friends in the dorm. She was from Switzerland and we quickly bonded over homesickness and fear of our respective roommates.

That first year, I couldn't handle the nonstop energy of teenage artistic expression, combined with the constant tension of audition-performance-audition-performance. Then, there was the actual school part. In acting class, this edginess worked in my favor. I was your girl if you needed instant crying or a good chair throwing. In class, I perfected the role of Hedda Gabler Having a Panic Attack. But I wasn't cast in anything that year, to my great embarrassment.

Still, that did leave many of my nights free in a half-empty dorm. Whenever I didn't have tech duty, I retreated to my room to sing along with musical theater recordings. This habit was discouraged by teachers, the point being that none of us was Patti LuPone and "practicing" along with her voice would only lead to poor imitation. I followed the rules when rehearsing my songs assigned for class, using only a cassette tape of recorded piano accompaniment. But alone in my dorm room, all bets were off. I flipped through my album of Original Broadway Cast recordings and spent the night singing myself raw with the kind of stuff that's only acceptable to sing if you're at musical theater boarding school, or you are, in fact,

Patti LuPone. I did the standards: *Les Mis*, *Into the Woods*. I went for smaller, cult hits like *Songs for a New World*. I wasn't above doing Disney. It is a fact that I was once punished for waking up a neighboring dorm by singing "Part of Your World" with my window open. It was not my first offense.

I couldn't binge on musicals when my roommate was home, so on those nights, I'd reserve the dorm television and pull out my *X-Files* VHS boxed set. There was a local deli that delivered pints of Ben & Jerry's, but the delivery minimum meant you had to order two at a time, which saved me from the embarrassment of actually deciding to order two at a time.

I went home for Columbus Day weekend and no one said anything. Mom seemed happy to see me. My stepdad asked about classes. Everything was normal, except for their faces. It was the first time I recognized the look—the one that all of my tribe knows so well. We fear it as we step out of cars to see long-lost friends, or walk into the family Christmas party, holding our stomachs in until we sit down and exhale. I saw them all see me, make note of something, then deliberately close up.

That weekend, Melissa came over to watch a movie on the beanbag chairs in our basement. I searched her face for the look but never found it, either because she didn't care or because she too was occupied with her own new school year. We split a bag of Reduced Fat Oreos, and I listened to her chat about her new maybe-boyfriend and the plans she was already making for college. College. I was inches into my sophomore year of high school and barely hanging on. College seemed like a terrifying, distant planet that I would never see until I'd gone through astronaut training.

The idea of a boyfriend felt just as remote. At the time, Walnut Hill had somewhere around two hundred students, and the heterosexual male population was the smallest minority on campus. The handful of straight guys were all dating ballerinas; the best that all the other straight girls could do was lust after their gay guy friends or take a stab at lesbianism and hope like hell that it took. I was good at the gay-guy crush thing, but even if I'd been interested in dating a girl, it had taken all my chutzpah just to try to be *friends* with some of them. It was infinitely easier just to hole up with Fox Mulder and two pints of ice cream every night. But Melissa's story of real-life car kissing and sexually charged AOL Instant Messaging made me wish I'd at least come up with a pretend boyfriend to talk about. I'd never felt so far away from a friend.

After Melissa left, I sat around with the Oreos, clicking aimlessly through channels and resent-fantasizing about her ever-more fabulous adulthood and my own worminess. Mom came through to fetch a load of laundry, and as she turned to head back up the stairs I finally said to her back:

"Do I look like I've gained a lot of weight?"

She stood on the stairs for a moment, her back still toward me. "Yes."

She went upstairs. I went back to the television, bathed in a new and nauseating truth.

I was really fat now. I didn't dare weigh myself anymore, but I'd slowly transitioned out of my regular clothes and into a daily uniform of black sweatpants and loose T-shirts. At school, it was easy enough not to see red flags like this—sweatpants were "movement clothing" required for all acting and dance classes. I had no parent eyeing my plate, and the few friends I had were new and not about to say, "Get a grip, fellow-classmate-I've-known-for-eight-weeks."

I'd known what my mom would say when I asked her, and I'd known how I would feel when I heard it: shocked and hurt and humiliated. That was the magic emotional formula that launched me into any diet. When I returned to Walnut Hill, rather than going back to Weight Watchers (how would I get to meetings?) or Eat

Right for Your Type (where would I find mutton?), I decided it was easier to do exactly what the skinny girls did. For the next three years, I did everyone's diet.

From Hannah Liebman I borrowed a Diet Coke habit that we both suspected and possibly hoped would lead to an Actual Coke habit by the time we got to college. Hannah was a star of the theater department and my sometimes-friend, particularly when it came to diet-tip sharing. She was talented and madly confident, but aware that her buxom body worked against her as a dancer; Bob Fosse left no room in his choreography for belly or boobs. I already knew I was not *Chicago*-bound, but I wanted the flat-panel body of a chorus girl anyway, and I gratefully accepted the little grainy pills she tipped out of an Aleve bottle and into my palm every afternoon. When Dexatrim was recalled for containing a stroke-causing ingredient (something like "phenynleflekrnenagucosamine"), we bemoaned the loss of our sleepless nights and occasional heart flutters, briefly switching to Dexatrim Natural (i.e., Dexatrim Boring). Then Hannah went on a family vacation to Mexico and came back with a purse full of possible stroke risks. Problem solved.

From Beth, a dance major in my dorm, I learned about sugar-free candy. Beth was diabetic and while she'd watched many of her fellow dancers suffer through the endless, cyclical grip of anorexia, she struggled with her own complicated health issue. She was long and thin and muscled, like the rest of them, but would never be as small as those furious pixies, the "bunheads," who typically played the Sugar Plum Fairy role in our annual *Nutcracker* run. She was a solid Snowflake, smiling in the second row.

Dancing all day while maintaining level blood sugar is a complex challenge that requires constant testing and dosing and math. She had candy and juice for low-sugar emergencies, but when she wanted to take the shuttle bus into town for a movie, she packed a bag of sugar-free gummy worms or diabetic-friendly peanut butter cups.

Beth's minifridge had a seemingly bottomless supply of food, so when I asked to try her gummies, she tossed me a whole bag. We were sitting on the floor of her room, studying for a Biology test.

"They're good!" I chirped, genuinely surprised.

"They're okay," she replied.

In truth, the candy was a little hard to chew, and the sorbitol sweetener left a bitter glaze in my mouth. Still, I pressed on:

"No, I really like them!"

"Just don't eat the whole bag. You'll shit your brains out."

Oh really, now?

I stocked up at the local drugstore and took to eating sugar-free candy after each meal, even if I'd had dessert (I'd almost certainly had dessert). It was the equivalent of a purge, except I didn't have to call it that. There was no scary, messy toil of vomiting, only many an uncomfortable evening on the toilet. My dorm was connected to an administrative building, so rather than use the very public stalls near my bedroom, I spent hours in the privacy of the staff bathroom, sitting and waiting, feet going numb, until I was sure it was all over. Why didn't other people know about this?! Of course, they did—they just didn't write sexy young-adult novels like *The Best Little Girl in the World* about it, because no one pictures the Best Little Girl in the World as a fat, anxious theater nerd, shitting her brains out in a bathroom stall.

The sugar-free trick backfired after a few months when I wound up having to rush out of class for a not-so-private session in an academic building. Our student bathrooms were coed, and the tops of the stalls were so low it was obvious they'd been purchased for an elementary school. One of the few close friends I'd made was Jon, a six-foot-four theater student with whom I shared an equal love of *The X-Files*, Ani DiFranco, and Stephen Sondheim—not to mention a class schedule.

It's moments like this that make me believe that God exists and is, in fact, a mid-'90s sitcom writer. Kelsey enters stall, drops pants, and sits down. Enter: Jon.

"Oh heeeey!" He peered down at me from a neighboring stall as I clenched my butt cheeks and smiled with the force of a thousand suns.

"He-heeeeey," I eked out.

"Oh God, I can't pee when you're looking at me," he said.

"So don't look at me!"

"Okay, okay. I'm looking at the wall." He stared at the tiled wall and then cracked up.

"I can't! You go first!"

"Ha. Ha-ha. I can't, either." Because I'll have to change schools, if not planets, after.

"Come on, please?!"

"Pee now, you pee now!" I didn't scream so much as growl into my lap, but the voice that came out of me was enough to reverberate off the walls and get Jon to start peeing immediately, then flush, wash his hands, and get the hell out in under forty seconds.

"Bye!"

Sorbitol, mannitol, and other artificial sweeteners can indeed cause apocalyptic diarrhea in most people, as well as bloating and the kind of cramps that make me reconsider ever having children.

Sugar-free, as it turned out, required moderation after all. I had weeks of life-changing constipation after quitting the stuff (again, where's *my* sexy young-adult novel?) and from then on only used it during crisis mode. I kept a stash of sugar-free gummies for post-pizza binges or the nights before auditions, but the magic of the first few months of toilet euphoria was gone.

From another dance friend I learned about working out in garbage-bag pants. From my junior-year scene study partner I adopted a grapefruit habit that went not unlike the sugar-free experiment. By junior year, Sydney and I had met and become best friends, so when she became an Atkins devotee, I followed her lead without shelling out cash for the book.

"Basically, no bread and all the nuts you want," she said. That's how I ended up eating almonds by the sackful for longer than I care to think about. In the grand finale of my high school diets, Sydney and I revived the low-carb concept the following year, and that lasted for a whole whopping week.

In between these fits and starts, I swung back to the Ben & Jerry's phase, taking emotional eating to new heights. This was the kind of stuff you only read about in the darkest of *Cathy* cartoons: sneaking into Chrissy's room to sneak nibbles of the chocolate bars she brought back from Switzerland; eating slice after slice of pizza by myself in a local restaurant while hiding from a table of fellow students; picking the dried-out icing off someone's birthday cake, which they'd left out overnight in the common room.

I did all this because the new diet was coming, any minute. It didn't matter that there was no one looking over my shoulder or that I didn't even want the next slice of pizza, my stomach already churning with nausea. When I lived in that cycle, I was constantly desperate for something. Food was both the fuel of that desperation and the white noise that blocked it out. I did it because this endless up and down left no room for me to feel anything else, and that was the only calm I knew. I did it because I had always done it.

We call fat people lazy. They're not. Fat people are zealous. They will cleave and push and fight harder than anyone. They have been in battle since the day someone poked them in the soft part of their belly or slapped the last piece of Halloween candy from their chubby hand. No one works harder at anything than a fat person works on a diet they believe will make them thin. They're not stupid, either—another hateful misconception that lingers in the bigoted corners of our cultural consciousness. At eighteen, I could have written a thesis on calorie content and ketones and insoluble fiber, in iambic pentameter if you wanted. They're not fat for lack of knowledge or effort. Some fat people became fat for a reason (medical, emotional, environmental). Others were simply born to be larger than you might like them to be. But all those chronic fat dieters are fatter for the dieting. They're fatter because they've been failed.

I failed each one of those programs because failure is built in by design. Sure, there are those among us who might drop baby weight with two months on the Zone, but those so-called success stories make up the teeniest, tiniest percentage. You have to look quite closely to see that asterisk: "Results not typical." The rest of us are lifers.

*

By the time I graduated, I'd found my footing in school. Grades had leveled out at slightly above average, and I'd been cast in several plays—usually as the grandmother or the sexless spinster, for obvious reasons. I still kept a small circle of close friends, but by senior year I was something akin to popular. Somehow I found myself senior class president and on my way to Boston University. And I was heavier than I had ever been.

On graduation day, I sat with Dad on the back steps of my dorm, freshly dressed in cap and gown. He was so proud of me; did I know that? He loved me more than anything in the world.

"I just hate to see you like this." He was almost in tears.

"I know. But I'm working on it!" I aimed for chipper but my voice came out strangled.

He nodded. "I want you to be happy. I want you to have a life, sweetie."

"Dad, seriously. I'll take care of it."

He smiled, the anguish in his face so acute. He looked at me like the parent of a murderer, standing by his monstrous child despite her crimes.

In those three years at Walnut Hill, I'd yo-yoed up and down the same hundred pounds. The years after that were much the same as I threw myself, heart and soul, into Jenny Craig, CalorieKing, even one hellish week with SlimFast. If the plan was in a book or written down for me by someone thin and intimidating, I'd commit with the devotion of a saint. Then I'd slip, true sinner that I was. But still I believed and returned to the next diet with a real and renewed faith. Yet, any weight loss I managed was fleeting. In the end, I only got fatter with every round.

It was all true, every terrible thought I had about myself. My mother had been right to be angry and disgusted by my stomach. Of course my father feared for my future, crying at the very sight of me. I was ruined.

Chapter 7

Carbs!

I'm going to have a cookie!" I called to Chrissy from the kitchen. She didn't answer.

"I'm going to have one of these cookies!" I called again. "Hey, is that okay?!"

Chrissy stuck her head out of the bathroom door and looked around to see what all the screaming was about.

"Dude, you *brought* the cookies."

She closed the door and I smacked the heel of my palm to my head, cringing at yet another socially awkward gaffe. Since I had started intuitive eating, everyone I came into contact with—baristas, the pharmacist—was subject to this new habit I had of making grand eating proclamations. But Harry and my friends bore the brunt of it.

My three closest friends were the ones I made in high school: Chrissy, Debbie, and almost-saw-me-pooping Jon. I didn't know if that was healthy or not, but it was nice to know there were three people in the world who'd known me as a fifteen-year-old and still liked me. Because the universe is a sitcom, we wound up spending most of our twenties within shouting distance of each other. Chrissy and Jon were roommates, sharing a big, white loft by the Brooklyn Navy Yard, and Debbie's apartment was just three blocks from mine. It was my actual deepest fear that one of us would one day move to another borough.

I'd come over to make dinner with Chrissy while Jon was out with his new boyfriend. It was an old routine: We'd catch up on each other's weeks while chopping onions for pasta sauce, then eat dinner in front of a horror movie or a saccharine romcom. Jon would inevitably come home in time to roll his eyes at the last twenty minutes of our movie, then we'd all sit around and gossip, breaking off pieces of Swiss chocolate bars from Chrissy's stash.

But, this time, I'd brought cookies myself. Creating a sense of "food security" was a vital step in the process. I made sure any food I had an inclination toward was readily available—especially if it was something formerly forbidden. The idea was that by making cookies constantly accessible I would stop my brain from treating them like manna from heaven. It was a pain in the ass, hauling cookies everywhere, but I knew it was a necessary part of the deprogramming.

By now I understood it was the diet cycle that had made me the kind of lunatic who'd pick the frosting off of other people's birthday cakes then turn around and live on green-grape rations for a month. It was a miserable trap I'd been stuck in for decades, and finally breaking out was the greatest thing I'd ever done for myself. So, why did freedom feel so awkward?

Those first weeks of intuitive eating felt too good to be true, but also crazy and out of control. Nothing was off-limits. I was a kid in the candy store, and the candy store was *everywhere*. With every food suddenly on the table, I'd be lying if I said the first thing I desired was a baby carrot. No, I'd been let off the leash and was grabbing for everything I'd slapped my hands away from for decades. Food security was only part of it. Above all, I had to learn permission to eat. That permission is the foundation of becoming an intuitive eater. It was now my job to realize I could eat anything. I was fat and I could eat anything. It was wonderful and fulfilling. It was alarming. It was also mainly carbs.

"Oh, I'm hungry!" I'd announced to myself at work in a little whisper-shout. "What do I want to eat?"

There's no rule about speaking out loud in intuitive eating, but in the early days when I still couldn't quite get my head around the concept, I found it helpful to talk myself through it like a gentle kindergarten teacher. "You want a hot chocolate? Well, let's get you one!" I might cheerfully mutter while passing Starbucks. "How does sushi sound for dinner? No? Eggs on toast it is." When you've spent your whole life being ashamed to eat at all, expressing those needs and desires is new and weird. (Talking to yourself is empirically weird, too, but you've got to pick your battles.) Eating a cookie in front of someone felt like breaking a rule, and asking for one, even from myself, felt criminal. I needed to bank as many moments of permission as possible. Vocalizing these instances (i.e., meals and snacks) was a radical act, even if it meant whispering to myself at work, or boldly declaring my intent to eat a cookie while my friend was just trying to use the bathroom.

"What do I want to eat?" I whispered to myself one early afternoon.

The answer was French onion soup and mashed potatoes, loud and clear. I opened Seamless, who no longer spoke to me as much, now that I was speaking to myself, and found a restaurant that had both. The day before I'd had pizza for lunch and pasta for dinner. The day before that had been similarly starchy with fried rice, corn chips, and rye toast in the mix. There'd been other food groups as well, but it was scary how much I desired carbohydrates. I was actually scared. I lay in bed at night wondering if I had made a massive, public misstep and now everyone would watch as I ballooned to even greater girth on a diet of intuitively eaten bread, noodles, and Triscuits. Holy hell, though, Triscuits were good.

*

"I feel like I'm physically addicted to carbohydrates."

Years of therapy had taught me that if you want to say something a little bit crazy and still sound like a reasonable person, start the sentence with "I feel." It's a great trick both for conflict resolution and confessing to an irrational belief that you've developed an actual addiction to crackers.

"Okay! Why do you think you're addicted to carbohydrates?" Theresa seemed game for this fresh lunacy I'd laid at her feet.

"Because I'm eating them a lot."

She looked down at the record of meals I'd handed her. I took a deep breath.

"Yeah, there are carbs on this list."

"It's too much, right? Like, it's crazy."

"What day felt the craziest?"

"All of them. Yesterday, I guess."

Theresa ruffled through the printouts where I'd listed all my meals and snacks over the course of the week. It was different from a food journal (that was why I called it an "eating record"), because a "food journal" was something I'd kept while on a diet. The point of recording my meals was now an act of exploration rather than regulation. Each time I ate, I noted down my level of hunger beforehand and fullness when I was done, using a scale of 1 to 10. I wrote down any feelings or struggles I had with choosing a particular food. *I really want a hamburger but I feel like I should have a turkey burger. I guess I have a belief that beef is Bad and turkey is Good.* I noted any discoveries I had with a particular eating experience. *Got a couple orders of fries to share with the table, then ended up panicking and eating them all. Lesson learned: order only my own damn fries next time.* It was helpful to see the patterns I'd fallen into over the years, as well as all the little anxieties I felt in different eating situations. Still, each time I handed over my eating record, I felt momentarily certain that Theresa would take one look and call the police. "She's gone mad! She ate cookies and frozen yogurt on the same day!" And yet:

"Okay, yesterday you had an egg-and-tomato sandwich for breakfast."

"Yes, on bread."

"Did you want the sandwich? Was it satisfying?"

"Yes, definitely." Breakfast was the easiest part of my day. Any dieter knows that clean-slate feeling that comes with a new morning. I crushed breakfast, intuitively speaking.

"For lunch you were at a six for hunger and you had pad see ew, then hit a six for fullness."

Her voice was entirely neutral, but I winced. I felt caught in the act, ordering Thai food with no excuse. It wasn't my birthday, I wasn't famished, and I had had breakfast. I had been just regular-hungry, and pad see ew with broccoli and chicken sounded great. In the notes I'd written "lots of broccoli," as if the extra greens would somehow negate my plate of big fat, starchy noodles.

"Do you have permission to eat carbs?" Theresa responded off my look.

"Yes, I have permission to eat carbs." I wasn't rolling my eyes, but I really wanted to be rolling my eyes.

"Because you don't sound like you do."

"I have permission to eat them, but I don't want to be a crazy carb monster, no!"

That was the moment I heard just what a "crazy carb monster" sounds like. Whether it was overeating or trying to restrict, obsessing about food was still obsessing about food. There was no crime in a two-carb meal or a pizza-and-pasta day. Sometimes, it just happens. And, sometimes, you've been terrified and tantalized by the thought of processed flour for so long that when you're finally allowed to eat it, you go a little crazy for a week. The trick was not to frantically jerk the steering wheel in the other direction, trying to correct. For once, I had to let go and trust that balance would come naturally, because I was not, in fact, a car.

That day in Theresa's office, I didn't really believe it yet. But I'd already taken the leap of faith. I had to stop fighting the fall.

I ate the carbs. I talked myself through every cracker and tortilla chip and baked potato (not just sweet potato—russet, the real deal). And I enjoyed them. I took lunch away from my desk and twirled udon noodles out of vegetable soup until I was satisfied, then I put the rest away and got back to my day. I made bowls of whole wheat pasta with fresh lemon and basil for Harry and myself, not because I wanted "healthy" pasta but because I enjoyed the grainy texture. I proclaimed each cookie with pride. When the freak-out thoughts came up, I appealed to the carb monster with reason: *If you can't trust me yet, trust Theresa.* And I waited. And one day, much sooner than I expected, I was hungry and the answer to that hunger was: scallops.

It took two weeks. Two weeks of teaching myself permission to eat carbohydrates, and my brain got the message. There was no need to hoard it and no one would take it away. I could eat scallops on a bed of sautéed spinach for dinner and enjoy every bite. There was no need to fear that it would be only lean fish and greens from here on out. Learning that, not just in my mind but also in my body, made the pasta and the scallops both so much more delicious. I could finally eat them both with a sense of calm. I could pick up my fork and put it down, push the plate aside and take it back. I could get second helpings or I could leave whatever I didn't want on the plate.

It was just the first of many firsts. I'd have to learn permission dozens of times: unlearn to fear dairy and French fries, and then go back and do carbs all over again. But I had an experience in my back pocket now, and I could pull it out to look at during the darker, tougher months to come. I knew that I was capable, a little less monstrous than I'd been a month before. It was the beginning of trust.

There was one more thing in my back pocket: my phone. In it, I wrote little discoveries and weekly goals during all my sessions with Theresa. *Prioritize dinner—don't skip. Do I associate Starbucks with depression? Consider.* During the Great Carb Freak-Out she said one thing in particular, which I quickly thumb-typed into an e-mail and sent to myself for safekeeping. I still look at it on days when it's exceptionally hard to just believe and let go. I share it with you not because it's gentle and kind and makes you feel good, but because it's true. Theresa's not a sentimental lady—she's a coach, and a woman of science. So, when you say it to yourself, say it in the voice of someone who's not fucking around:

"No one is broken. I've never met anyone who was broken."

Chapter 8

The Cool Table

By my late twenties, I'd blown through half a dozen IKEA dressers, none of which could bear the emotional weight of my T-shirt collection. Each time I tried to purge that middle drawer, I found another too-small top I was saving for the future, or a threadbare tank that still smelled like the past. But times had changed, and now I was letting go of both those things (right?).

One night, I scooped out that jammed middle drawer and began tossing items across the room. Urban Outfitters button-down with fringe down the middle? Gone. *Godspell* T-shirt, circa second grade? Probably not going to fit into that without a time machine. I'd only gotten through the sedimentary level before I found the baseball tee.

It was chilly in my bedroom, one of those weird, transitional nights where it's cold enough for a jacket, but not cold enough for the radiator to kick on. I took off my fuzzy sweater anyway, and pulled on the gray and green XXL top, sniffing the collar. It didn't smell like anything but the fiberboard drawer, but that sucker wasn't going anywhere.

*

Since that first diet at age eleven to the last at twenty-seven, my successes had been moderate: ten to thirty pounds. Only once did I pull off transformational weight loss—magazine-cover, before and after photos weight loss. It was the most strenuous diet I'd ever attempted, and by far the most instantly effective. I'd gotten that baseball tee the week it started, and a few months later, it was down to my knees.

The summer after high school I landed an internship at the most important corporation in New York, America, the universe, the mind of God: the production office of *Sex and the City*. In 2002, there was no higher calling than to fetch, carry, copy, and file for those be-heeled ladies and the staff that put puns in their mouths. I'd been out of high school for approximately twenty-six hours before reporting to the wildly unglamorous production office in Long Island City, Queens.

My first impression was how overdressed I was. After three years of living in jazz sneakers and a promotional *Chicago* T-shirt, I'd opted to wear a pencil skirt with a button-down and the kitten-heel shoes I hadn't seen since my prep school interviews. As it turned out, I'd have been better off in my jazz sneakers. Production interns don't wear heels. Stupid production interns do.

Getting off the subway on a sweaty June morning, I walked three blocks in the wrong direction, turned back, and then paused in front of an open garage where two mechanics were chatting under a raised car.

"If I keep walking this way, will I hit Twenty-Second Street?"

They stopped talking to look at me, nodded briefly, then went inside. Most New Yorkers like to show off their knowledge of streets and subway routes, but some have seen one too many interns. I reflexively yanked my shirt down over my stomach, and turned to keep walking, when a short blue bus pulled up alongside me, immediately discharging a large group of men—some old, but mostly quite young, and all in widely varied attire. It was at this point that I noticed the large block writing across the front and back of the vehicle: NEW YORK CITY CORRECTIONS DEPARTMENT: RIKER'S ISLAND.

I spent a full minute gaping like the stunned, suburban fish I was; it was then that I realized in my entire life spent in and around New York City, I'd never once been to Queens—unless you counted the airport. I turned away and headed in the direction of what I hoped was Twenty-Second Street.

"Hi, sorry, you don't have a desk."

This was Mike, one of many guys in baseball hats who would tell me what to do for the next three months.

"Oh, that's fine. I don't need a desk or anything," I answered automatically. I would sit on the floor as long as I could spend the rest of my life bragging about the summer I spent sitting on *Sex and the City*'s carpet.

"We'll figure something out. Follow me."

Mike showed me around the production floor, pointing at different soundproofed rooms and tables littered with scripts and empty soda cans. Here was a line of potential blondes the *Sopranos* team was auditioning in one of our conference rooms ("our!"). Here was costume designer Patricia Field's wardrobe room and a pile of bras that needed to be returned (bras!). At some point I felt the beginnings of a blister as my left heel rubbed against a shoe it hadn't worn in four years. But I power-limped across that entire floor, because I had only two goals that summer: to lose weight, and to make everyone at this job love me more than their own children.

Finally, we entered a large kitchen-cum-copy room. On the fridge was a photo of Elizabeth Taylor and Michael Jackson. Against the wall were hundreds and hundreds of multicolored scripts, stacked nearly to the ceiling.

"So, I guess we'll start you here."

"Where?" I asked, looking at the Liz Taylor–Michael Jackson photo.

He gestured to the wall.

"These are the scripts we've already shot this season. We need to get rid of these copies for security—eBay and everything."

"Okay, great!"

A bonfire, perhaps? A landfill? I was full of ideas already!

He pointed to a small personal office shredder next to the Xerox machine. "You know how to use these things, right?"

Nope.

Four hours later I was sitting on *Sex and the City*'s carpet, about twelve inches into the thirty thousand inches of script I'd shred that summer. By the time Mike came back to check my progress, I'd read the line, "You have slept with eight men and we're still on appetizers" six times and wasn't even close to sick of it.

"How's it going?"

"Great!"

"So, listen. Around two, can you set up some snacks on the kitchen table?"

"Of course. Just, whatever's in the cabinets?"

"Yeah."

"I can do that."

He didn't leave.

"So, listen." He locked eyes with me and reached into his pocket. "I'm going to give you the key to the chocolate closet."

He held out the key, a little. I got off the floor, though his tone seemed to indicate that perhaps I ought to kneel.

"Okay."

"We don't usually give interns the key to the chocolate closet. We've had some problems. Be careful, all right?"

I assured him I would be. I did not take this responsibility lightly. I respected the chocolate.

"Do not share this with anyone, and put anything that's not eaten back in the closet by the end of the day. Then you *lock it*. Listen, seriously."

He gave me the key and took off. I looked around the kitchen trying to identify this hallowed cabinet. Immediately my eye caught the tall, skinny white closet in the corner, separate and padlocked.

I approached, glancing once over my shoulder, lest Mike appear to steal back his precious. I slid my key into the lock and opened the door.

✳

"No carbs and no refined sugar. You're done with those."

"Okay." I nodded, hard.

Judy sat behind her desk in a small, elegant office high above East Sixty-First Street. Just behind her was a knockout view of the Queensboro Bridge. Judy terrified me. People with bridge views mean business, and Judy had earned that window.

"You can start the day with some Fiber One, but no more than half a cup." She looked up from her large, yellow legal pad and locked eyes with me: *You got me?* I nodded and threw in a hearty thumbs-up for good measure. Judy went back to writing out my meal plan. "You can have an apple with that, too, if you need one."

I'd found Judy through my doctor, and though her respected roster was jammed with clients already, I'd managed to squeeze in a quick appointment within days of calling. I'd lost weight with nutritionists before, responding well to one-on-one instruction from scary ladies writing out meal plans specifically prescribed for my brand of fatness. So, upon arriving home from Walnut Hill, my first order of business was to get myself into an office like this, and find a new scary lady with a notepad who would write down exactly what and when and how I should eat, forever. Judy had, by far, the scariest demeanor and the biggest notepad of any nutritionist I'd ever met. I was thrilled.

One thing Judy and my doctor both agreed on was my blood sugar. In high school, I had been diagnosed as having a borderline case of insulin insensitivity, probably as a result of polycystic ovary syndrome. It's a relatively common issue among women, and my case was largely asymptomatic, except for the insulin issue. What it meant was that I wasn't exactly borderline diabetic, but I was borderline borderline diabetic. It wasn't clear to me if my weight was the cause or the result of this issue, but everyone agreed that going on a diet would fix it. Over 220 pounds, I was bloated with boarding school and all the big fat feelings I'd eaten there. I deserved this ass kicking, and Judy delivered.

"When I say four ounces of white-meat chicken," she said, scribbling out my lunch plan on her pad, "I mean four ounces. Measure it before you eat. It should be about the size of your palm. Well, not yours, but my palm."

I glanced down at my hands, which were apparently the size of personal pan pizzas. I looked back up at Judy's, held up in a tight, narrow high five, as if saluting a dictator.

"Got it."

She moved on to the afternoon and evening, detailing the handfuls of raw almonds I could snack on at 3:30 p.m. and the dinners I could finish with a half cup of fat-free, no-sugar-added frozen yogurt, or a side of ten to twelve raspberries.

"What about grapes or other berries?"

Judy's pen stopped abruptly. She turned a gaze of flattened anger up at me.

"Grapes are just sugar. You might as well be eating a pile of gummy bears."

"Oh, I'm sorry." I really was.

"Kelsey, you're young." She put down her pen for a moment, and I braced myself for more eye contact. "This is only going to get harder and harder. When you're twenty-five or thirty-five, losing this weight will take much longer. You need to do this now. I beg you."

She begged me. Judy, with her bridge view and notepad and four-ounce palms, was calling to me from the other side of something. I was suddenly that schlubby not-as-rich-kid in the sixth grade, being given my one shot to hang with the size-zero girls. I really could be one of them. I just had to make an effort, lose the belly, and figure out how to 'do stuff with hair accessories. Or I could languish. I could be a dumpy twenty-five-year-old and a lonesome thirty-five-year-old, and after that, who knew? Sweatshirts? Bed sores? An actual death by chocolate?

"No grapes. Understood."

I spent the rest of the summer shredding scripts and being called "Chelsea" at *Sex and the City*, happy to earn my trod-upon-intern stripes. Every morning, I'd pass the Riker's discharge bus, the stream of newly released inmates a cheering reminder that I was on time for work. I had a desk by that point, but the kitchen-copy room was where I spent most of my time. Each morning, I'd put out breakfast cereal at 9 a.m., shred and file for a few hours, then pick up and deliver lunches down to the set. At 2 p.m., I'd unlock the chocolate closet and release its bounty upon the office.

Mike was right to speak its name with such fearful reverence. Inside this closet were tubs of Hershey's miniatures, bulk bags of fun-size candy bars, and box after box of Oreo snack packs. Evidently, it wasn't just me who had a problem with sugar. Before they thought to buy a lock, this closet had been savagely pillaged all day, every day, leaving the poor bastard who'd preceded me to constantly restock the thing. It had become an actual budget problem.

I never ate a single thing from that closet. Each afternoon, I'd arrange a cornucopia of treats on the kitchen table, artfully piling cookies and chocolate bars to the delight of production assistants and postproduction assistants, who would blearily stumble out of edit suites to grab a cache of sugar from my generous heap of plenty. I myself was satisfied with the sanctioned tablespoon of peanut butter Judy had prescribed in case of emergency. Well, "satisfied" wasn't quite right, but seeing as every afternoon at 2 p.m. felt like an emergency, I was blowing through half a jar of peanut butter every week.

I kept it in the bottom drawer of my desk, Don Draper style, and reached for it the instant I was finished with my chocolate-closet duties. I'd level off a tablespoon and allow myself a lick. Then I'd place the spoon into a paper cup and push it to the far corner of my desk. *Shred, file, copy, and repeat.* If I was going to make that tablespoon last all afternoon, I had to make every lick count. But, as soon as that cup hit the corner, I'd be desperately fighting the urge to grab it, grab the whole jar, and scoop it all into my face with one bite. I literally fantasized about this scenario. What would it feel like to have an entire mouthful of peanut butter? I hadn't had sex yet, but surely, peanut-butter mouth would be better.

The day after my appointment with Judy (and the Final Pig-Out dinner of oily pasta and Carvel Flying Saucers that I'd eaten that night), I'd begun her strict regime of low-carb, low-fat, high-protein, and absolutely-no-refined-sugar. This was how grown-ups ate. This was how you crossed the boundary from childish loser to lithe, adult sophisticate. The secret was simple: You just had to be hungry, all the time. People like the staff and crew could raid the chocolate closet every afternoon, but those four iconic women in front of their cameras existed in that other realm. It was part of their job to be thin; that was how we wanted them, and so they were. When I thought of it as part of my job, sticking to this ascetic regime was simple. Not easy, but simple. With every lost pound I felt closer, not to the

famous actresses, but to famous-actressness. It wasn't about my own
fading acting aspirations so much as my new dream to just be someone better. I could figure out who that might be later; the important
part was she would be thin. So, with pleasure, I packed up containers
of apple slices and broccoli snacks (not carrots—too many carbs) that
I could bring on my commute into the city.

Mom agreed to pay for a nutritionist, but she'd seen it all before. She'd
long since given up policing my eating, having watched me try and
fail so many times to pull myself together. I was grateful to live without her open criticism, but in my heart I felt more like a problem she'd
washed her hands of. And as the years went by, my weight became a
mere irritation, trumped by bigger, louder problems growing in our
home. It was fine, though. I would be thin and she would be well.

Mom walked through the kitchen one night, a tall acrylic tumbler in one hand and a pack of cigarettes in the other. She no longer
hid the smoking habit she'd taken up sometime in the last year ("A
lot of people started smoking again after 9/11"). Sloshing around
in the cup was another secret we weren't allowed to talk about.

I didn't know for sure when she had stopped going to AA nor
when she'd started drinking again. Earlier that summer, we'd been
at a neighbor's pool party, when I'd looked up from the water to
see her standing by the grill and tipping back a Mike's Hard Lemonade. The sight so stunned me that I plunged back underwater
as if to wash it away. That night I'd gotten up the guts to ask her
if what I'd seen was true. That time she was contrite, promising
that she would stop—soon. Instead she'd become a sloppy sneak,
hiding the wine in opaque water glasses. More than once I'd found
the cups half drunk around the house, and approached her with the
evidence, upset and afraid. But she wasn't sorry anymore. She was
enraged at being caught, and at me for catching her.

That night in the kitchen, I knew better. If she saw me so much as glance down at the glass, her fury could last for days. But though I kept my gaze level, I'd been watching her all summer from behind every corner. It wasn't just the drinking and the smoking. She seemed to vibrate with tension and was never fully present in the room, even when she was right there, talking to me. I stayed up late, peeking out the window for glimpses of the flashlight she used when she gardened all night. I listened at the bathroom door when she was in the tub in case she'd nodded off. Only once did I have to burst through the door and blow my cover, waking her up with a childish scream. I'd felt the ice grow thin beneath me since catching her that time, and now as she stopped to survey me in the kitchen, I turned nervous and smiley. She paused for a moment to ask exactly what I was doing.

"Making breakfast for the rest of August!" I had pulled a stool up to the kitchen counter, turned on last week's episode of *Sex and the City*, and got out the measuring cup. Opening box after box of Fiber One, I carefully portioned out half cups of cereal into small Ziploc bags, then laid them out in rows of five.

"And you have to use three *hundred* bags to do it? Don't you think it's rather wasteful?"

I paused, looking at the heap of litter I'd generated. Behind me, the TV chirped, "You have slept with eight men and we're still on appetizers!" and my gut did a sick flip.

"I'm sorry."

She pursed her lips, exhaled hard through her nose, and headed out to the front porch.

During my last week at *Sex and the City*, Mike popped by my desk just as I was beginning my afternoon liaison with the peanut butter jar.

"Hey listen, you wanna go downstairs tomorrow?"

Downstairs meant the set. I'd poked around plenty during off hours, sticking my head out of Carrie's window and even sitting in Aidan's chair for ten seconds, until a lighting guy walked by and paused to make deeply pitying eye contact with me. During shooting, I only made brief trips to the stage, delivering documents or someone's dinner, then mouthing a silent *You're welcome* and tiptoeing out of the room while thirty feet away, Charlotte fell in love with her divorce lawyer, even though he was bald.

"Really?" I asked Mike. I knew what he meant.

"Yeah." He shrugged. "Everyone gets a turn."

Being an extra was the unofficial intern perk. I'd already been given a slew of *SATC* hats and shirts, including the beloved baseball tee, but this was the real prize I'd been waiting for. Many of my fellow script shredders had opted out simply because being an extra is fist-eatingly dull. But I was up for anything that meant standing ten feet closer to the fantasy. The next day, as instructed, I arrived at the coffee shop set wearing a colorful but not-too-bright dress and waited with the handful of background actors hired for the scene. I waved a sheepish hello to Gary, the assistant director in charge of extra coordination. He didn't know my name, but he waved a friendly reply, recognizing me as the girl who brought the Krispy Kreme delivery every Friday.

"You're down here all day?"

"Yeah, I'm taking my turn." I gestured to my dress and heels and the fact that I wasn't holding donuts.

"Great. We'll definitely get you in there."

Of course he would. All the other interns who'd opted in got their chance to shine, blurrily in the background. Anyway, it was a small group of extras that day: just me, four women, and a couple of guys in suits. We all loitered patiently while the scene was lit, then shot from one angle, then relit for the next. With each setup, Gary came out and surveyed us in a loose lineup, pulling one or two new bodies into the scene. Shoot, cut, reset. We sat, we stood, and we sat back down again, trying to pretend that this whole thing felt nothing like picking teams for dodgeball. During the fourth hour, one of the suit guys decided we were friends.

"Are you an actress?"

"Sometimes."

"What roles do you usually play?"

I thought of Dave and Maureen back at Rainbow Management saying I was best friend or girlfriend material.

"Best friends, mostly."

"Yeah? I thought you'd play, like, biker chicks." He vroom-vroomed an invisible bike in front of him. I gave him a chuckle because it felt like he was waiting for one, and instinctively folded my arms in front of myself. Only then did I look around and start to do the math. There were just a few of us left to be placed and the scene was almost finished. I sat down on a cooler and realized what was happening. My outfit wasn't the problem. The other extras were dressed just like me, but they were also thin. It hadn't even occurred to me, because how could it possibly matter? If I showed up on screen at all, it would be as a passing blur in the distance, or the back of my left arm. But with each line-up, Gary looked us up and down and asked someone else to step onto the set.

"I can change?" I offered. I had four other outfits folded in a duffel bag, just in case.

"Nope, you're fine, it's not that. We'll get you in there, don't worry!"

Gary never picked me. I packed up and headed for the subway, deciding never to tell anyone about this stupid day that I'd gotten all excited for, as if it signified anything at all. I cold-comforted myself with the knowledge that plenty of extras who get called in never wind up being placed in the scene. It happened on sets every day. Still, on that particular day, I was the only one who wasn't. Maybe it wasn't "that." Maybe it wasn't anything. But when you stand around all day not being picked, it's hard not to imagine what made you so unworthy of sitting, out of focus, behind the cool kids' table.

Chapter 9

The Gun on the Wall

The afternoon I moved into my freshman dorm at Boston University was hotter than any other day that summer. Elevators clogged with families and moving dollies dinged constantly outside my open door.

My mother and Steve had left hours ago, after Mom had been getting visibly antsier by the minute. I was equal parts anxious about her agitated state and glad to be free of it—now I could nest. Up went the 8×10 stills and miniature posters from movies like *Say Anything...* and *Love Story*. Out came my new sets of jersey Twin XL sheets. I put on an audiobook of *She's Come Undone* for company. I'd read or listened to the book at least three times before, and it was comforting to travel through the sad, familiar story as I unpacked my stash of Fiber One, fat-free vegetable soup, and the whole peeled tomatoes I ate straight from the can. The entire bottom drawer of my dresser was devoted to diet-friendly foods, and beneath that lay my scale.

My new roommate, Jenna, was just one of the things that made this place not my high school. She was bright and cheery, a Midwestern cheerleader with three older sisters and parents that hugged and teased and left their baby with tears in their eyes. My last roommate at Walnut Hill had been a riot grrrl devotee who videotaped herself tripping and then watched it repeatedly for her own amusement. Jenna was more into Mandy Moore.

"Do you want to come to the dining hall with me and Casey?"

Who was Casey? She had a Casey already?

"No, that's okay. I'm going to get organized." Read: I'm going to measure out cereal baggies and watch *Mulholland Drive*.

My entire freshman-year social life can be summed up by that exchange.

Over the next few months, Jenna developed into her college self, going to parties, finding a friend group, and making tipsy conversation with guys. Straight guys! For all that talk about straight, white males running the universe, it was a demographic I hadn't had much contact with since I was fourteen. Just before my Walnut Hill graduation, I'd gotten in an argument with Sydney over whether or not all guys wore makeup.

"A lot of guys wear eyeliner, right?"

"Not really, honey. That's just here." She'd spent two years in "real" high school, and had even had physical contact with a straight guy. The two dry-humping sessions she'd had essentially made her Anaïs Nin in my eyes.

"But *all* guys wear concealer at least?"

"No, dear."

It was part of the reason I'd chosen BU over the small, liberal arts colleges everyone assumed I'd opt for. At a school with over twenty thousand students, at least *some* of them must be males who were interested in females, and statistically, I'd have to hit it off with one of them. According to every movie ever made, that's just what happened in college. Soon enough, I would surely be fumbling through my first relationship with a sweet but goony guy who liked my taste in cinema and who would introduce me to things like sex and Goldschläger. We'd break up by Christmas and I'd be on to the next dude, eventually meeting The One with whom I'd be sharing off-campus housing and pregnancy scares by senior year. Roll credits.

But in order for that to happen, I needed to leave my room. Leaving the room was not my thing. Making new friends seemed exhausting, and I was tired enough with my new academic schedule and the time and energy it took to manage my diet in the face of the dining hall's curly fries. Furthermore, I was scared out of my mind. I was intimidated by the innate social skills of Jenna and her fellow fun havers. (I was also scared of alcohol, having had yet to discover the social lubricant of cheap Chardonnay.) I was anxious about making party conversation or hallway chat before class. And guys? It's taken me ten years to realize that I was, in fact, more scared of the freshman males of Boston University than of the newly released inmates on the Rikers Island bus.

Then there was my mom: a nugget of worry in the back of my mind that grew larger every day. I'd gotten her on the phone once since I'd started school, but neither she nor anyone else at home had called me to check in for three weeks.

It wasn't so different from my years at boarding school. Typically, I'd leave two or three messages asking her to call me, eventually leaving one with an urgent, specific reason ("Can you please call me back this time? I just have a quick question for my medical form, and I need to turn it in tomorrow.") Within a few days, my phone would ring, and I'd hear her voice, casual and rushed: "Hey baby, what's up?" Then, I'd have to fabricate a question about my medical history on the spot.

But now there was only silence. I tried at different times of day, even in the middle of the night, but each time I only got my sister's recorded voice on the answering machine, asking me to leave a message after the tone.

My Walnut Hill friends were off having their own wonderful and terrible college experiences, though we kept tabs with e-mail and the occasional four-hour phone call. Each time, I hung up feeling farther away, resentful of their new lives and friends and haircuts.

Anyway, who had time for friends? I'd just make new thin-person friends as soon as I got skinny. For now, without the burden of other humans in my life, things were going great. My diet was going great. Every morning I'd wake up, weigh myself, pee, then weigh myself again. The number was always lower than the day before, and even if it was just a quarter of a pound, I could breathe easy. Plateaus were death, so I decided I wouldn't even hit one. On the best days, like the morning I dipped out of the 190s and into the 180s, I would literally jump with delight, mutely cheering on my success so as not to wake Jenna, who was sleeping the sleep of the not-crazy. It is a fact that I once spontaneously high-fived myself in the mirror.

After my morning weigh-in, I'd dress in silence, grab a baggie of Fiber One, another baggie of vitamins, and an apple. The key was making breakfast last until midmorning, or I'd be famished and crazy by lunch. Throughout my morning Rhetoric 102 lecture, I'd nibble on the little brown cereal twigs, which only fueled the existing rumor that I was eating actual rabbit food.

Lunch was usually a vegetarian burrito (no rice, no sour cream, tablespoon of guacamole, all of which I mentally reported to Scary Judy) and a huge bowl of raw tomatoes drenched in balsamic vinegar. That dining hall burrito was, by far and away, the culinary highlight of my life. I felt sincere excitement at feeling its substantial weight in my hands. I ate the whole thing in a matter of seconds, once I got to my table and laid out my lunchtime companion, *People* magazine.

I'd worked out a class schedule that left most of my afternoons free, so after lunch I'd head back to my dorm room for a few solid hours of reading or, more often, lying belly-down on my bed watching reruns of *South Park* on my laptop until Jenna came home and told me about her day, one which did not revolve around rabbit food and cartoons. Then, of course, it was time to work out.

"What's that weird smell?" Jenna asked me one day, looking up from the textbook resting on her lap. We were having a study night together, our weekly ritual that culminated in *8 Minute Abs* and a reward episode of *Will & Grace* on our teeny TV/DVD player. That weird smell was my side of the room. I'd started going to the Bikram yoga studio two blocks away for a nightly class every day of the week. The practice, held in a room heated to 115 degrees, consisted of twenty-six poses performed facing a mirrored wall. It fit my bill perfectly: comfortably repetitive, physically challenging, incredibly uncomfortable at times—all in front of a mirror in which I could stare at my shrinking, sweat-soaked body parts. When I left, it was not with a calm, clear mind, but with the relief of a child leaving the dentist's office. I loved and dreaded it in equal measure, and soon enough was going twice a day. I was officially abusing yoga.

The benefits of hot yoga abuse include constant thirst, trembling muscles, and a laundry-bin stink you can no longer hide from your roommate, no matter how many scented dryer sheets you stash around the room. But I was losing weight even faster now. I'd first met with Judy in June. By November, I'd lost sixty pounds.

The morning I hit that milestone, I looked up from the scale and around my empty room, beaming with joy at no one. Jenna was gone for the weekend. The whole floor was still and sleeping at 8 a.m. on a Saturday. I wanted to call everyone, but there was no one to call. Instead, I celebrated with *Will & Grace*.

*

A week later, my phone rang. It was early in the evening, and I was half working on a paper, half chatting with Jenna and her friend Chris while they finished a pizza on her bed. I remember that I was drinking a Diet Coke. I remember that Chris was wearing a baseball hat. The whole room smelled like greasy leftovers.

It was Steve. "Hi. Did Mom call you?"

"No. I called her yesterday, but never heard back."

"But you haven't heard from her today or tonight?"

"No, why?" My whole body began to throb, each follicle and pore twanging with alarm.

Steve gushed a pressured sigh into the phone. "She took off this afternoon. She was upset."

"What do you mean?"

"No one's heard from her. She left a message on the machine. She was very upset."

"What did she say in the message?"

Jenna looked up at me, a question on her face. Chris poked her in the side and she swatted vaguely at his hand.

"She said she had to leave."

"Where?"

"I have no fucking idea, Kels."

"Did something happen? What else did she say?"

"Nothing. I have to go. I'll call you back."

My fingers gripped white around the phone as he disconnected.

"What happened?" Jenna asked. I let her question bounce around in my head.

"My mother is missing."

"What?!"

"She left this afternoon and no one's heard from her."

"Are you serious?"

I nodded and turned back to my laptop, staring at my last paragraph. Without noticing, I'd begun to take quick, shallow breaths. My scalp and face prickled with heat.

"Kelsey, oh my God. What does that mean?"

Slowly, Jenna got off the bed, and came over, putting her arms around my shoulders from behind. The gesture felt so intimate and generous that I felt a dull nervousness over how to respond. I patted my fingers against her arm, expecting them to loosen, but she held on.

"She left a message saying she had to leave. She was upset."

"Come on, hey," Chris jumped in, stepping over the pizza box. "She probably got in a fight with your dad and took off."

I stared at my computer. I could smell Jenna's conditioner as her hair brushed my shoulder.

"He's my stepdad."

"Yeah, just calm down. She's pissed at him and went for a drive."

I looked up at this complete and total fucking idiot. He smiled into my face, a shitheel doctor hushing a fussing child.

"Relax."

My mother used to whisper "Mommy always comes back" when I was little and could hardly bear to see her leave for a trip to the grocery store. Fiendish though it may be, I cannot help but wonder if both of us feared that one day she might not.

The night that Steve called, I paced the bedroom for hours in silence while Jenna slept, certain beyond a doubt that Mom was dead. She'd driven off the Bear Mountain Bridge, drunk or simply crazy. She'd tipped over the edge and into the madness, and I wasn't there. It wasn't exactly my fault. Deep down, I knew I had no power to make her better. But if I had been there I could at least have hidden her car keys.

At 5 a.m. the next morning, I took the first train back to New York. By the time I arrived in Croton, she had called home again. She was alive. But she wasn't coming home. She needed to not be home for a while. Two days later, Steve brought her back, all smiles, and my siblings and I clambered to get our arms around her. They were the other reasons I was guilty. They were only nine and ten years old, and who knew what they'd been through, while I'd been up in Boston eating canned tomatoes? There would be more to go through, for all of us. This was the beginning of a tenuous era in our lives. There would be hospitals and hope and more gut-punching phone calls. But never again would it feel quite like this. Her smoking and drinking that summer; her eyes that looked everywhere but straight ahead. It was the gun on the wall in our house. What a terrible relief when it finally fired.

Two months later, back at school, I woke up and rolled over in bed, checking the light outside my window. It wasn't quite dawn, even earlier than the yoga class I might attend if I were still going to yoga in the morning. I pulled the phone out from under my pillow, where I'd held it in my hand all night like a tiny, plastic security blanket. *Thank you, God, no messages.*

Once, I'd dreaded that silent phone, each unreturned call adding to my litany of worst-case scenarios. At last, one of them had come so absolutely true, and I knew I had been right to worry and pray and keep vigil at her bedroom door all those years ago.

Now I kept the phone just as close, but willed it not to ring.

I shuffled to the bathroom, allowing myself only a brief, sidelong glance in the mirror. I'd slept in the XXL *Sex and the City* baseball tee, though it no longer fit like a nightgown so much as a slightly too-big shirt. No weigh-in today, but I would start again tomorrow, definitely. I would go to the supermarket and stock up on all my safe foods, then hit a yoga class tonight and go straight to sleep with a Benadryl to knock me out. I would claw my way back into the zone, and lose the remaining forty pounds, starting tomorrow.

By spring semester, I'd gained twenty.

Chapter 10

Reruns

I beg you to do this, Kelsey."

Four years later, Judy looked exactly the same. I'd come crawling back to her scenic office, three months after graduating early from BU with a film degree and not much else. By my final year, I had finally made three friends, but my social skills had never really developed past the point of leaving my room, and I could count the number of parties I'd attended on half a hand. There had been no romances with well-meaning, doofy guys, and though I'd learned to drink, I mainly did that alone, with a movie playing on my TV for company. For the most part, I was good at classes. I just wasn't good at college.

My last summer internship led to my first real job, an assistant position at an independent film company. The pay was minimal and the hours were nuts, but such was the life of these, the coolest of the cool kids. *Sex and the City* was for high school. I was a postgrad now. I'd taken courses on Jim Jarmusch and watched the entire Kiéslowski canon in a month. I had new icons to emulate: Sofia Coppola, Charlotte Gainsbourg, and whoever had the weirdest, most naked performance at Sundance that year. I had the right taste and knowledge, and I knew what names to drop. But there was still one thing I needed to join that crowd—or around a hundred things I needed to lose.

"What happened?" Judy tilted her head, dismayed.

"I don't know. College."

Judy whipped out her legal pad and once again begged me to follow the food plan and lose the weight, once and for all, *please*. I looked down at my hands and remembered what she'd told me years ago: It would only get harder as I got older. Already, I knew she was right. I'd resisted this appointment for weeks. But Judy's plan had gotten me as close to thin as I'd ever been, and I needed to get back in her zone and stay there. She tore the paper off her pad, scribbled with food rules identical to the ones I'd broken back in college, and handed it to me with a grim smile.

"Just do this—don't think about it too hard. Just do it so you can get on with your life."

I nodded. I knew, at last, what life I wanted and who I wanted to be in it: my boss.

Cal was a young director, already famous in certain circles and associated with people who were famous in all circles. She and her friends were part of the particular subset of socialites who had nice apartments and thousand-dollar handbags, but never any cash on hand. They always had tickets to Fashion Week, but sat in the second row. Then they went to dinner with the people who sat in the front row. I know, because I made the reservations.

"Wine time!"

Cal and I met in her Tribeca loft most afternoons to work out her schedule and go over my to-do lists (buy more mustard bath powder, book facial, drop shoes at the shoe guy). While working at the production company, I'd assisted her on a film, and when shooting was over, I simply refused to stop assisting her. Working on a set is bonding, and I'd bonded to her like an orphaned baby monkey. She was the older, savvier, funnier, famous-er version of the self I hoped to become. And she liked me just enough that I would have done anything to make her like me more.

"The usual?" I asked.

"Yep."

The usual. I loved that we had a usual. The usual was a bottle of Côtes du Rhône, whatever they had around fifteen dollars. I'd call the wine store to deliver two bottles, then take a cigarette out of Cal's pack.

"Do you want a snack?"

She pulled a bowl of grapes out of the fridge. Just a nice little ceramic bowl filled with already washed grapes. Like everything else she did, it seemed impossibly elegant. I could barely be bothered to take grapes out of the bag, let alone rinse them and put them in a bowl. If I ate grapes, that is.

"I'm not allowed to eat those."

She looked at the bowl then raised a threaded, auburn eyebrow.

"Aren't we about to drink wine?"

"Well. I guess, yeah."

"Made of grapes, you realize."

"It's fine."

It was fine because I didn't plan on eating anything else that day. Once Cal called "wine time," the workday was done and we'd spend the next few hours drinking Côtes du Rhône out of the mismatched gold-leaf cups she'd picked up in Marrakech.

"I don't want to live here anymore," she declared, looking around the apartment. "Do you want to live here?"

"Really?"

"Yeah, I mean, I'm in Paris half the time anyway. You could just sublet in case I ever want to come back."

My stomach clenched at the thought of Cal moving away permanently, but the thought of living in her perfumed home, walking barefoot across her splintery hardwood floors to pull a bowl of freshly washed grapes out of her fridge, thrilled me. Future Me would be able to eat grapes. She would be able to eat everything, but not be bothered to eat much of anything. She'd subsist on nine-dollar yogurts and sparkling rosé. She'd sweat out a hangover with a spin class, then meet a friend for coffee but order a tea. She'd be Cal, but with dark blonde hair instead of dark red. (Unless, maybe, dark red would look good on me.)

Like most nights, 8 p.m. marked the end of wine time, and Cal and I polished off our final glasses while she put together an outfit for the evening. Cal had a chic little wardrobe made up of gifts and friend-discounted clothes. My own was greatly supplemented by a bounty of her castoffs: battered Marc Jacobs totes, a chartreuse scarf that flattered no one's skin tone but that cost more at retail than my rent, and a pair of platform heels that almost fit. They would fit, surely, when I was sixty pounds lighter. Perhaps losing weight didn't take your feet from a size 9 to a size 6.5, but I kept the shoes neatly perched in the front of my closet, just in case.

I hung around while Cal groomed herself for her night out, keeping up a chatter of tales from my little life, or what small part of it didn't involve her. I'd recently moved into an apartment in Williamsburg which I was sharing with Sydney and her boyfriend, Jeff, both freshly graduated from acting school and not quite employed. My phone buzzed in my hand, and I looked down to see a text from my friend Debbie: *Dinner tonight?* I ignored it, not wanting to get distracted by a text conversation while I was hanging out with Cal.

"Are there any more cigarettes in there?" Cal nodded to the pack of American Spirits on her dresser, which I knew to be empty because I'd taken the last one.

"I can run out for more."

"Did you finish them?"

"I'm sorry."

She smirked at me in the mirror.

"You know smoking doesn't actually make you thin, right?"

I laughed. I laughed whenever I felt caught, and it was often.

Once, she'd let me tag along to a fancy friend's Christmas party and caught me ogling the Oscar in the corner ("Do you want me to take your picture with it?"). Another time, I'd made a dumb, new-kid joke about cocaine in the gift bags at Sundance, and she turned to her boyfriend and said, "Kelsey's perfect, did you know?"

I watched Cal finish the final stages of her routine. She never brushed her hair, only flipped it around in a mist of soft-scented serum, and her face was bare, save for a red-velvet mouth, but when she was done she looked like a character who'd stepped out of Joan Didion's Corvette: rangy and tall and an hour late for the party, but who checks the time? My phone hummed again and I pushed it quietly into my pocket.

"I like that dress." I liked all the dresses. This one was black, tight in the middle and drapey on the top.

"Yeah? I was going to donate it."

"No way, I'll take it!" Cal eyebrowed me again and I rolled my eyes, laughing extra hard. "Come on! For inspiration."

"Lady, there's no greater wardrobe than just being thin. I know we're not supposed to say that, but it's just the truth. You don't need this dress. When you're skinny you'll be able to wear track pants and look amazing."

"I know, right?"

"You'll get there, I can tell. You already have half the ass you used to." She turned around and squirted my head with her perfume. "You'll go full-blown Nicole Richie, and then we'll have to reverse you!"

Cal and I walked down the narrow steps of her building and into the thick evening air breezing in, sluggish and mineral, off the Hudson. She looked down the block for a taxi. I waited. Some nights she invited me along on whatever plans she had. I'd come home hours later wondering: *Should I tell my friends about spilling a drink on Kirsten Dunst's shoes while crawling around on the floor of the Mercer Hotel looking for the tube of lip balm that somebody threw across the table to make a point about tipping? Or was that the kind of thing where you had to be there?*

"Where are you headed?" I asked, fishing for my invite.

"Just an opening thing."

"Nice!" I couldn't contain my exclamation points around her.

"You have plans?"

I thought about Debbie's text floating in my phone. "Dinner with friends at this new pizza place," I decided, thinking of the restaurant we kept talking about going to. "They make their own mozzarella."

"Ooh, glad you steered clear of those grapes!"

I laughed like the idiot idiot *idiot* I was. A cab pulled up beside us and Cal squeezed me tight. Her late-'80s implants crushed my chest but I'd never be the one to stop hugging first.

"'Night, sweetie." She blew a quick *mwah* into the air and hopped in the cab. "Enjoy your weekend."

Softly drunk, I walked toward the L train reviewing the evening in my mind. Had I said anything extra stupid? How was her mood when we said good-bye? Had I pushed the boundaries of our weird professional friendship and become an annoyance yet? Or was I still in?

I took out my phone to answer Debbie's text at last: *Sorry, just saw this! Crazy day, I'm so beat. Dinner tomorrow?*

I popped into Tasti D-Lite before getting on the subway, ordering a medium vanilla which was really a *huge* vanilla, and covering it in raspberry sauce. None of this was on Judy's list, but at least it had *lite* in the name. And raspberries were fruit. Anyway, I'd been good so far that day, eating a plain old chicken breast with Brussels sprouts for lunch. I ordered it the same as Cal—no sauce, and just a splash of vinegar on the greens. True, I was filled with grape-based wine, but wasn't it better, then, to eat something so I could get up early, not too hung over, and hit the gym? Or maybe I'd just work out tonight? I wasn't that drunk.

I sat on the train making promises to myself, while spooning cool gobs of the soft-serve into my mouth and listening to an audiobook of *The Sheltering Sky*, a title Cal had explained was mandatory reading. Exiting the train at Graham Avenue, I stopped at the deli and bought a bag of sweet potato chips, crunching through them on the five-minute walk home, then dumping the empty bag into a trash can before heading into my building.

The living room smelled like Mexican takeout as I passed through, calling a hello to Sydney and Jeff through their closed door. I kicked my shoes off and into my bedroom, then toe-heeled into the kitchen. In the refrigerator was a pot of leftover tomato-y chicken and rice, which I'd made the Saturday before, when the three of us had stayed in the apartment all day watching a *Law & Order: SVU* marathon. It was cold and tasted like the fridge, but I wasn't going to eat an entire serving anyway. I leaned back on the counter, listening to the laugh track from Sydney and Jeff's television. Most nights they caught the reruns of *Fresh Prince of Bel-Air*, and sometimes I stood in the doorway, watching with them. Not tonight, though.

I picked cold hunks of chicken off the bone and nibbled lightly until the pot was mostly empty, but not so empty that I couldn't cover it with a lid and put it back in the fridge. I washed the cold greasiness off my hands, then scrubbed my face hard with a grainy, peach-scented soap.

In bed, I turned on the television and chose a *Sex and the City* episode at random from HBO On Demand (I only ever watched reruns), then curled up sideways on my unmade bed, finally, absolutely full. I was more than full, in fact. I was nauseated and growing more so by the minute. Ten minutes into the show, the discomfort became impossible to ignore. *I won't be able to sleep*, I thought. *Then tomorrow I'll be too tired for the gym and too dazed to work on my screenplay. And forget having dinner with Debbie.* The day would be shot. Then there was the scarier thought beneath my worries, too sick and jittery to really think: All day, I would have to bear the burden of that soft-serve-potato-chip-cold-chicken incident.

I hadn't intended any of it. It had been a series of accidental slips, little inklings I'd have consciously ignored had I been fully conscious. But I was tipsy and afraid, caught up in what a mess I'd made of myself. I was almost twenty-four years old and no thinner, no wiser, no closer to a single goal, than I had been in high school. I hadn't grown at all, but got fatter by the minute. And here I was, eating my way out of the best diet I'd ever been on. I saw Judy's face and Mom's face. I saw my father's sad, earnest eyes, watching me step out of the Jetway during our visit last year as I tried to hide my belly with my overnight bag.

I took the towel from the back of my door and headed for the bathroom, fast. It wasn't just my stomach now; every cell in my body felt nauseated and shaky. The back of my neck burned and my fingers felt dumb and clammy as I pulled my hair into a sloppy bun. I didn't vomit to get rid of the food, but of this hateful cacophony of feeling, flooding out of my nasty brain and all over me. I never could stand a stomachache, and was always terrified of throwing up as a child. The act itself was a momentary nightmare, my body absolutely out of my control. But in these moments when I did control it, taking deep, preparatory breaths, then applying the lightest tickle to that hard spot in the back of my throat, it was a manageable terror. And, when it was over, oh how instant came the calm.

I didn't do it often. At most, I allowed myself this ritual maybe twice a month. But any more than that would have been a problem with a name. As it was, I only vomited to relieve the worst of the stomachache nights. I was sick, I told myself (and my roommates). Perhaps I'd eaten something funny earlier in the day, or maybe it was just tension and alcohol, but what twenty-three-year-old wasn't stressed and drinking too much? Either way, if a person vomited they were sick—sick, and off the hook. That's the rule of puking.

All I had to do now was clean up. I sprayed bleach all over the bathroom and then scrubbed myself down in the shower. A shower made everything feel better. Back in my room, I made up my bed and tucked myself in neatly with a glass of ice water and a bottle of Tums. I didn't have to do anything but feel better. I didn't have to worry about anything but rest. I had license to cancel dinner with Debbie the next day, guilt free. *Ugh, was up all night puking,* I'd text her in the morning before I spent my Saturday watching television in bed, maybe cleaning my room if I felt up to it, then watching a movie on the couch with Sydney and Jeff, if they were home. If they weren't, then fine, more couch for me.

When I did manage to leave my messy nest, I gave my friends the highlights reel of my nights out with Cal. It was a good one; I spilled drinks on some *pretty* famous people. But the long, numbed-out nights between my bedroom and my bathroom and Tasti D-Lite were the real story of my twenties—or as real as every trip to Paris and dinky credit at the end of an independent film. Kelsey Miller: Assistant to the Director. I told that story to everyone. Kelsey Miller: Ice Cream-Puker, Couch-Sitter, Chronic Plans-Canceler. That story sat balled up in my belly, and I kept it well fed.

In truth, it was another secret that had been keeping me sick for years. It was the only one I could not tell, too lethal a poison to release. But every day I felt it rising higher in my throat, so close to spilling out of me. Any day now, I would open my wretched mouth and ruin us all.

Chapter 11

Telling

The first time William grabbed me, I was eight years old. It was the end of another dinner party at our house, the adults gathering coats and deciding who would drive, while I made the rounds for goodnight hugs. Good nights were mandatory for me, a huggy kid. I found him in Mom and Steve's darkened bedroom and reached up. He put his arms around me for a quick hug. Then, as if by natural impulse, he reached down and clamped his hands over my butt, so hard it made a slapping sound. He pulled me in and pressed me against his crotch, squeezing my bottom in a rough, whole-handed clench. I was wearing my favorite nightgown—a frilly, floor-length shift, perfect for wandering the house in my *Secret Garden* fantasies. The fabric was overwashed and thin, and I felt naked against his body. He leaned down into my neck and growled, a hungry "Mmmm."

It was over in seconds. He planted a wet bourbon kiss on my face and released me. I felt nothing. I felt hands everywhere. I stumbled out of the room on dumb feet. In my bedroom, I took off the nightgown, now reeking with the smell of grown-up party and someone else's body, if only in my mind. I wanted to wash his bourbon breath out of my hair, but more than that I wanted to sleep. My brain was still awash in panic, waves of whiteness pulsing across each thought. And my body was somewhere else.

I'd seen him do the same thing to his wife. At the end of many nights, she'd laugh and brush his tipsy hand away, rolling her eyes at this silly husband of hers. He must have simply thought I was her—that's all. Because it was dark. Because he was a little more than tipsy tonight, and I was a little too developed for a girl my age.

His name wasn't William, but his real name doesn't matter. What matters is that his was one of the most familiar faces in my life, and he is an unavoidable presence in my story. He'd been a close family friend since our Sleepy Hollow days. In another family, I might have been instructed to call him "uncle," but we rolled our eyes at such formalities between children and adults. I'd known and trusted him for my entire conscious life. So, I knew it had to be an accident, and one that I could have prevented. Why hadn't I jumped back and turned on the lights? Why had I asked him for a hug in the first place? Drunk people didn't know what they were doing, and if I told somebody now, it would be so embarrassing. Either way, it was a one-time case of mistaken identity, and next time I'd know to keep out of the way.

This became the little litany I ran through each time it happened. Though it kept happening, it never got much worse than that first incident, and I had an excuse at the ready every single time. He'd confused me with his wife again. He had so much to drink that he didn't realize where his hand was. Or else he was being affectionate and it was my own disgusting mind making something out of nothing.

After all, my clothes were always on, and his touch so fast and sloppy. With little effort, I could shrink the incident down into meaninglessness—an accidental collision in a darkened hallway. It was nothing like what happened in books or movies. There was no creeping into my bedroom at night. No promises of candy.

I got good at keeping out of his way. I'd see his eyes turn glassy and leave the room. If his friendly shoulder squeeze began to drift downward, I faked a coughing fit. I learned to cover up so his eyes, forever dropping to my breasts, would land on an oversized sweatshirt. Sometimes he'd quickly pop into the bathroom while I showered, ("Oops, I'm not looking! Just need to grab a tissue!"), and I'd crouch low behind the translucent shower curtain, holding my knees to my chest.

By middle school, it was instinct. At every party, dinner, and holiday, I knew where he was in the room. I was vigilant enough for the both of us, though he was never careful. A couple cocktails into the evening, his hands might wander right out in the open.

Sometimes we were mere feet from my mother, in a room full of people, none of whom seemed to see a hand where it shouldn't be, and thank God for that. Because, hadn't Mom told me that my lipstick was too flashy? Hadn't I picked this skirt because it made me look grown-up?

Occasionally, I'd slip, mistime my entrance and wind up seated next to him on the couch. Nine times out of ten, it wouldn't be so bad. He might just put an arm around me, rub my shoulder soft and slowly, and ask me about school. But sometimes—just a few times—he'd lean in toward my face with a goofy smile, then close his eyes. Was it friendly? Familial? *It must be, of course*, I always told myself. But then I'd remember the grabbing and the staring and suddenly realize he was far too close. Wriggling out from under his arm and jumping off the sofa, I'd produce a high-pitched laugh, while his face melted into the pout of a sour, rejected frat boy.

That's how I described the incidents to my therapist, years later: "It was just like being a girl at a frat party when it gets a little rowdy."

"Except kids don't go to drunken frat parties," he replied. And I nodded in that way you do when your therapist points out how obviously shitty your childhood was.

I was three months out of college by the time I started saying it out loud. Though already living in Brooklyn, I went home many weekends, in part to stock up on toilet paper, but mostly to see my mom. Her manic cycle of ups and downs was still the extreme weather pattern in my life, and though I feared what I might find whenever I went home, not knowing was far more terrifying. Not even the worry over crossing paths with William could keep me away, and I inevitably did, each time. He might come up behind me while I dressed a salad for a dinner party, and put a hand low around my hip. I'd squeeze out sideways before it could move any farther, before this became another moment I had to try to forget. Those white waves of panic returned as if on cue, pulsing out that awful, necessary numbness through my body. I'd jump away to open the refrigerator and dig around for a jar of imaginary mustard. He'd click his tongue and open his mouth in exasperation.

"I can't say hello to you? What?"

"What?! Nothing!" I'd chirp into the fridge. Grumbling, he'd slouch out of the room.

By then, the truth was leaking out of me. During late-night conversations with Chrissy or Debbie, I might blurt out a casual reference to that first incident: my nightgown, the painful squeezing, how crazy drunk he must have been to mistake a kid for his wife, gross! They didn't laugh, though. They sat in shocked and awkward silence; unsure of how to navigate the little grenade I'd tossed into our evening with such nonchalance. It was that silence I both dreaded and desired. I thrilled at the discomfort in their eyes. Finally, finally, somebody noticed.

It was their solemn faces that gave me permission to tell, and then I couldn't stop. I was spilling out the secret in clumsy puddles wherever I went. Four glasses of wine at my writing group and out it tumbled, turning three astonished sets of eyes in my direction. One night, I stayed up with Cal, swapping asshole-parent stories and childhood-trauma tales. She nodded at my rushed admission and lit a cigarette. "You know, pretty much everyone's been molested, though."

"Oh, of course, of course!" I hastened to apologize, like I did whenever anyone shrugged it off or simply nodded. Then I'd complete the humiliating routine of grabbing my purse, saying *Sorry*, heading out the door—and *I'm sorry*, again—then drafting the official so-sorry-so-embarrassed e-mail on the subway.

When someone replied instead with an open, concerned tone, I melted into tears. I overstayed my welcome at many a dinner table, hysterical with relief. After those nights, I drafted a variation on the so-sorry e-mail, adding a few dozen thank-yous.

Telling people felt like a gamble, but one I could no longer stop myself from doing. Rewatching *The Ice Storm* with Jon one night, I felt the panic rise.

"Turn it off, this is so fucking stupid!" I told him.

"Well, excuse me, film school."

"Seriously, why are we watching this?"

"Because it's dark and moody and really great? And you picked it?"

We spent the rest of the sweaty summer evening on his roof, sharing cigarettes and tall glasses of ice water as I uncoiled and began to speak.

We'd rarely had this kind of talk. Jon and I could spend whole weekends arguing the feminist ramifications of *The Piano* versus *The Piano Teacher* versus *Showgirls*, vent about work problems, or conjugate a text from his latest not-quite-boyfriend, but it took ten years and an Ang Lee movie for me to get real with one of my oldest, closest friends.

"I'm sorry," I concluded, noting his silence.

"That's okay." Jon shrugged, but not in the dismissive way that made me want to disappear.

"You're, like, *never* going to invite me over for a movie again."

He shook his head a little but didn't tell me to stop. He didn't turn concerned and sympathetic, or fill the silence with a joke. In the quiet, I looked up and he didn't look away.

"I'm still here."

Eventually, I shared the story with my father, but only after months of worry and hesitation, knowing just how deeply it would wound and shock him. But when I finally blurted it out across his dining room table one weekend, his face melted into anguish. He looked down and nodded.

"I thought maybe that was what was going on."

"You did?"

"Yeah," he sniffed. "When you started gaining weight and everything."

He got up and kissed the top of my head with shaky tenderness, whispering his sorrowful apologies. I could hardly bear the weight of his sadness in that moment. It wasn't until weeks later that it occurred to me: *You thought maybe this was going on?*

*

There was one person I could never and would never tell. All throughout this klutzy phase of telling the truth in bits and pieces, I kept a mouthful of caveats between the two of us. "The William stuff," as I always called it, could hardly be defined as real abuse or, Jesus, *molestation*. It wasn't as bad as what happened to other girls. Yeah, it had screwed me up a little bit, but that was what therapy was for. Telling her would only make things worse, I was sure. And I was right.

In the end, I told my mother only because she finally asked. I can't think how the conversation started. Maybe we were talking about sex or dating. She was never the kind of mom who would harangue me over not having a boyfriend, and she rarely treaded into the territory of my blank romantic life. I still don't know just what she knew or how long she'd known it, but one sticky September afternoon, the question came loose.

"Did William ever…" The two of us sat on the front porch of our house in Adirondack chairs, tacky with humidity. She ashed her cigarette into a ceramic turquoise dish and took a breath. I looked out across the yard in disbelief that the conversation I'd waited fourteen years for was finally going to happen while the lawn guy mowed the grass.

"Did William ever touch you in an inappropriate way?"

My heart beat the white waves out across my chest. But there was only one answer.

"Yes."

She squinched her eyes closed and tucked her chin low into her chest, a flinch in slow motion. She exhaled a long breath through the O of her lips, and every nerve inside me throbbed, watching the bomb land, the force of its terrible impact, ravaging my mother and rendering her silent.

"It was just a few times, mostly just grabbing. That's all." Anything, anything that would take it back, a little. But it was too late. The truth lands hard and the landscape is never the same afterward.

Finally, she spoke.

"It's going to take me a while to process this. I want to respond the right way and I can't right now. I hope you understand. It's too much. It's too much." She lifted her hands, pressed the palms to her chest and shook her head hard: a brief, blonde hurricane.

"Of course," I soothed. I wanted to reach for her and I wanted to run. She returned to her cigarette and stared out at the yard, the lawn mower rumbling in the distance. I looked to see if her hand shook when she took a drag, but she was all too still. I got up, the moment no longer mine, and retreated into the dark, cool house.

For a few days, I waited for her response. I suppose I thought there would be another talk on the porch, her carefully chosen words offering just the balm I needed. But it never happened. It was my bomb to drop, and me who had rendered her stunned. Why on earth had I expected anything but fallout?

Often, I remind myself of that caveat I gave her: It *was* just a handful of times. It was *just* grabby hands and staring and almost-kisses, which I'd *always* managed to duck out of. Having practiced since the age of eight, I was good at stopping an "incident" while it was still minor. That way it could always stay ambiguous in my mind. That way, I could sit across from him at the Christmas dinner or birthday party, and forgive myself for fighting the urge to get up and run and run until I catapulted right off the earth. Because one of us had to behave themselves or this semblance of normalcy would collapse. If I didn't act polite and unbothered, William would sulk and people would ask questions, and, oh God, everyone would know. They would have to look directly at what they'd looked away from, over and over again.

I didn't want to be looked at. As I grew into and then out of adolescence, I still daydreamed of being beautiful, flat-tummied and B-cupped. Theoretically, I wanted to be noticed, but not yet—not until I was thin. It would all have to wait until I was thin, because this body was damaged and repugnant. It was disloyal and obnoxious, this body that had made me into a woman before the age of ten.

Each time I tried on a fitted blouse, I'd remember my mother's side eye that time I came out of my room dressed for school in a V-neck:

"Sorry, babe, you're just a little too busty for that one," she said, and stuck out her chest, aping a cartoonish sexy walk I wasn't doing. "Oh, I'm kidding! I'm sorry, jeez Louise!" she called after me, when I hurried off to change.

Even worse, I'd remember the humiliation that happened if she didn't catch me, but William did: the summer I was twelve and he cracked a joke about my "porn-star-cheerleader look"—a pink plaid Delia*s skirt and matching sweater that I'd picked out for a party at the country club. He put a just-kidding arm around my shoulders and laughed too hard at his own joke, until the others laughed along with him. If he'd had one less bourbon, maybe he wouldn't have said it. Or, maybe if my top wasn't so bright.

This is the sickness of abuse—the infection he gave me when he took that first handful of my childish flesh.

Motherfucker. You made a liar out of me.

Even here, in my own pages, I cannot tell the whole truth, burying his name in anonymity. I tell myself that to expose him would hurt innocent others, and so hiding him is a generous act. But that's only part of the reason. Mostly, it's because I am afraid, still. Every time I tell someone, a wretched voice comes shrieking from the corner of my mind: *Are you making too much of this? Are you just looking for attention, little girl? Why must you rock this boat? Can't you see it's hard enough for everyone without you opening your big, fat mouth about a few over-the-clothes touches?*

That's the voice that keeps me quiet, and for that I am ashamed. I want to be braver. What happened to me was nowhere near as bad as what happened to so many other women who *have* named names, and I feel like a coward in their company.

Because, even after all these years of processing and self-helping myself out of the hole, I still sometimes wonder if my blouse was too bright. I still see my mother's face seize up on the porch that day, and wish, for a searing second, that I could un-tell her.

It is still a thing I rarely name. It's always been "the William stuff," when I mention it to friends or therapists, or the guy who didn't understand why I suddenly went cold, why I couldn't just relax and he wouldn't put his hand there again, no pressure, he promised. Nameless or not, I have to tell, because this is a thread inside the messy, knotted fabric of my story with food. It's one of the things I buried in cold lumps of mashed potato, eaten in sneaky fingerfuls by the light of the refrigerator. It was the undertaste in every numbing bite, barely there but undeniable and caustic to the tongue. It's the shame I covered in extra pounds, the features of my face obscured as I sank deeper into my flesh.

In that attempt to hide inside myself, though, it seemed both me and my secret became all the more visible. My parents never managed to see the hands on my body, but they stared in horror as that body grew before their eyes. Friends must have heard it in my weepy voice, so desperate for their validation. And, surely, every guy I ever liked could see it written all over my nervous, moony face. The secret was as obvious and present as the belly I tried to cover with tightly folded hands. Hiding was a futile struggle. The only remedy was to tell.

Chapter 12

The Mushy Stuff

A ll that said, I *totally* wanted a boyfriend.

My measly romantic history didn't start until my middle to late-ish twenties. The only exception was Jacob Rensch in ninth grade. He'd been my boyfriend in name only, for ten days, and he went to another school. He was real. But everything else about the relationship was pretty much imaginary. We hung out in person twice before our e-mail breakup, which I recall as the greatest relief of my life. I got to soak wistfully in the bathtub and write three-chord songs on my acoustic guitar, just feeling as hard as I could. At that point, all I really wanted out of a relationship was the excuse to wallow when it ended.

My midtwenties self had plenty of good reasons to excuse and explain away the fact that I didn't date. High school and college were supposed to be the relationship training ground. But the male population of my small boarding school had been almost entirely gay. So, by college, I had no experience in flirtatious socializing with males of any kind, let alone the loud and typically beer-soaked males of a large university. Anyway, I was far too occupied with internships, dieting, and hiding in my room to go out there and try to wow 'em with my dazzling knowledge of early Sondheim and *My So-Called Life* trivia. I'd skipped the dating practice and decided I'd figure it out later, in the real world. Then, I took one look around New York City—my chosen corner of the real world—and thought I'd just keep lying low for a while. It wasn't really "hiding in your room" when you had a whole apartment, right?

The truth is, I never dated because it seemed absolutely terrifying and awful (and, it kind of is). I told myself I was focused on my job and my friendships and all that. I was, but also I was just plain scared—of rejection, of attachment, of all the singular humiliation that comes with putting yourself out there and saying, *I like you. Do you like me?* Oh yeah, and when I was a kid, someone I trusted messed with me in a sexual way. There, am I off the hook?

When I'm ready, I thought. *When I'm thin.* After *The Secret* came out and the entire world became briefly obsessed with vision boards and manifesting, I wrote a thousand-word letter to the universe describing the perfect life I would have and the perfect guy I would meet. He would understand my history and my lack of experience, and adore me anyway. He would just *get* me, and his love and acceptance would be a panacea that cured all my anxiety, emotional eating, and body shame—oh, but I would already be thin when I met him, obviously. The universe had to make me thin *first*, but that was a whole other manifestation letter. That one read something like: *SKINNY PLEASE NOW. Love, Kelsey.*

I don't know if it was the letter or the fact that I finally signed up for an OkCupid account, but somewhere around my twenty-fifth birthday I dipped a tentative toe into the dating pool. Even if I had manifested the guy of my dreams, he probably didn't have my address, and anyway, my buzzer didn't work. So, fine, *fine.* I'd try leaving the house.

The great thing about dating is that nobody is good at it and everyone hates it. If nothing else, that's one thing you always have in common with the person across the table from you. I was relieved to discover that starting so late in the game only made me slightly more terrible at dating than everyone else. That said, if your heart's not in it, Internet dating can feel like a miserable temp job where the only highlight is online Sudoku breaks. But I kept at it. I didn't need to find The One, but I needed to have dated *some*one. I needed to be able to say, "this guy I went out with," and then tell a funny story about a futon. I couldn't go to another party with friends and not be able to join the conversation about whether you should call or text the next day. And, seriously, I needed to have had sex. My lack of physical experience was rapidly becoming another big, bad secret I sat on. It felt okay being a virgin in college. It felt okay-not-great being one at twenty-two. By twenty-six, it felt like a national emergency. OkCupid wasn't cutting it; I needed to get FEMA on this.

I'd had a few groping experiences toward the end of college, thanks to the miracle of alcohol. And there were a few more during my online-dating phases, which ebbed and flowed for a few years, like a tide controlled entirely by my dieting cycle. When I was off the wagon, I barely browsed the websites and ignored any incoming messages. When I was in the diet zone, I seized the skinny day. Even if my body was only slightly less fat, it was on its way to thin, and therefore I was allowed to let someone else see it. Or, parts of it. Though only if I had full creative authority over all wardrobe and lighting and set direction. I was a maniacal auteur when it came to naked time.

Yes, everyone is bad at dating, but it's particularly clunky when you're a twenty-seven-year-old virgin who hates her body and will only leave the house if she has enough Points left for the day. I went on plenty of first dates, and a handful of second ones, but whenever things got remotely intimate, I immediately lost any modicum of cool. If the guy looked into my eyes too long or reached for my hand, I went on autopilot. I simply couldn't tolerate the tension of are-we-gonna-kiss-or-aren't-we, so more often than not, I just went for it myself. Even if the guy initiated kissing, I almost always let it escalate to street-makeout to cab-makeout to couch-makeout to topless. It had nothing much to do with desire. I couldn't bear the closeness of his eyes looking into mine, but I could take my shirt off, no problem. I was just doing what everyone else did, but faster.

"You know you don't have to make out with everyone, like, immediately. Right?" Debbie asked me one night, as we smashed up avocadoes for one of our traditional guacamole-and-embarrassing-movie nights. Whenever I was out on a date, I would wish I could just be home, eating snacks with Debbie and watching *How the West Was Fun,* starring the Olsen twins.

"Yeah."

"You don't even have to kiss them or anything."

"Of course, I know that." And, of course, I did. When I had this conversation with any of my friends, they all seemed to think I was succumbing to pressure. I was, but not the kind they were thinking. None of the guys I dated ever forced me into so much as hand holding. The pressure that pushed me was all in my own head. I *had* to catch up. I had to hit some milestones so I could just chill out and quit panicking about everyone else moving in together, breaking up, considering if and when they should have kids. Kids?! When I'd never even purchased condoms?! Yeah, sorry friends. I'll make out with everyone, everywhere.

But then I'd leave. Because, as soon as a guy touched me, my body floated away. It was that same, familiar feeling I got when William first grabbed me: a deadened, automatic separation from myself. I went through all the motions, but it felt like an unconscious habit; like washing a sinkful of dishes, while my mind went on to the next chore, just wanting to get it all done. Eventually, I learned about "dissociation," and how it's not an uncommon experience during sexual contact for people like me.

It always ended the same way.

"I haven't had sex with anyone," I'd blurt out of the blue.

"Oh. Okay."

End of date. Whether or not sex even came up, I routinely dropped this lead balloon on our evening—sometimes even throwing in a casual reference to childhood sexual trauma, just to be sure I killed all remaining boners. Then, I put on my shoes and went home to shower and watch *My Girl 2* in bed with a bag of cookies. All of it—the cab home, the hot shower, the cookies, the sweatpants—composed my ritual of simultaneous punishment and reward. I was embarrassed, certainly. But mostly I was relieved that my embarrassment was so great and so justified that I could forget the whole night ever happened, and never have to worry about hearing from the guy ever again. In the big picture, these dates only made my anxiety about never having had a relationship even more extreme. In the short term, I just had to run.

It took a couple years and a billion more hours of hashing out the William stuff in therapy, but eventually I let go of the Makeout-Flee system and started dating like a slightly less crazy person. And, one week after my twenty-eighth birthday, I finally had sex. Turns out, the only real problem with losing your virginity at twenty-eight is that when you text your friends at 3 a.m. to tell them, they're all already asleep.

Like all the guys I went out with, I met Jared online. He was a really nice guy with a crazy schedule and a recent ex-girlfriend and no hesitation in telling me he wasn't ready for anything serious. While some women might have considered this a deal breaker, it sounded just about perfect to me. The timing was right, too. Thanks to another round with Weight Watchers, I was at my lowest weight in years, right at the peak of the New Diet Buzz. Fearing that I'd turn fat again at any moment, I moved fast. He had no problem with that.

When I gave Jared the whole I-haven't-had-sex-and-here's-why spiel, he didn't panic. He asked a few questions. Yes, I had done "other stuff"—the kind of stuff that would make a lot of people consider me not exactly virginal. But the whole intercourse thing still felt like the big box I hadn't checked. Again, he clarified where we stood in terms of casual dating, and again I asked myself: *Is this okay?* And it really was. I wanted a real boyfriend sometime, definitely. But at that moment I wasn't ready for a relationship, either. I needed something simple and flexible in order to get ready for the real deal. I'd missed out on all that careless sex in high school and college, and now it loomed too large in my mind. I had to have sex without it being meaningful sex, in order to realize that sex wasn't the most meaningful thing.

Jared and I hung out every couple weeks, seeing movies or grabbing dinner, then going back to his place. After each time, I left with a low-level nervousness about whether or not it would be the last. But we'd been so up-front with each other and we were so loosely attached that it felt like the first half of all those movies where the couple tries to just sleep together without entanglement—minus the second half where everyone ends up crying and/or married. People refer to "fuck buddies," as if that scenario is every commitment-phobic man's fantasy. Guess what? Women can be scared and horny, too.

Truly, I don't know if that's the right term for what Jared was to me. In my heart, he is the one who eased me into the world of real dating and eventually taught me that what I wanted was something real—good, bad, and complicated.

Then I met Harry, and things got real, fast.

The story of how we met is partially magical coincidence and partially a product of the cold, calculating hand of social media. One winter morning, just weeks after I started seeing Jared, I got an OkCupid message from a cute guy with glasses and a neatly shaved head. I recognized the picture from somewhere, and five minutes of Facebook research revealed his name was Harry and he was an old colleague of my friend Jon's. (Jon's verdict: "Good guy! Kinda quiet." This was all he could give me after they'd worked together for three years. Dudes are the worst at this.)

It was a pretty perfect message as far as online dating goes: brief, dry, not generic and not icky. Seventy-five percent of the time, I got messages from dudes saying things like, "Hi, I like Kiéslowski, too. By the way, do you have huge calves?"

But, nice as this guy's message might have been, I just wasn't looking to jump back into the online-dating hustle at that moment. I already had Jared to *kind of* date, and more important, I had work to do. For months, I'd been trying to break out of assistant limbo and into a writing career. All of a sudden, I was busy with new freelance writing gigs and applying for every Internet-writer position I could find. By the time I was hired at Refinery29 that spring, I'd let the message slip my mind entirely. I barely had time to *kind of* date, let alone juggle.

A few months later, though, I found myself chatting with a dry, not-generic, and not-icky guy at Jon's birthday party.

"I'm Kelsey!" I called over the din. We were smushed into the crowded nook of an East Village cocktail bar.

"Gary!" He called back.

After that, I have no idea what we talked about. I was too distracted by the manic little cheerleader bouncing around my head, shrieking, "He's cute! He's talking to you! You've been chatting for more than five minutes ohmygodohmygod!" Naturally, I had to get out of there.

"I'm going to go!" I yelled, in what I hoped was a friendly way.

"Oh."

"I mean, I'm just going to go get another drink!"

"Oh, okay!"

I never came back. Whoever he was, he was too cute for comfort.

*

The next morning, it clicked. While catching up over hangover bagels, I told Jon about meeting his friend Gary, and how I had totally talked to him for five whole minutes.

"Who? Do you mean *Harry*?"

"No no, Gary. The guy with glasses in the white button-down."

"Yeah, that's Harry. I don't know a Gary. Who's named Gary anymore?"

That's when I finally figured out that Harry-not-Gary was the guy who messaged me on OkCupid months ago. And, that meant he thought I was cute, at least online. He'd talked to me for five minutes in real life, which meant he thought I was cute *and* not incredibly boring.

I sat staring agape at my bagel, putting the pieces together like a detective whose case just cracked wide open.

"He's a really good guy," Jon affirmed.

Given the evidence at hand, and the fact that I'd been the unresponsive jerk who'd ignored his message months ago, I decided to go ahead and add Harry as a Facebook friend. Next, I took it a step further, sending him a carefully crafted bashful message, saying something along the lines of, "Really nice talking to you the other night. PS: Sorry I ignored you." And, because he was indeed a good, not-generic, not-icky guy, he responded by asking me out. We had our first date a few days later at a Japanese restaurant in the East Village. After a couple hours of talking I found myself so nervous and excited by his sweet, subtle humor that I pulled the old make-out trick. We kissed on First Avenue, then in a taxi, then at his apartment. When I finally pulled away and told him I had to go home, he smiled sadly.

"Really? Why?"

"I want to see you again, okay?"

"Well, good, because you're gonna."

He pulled me back in close and locked eyes with me. Not for a second did I want to look away.

Ending things with Jared wasn't horrible, but it was sad. We both knew we could've been friends in other circumstances, but in the end, we just let go. Loose and intermittent as our fling was, it was still a connection and severing it hurt. But, even if there hadn't been a Harry, I knew it was time for me to stop dating in limbo. I was finally ready for the real deal.

And the real deal was *great*. It was hand holding and long talks and then running home to text my friends about the hand holding and long talks. We catapulted into love, taking each other on little adventure dates and half-seriously planning weekend trips. In mere weeks I moved past the phase of will-he-text-me-back anxiety and into the ease of knowing that he would. Harry was a rock, right from the start. There was no hesitation and no games. I was almost disappointed to discover what a straight shooter he was. Having grown up in a post–*Sex and the City* world, I expected narcissism, manipulation, or at the very least, a debilitating mommy issue we'd have to work through in order to get to the good part. But Harry came as advertised: a good one.

If Harry was happy with things moving fast, then I just wanted to go faster. We were both so bonkers for each other, I figured why not? Bring on the milestones! We had our first date in June, and by August, I'd dropped the L word. I raised the question of boyfriend-girlfriend status, oh, four thousand times, and though he knew we weren't there yet and wasn't in a rush to be, Harry never balked. In these moments, his calmness was what brought me back to earth—if only for a moment. I remembered this wasn't the kind of woman I was, and definitely not the kind I wanted to be. This was the behavior of a loopy teenager—not the independent adult I'd become over the last ten years, while my friends had paired off.

Still, if Harry brought out the giddy in me, he also brought out the frantic, high-speed maniac. The September night we finally became official, he leaned over in bed and mumbled in my ear:

"So, would you maybe wanna..."

"Say it!"

"...be my girlfriend?"

(Here again, I'll remind you that your adult friends may not appreciate 3 a.m. texts, no matter how exciting your news is.)

Of course, there's a downside to being with someone so demonstrably perfect: It really highlights your own imperfections. Despite the fact that Harry seemed to adore me as a whole, I knew there were things about me that he couldn't *actually* like. For instance: every part of my body.

It went well beyond turning the lights off and turning my back to him when I undressed, though I did both those things so frequently that one night he just went ahead and turned the lights off for me.

"Why do you want to turn the lights off?" I asked.

"I don't. But you always do, so..."

"Oh. I thought maybe you didn't like looking at me."

"What? That's crazy."

"I'm not crazy, I'm just uncomfortable!"

"Right, so I turned them off. Should I turn them back on?"

"No! Sorry! Thank you! I'm not crazy!"

Ah, the old I'm Not Crazy defense. I could have written a hundred analytical essays about the vitality of new wave feminism, but the second I became somebody's girlfriend, it was all, *I'm not crazy! Do you still love me?! I told you to turn the lights off, please and sorry!*

It turns out, you can love someone before you love yourself. It's just really uncomfortable for both of you. As Harry and I got closer, the issue of my unlovable body grew even bigger between us.

I felt my weight slowly creeping up in those first few months. There's just not as much time for relentless workouts and Points calculation when you're occupied with the full-time job of falling in love. And, the shameful truth, I came to realize, was that I had believed all those inane celebrity-interview quotes about how when someone loves you just as you are, all your food and body image issues just evaporate, absorbed by a cloud of a lover's acceptance— the greatest diet of all. I don't know what PR rep started this bull-shit rumor, but it seems every actress is obligated to repeat it at least once a year. It's just one of those mandatory quotes like, "I love French fries!" and "I don't believe in plastic surgery." Maybe it's all true, but I've never read a male celebrity profile that opens with a line about how pleasantly surprising it is that he ordered whole milk in his latte.

So, I waited for the power of love to heal my every self-doubt, growing more frustrated by the minute. I wasn't the only one. Going to sleep at night had become something akin to a wrestling match played entirely in the spooning position.

One night at his place, Harry cuddled up behind me and wrapped his arm around my middle: the danger zone. I reached for his hand, pretending an affectionate squeeze, then casually moved it off my stomach and onto my thigh. He played along for a minute, but while nodding off, his hand drifted back to my stomach—my flabby, floppy, stretch-marked stomach. It was my most unacceptable body part, the one I avoided all contact with. I thought I'd made progress the time I let him give me a raspberry, but the revolting, whoopee-cushion sound of it made my whole body cringe. I simply couldn't let him touch it while I slept; how would I suck it in all night?

The moment his hand fell back to my abdomen, I yanked it off and up to my chest. There. Surely, he'd prefer a handful of breast to belly. Harry sighed.

"What?"

"You never let me touch your tummy."

"Well, sorry. I don't like it."

"Why?"

"I just really don't like my stomach, okay? I don't want you to touch it."

Harry sat up. I turned onto my back, looking up at him in the dark.

"I don't want to, like, force you into anything. But I just don't get it. I've seen your body. I've seen your stomach."

"Why do you have to touch it, though? Why is it so important?"

"It's not so important, it's just... I don't know. We've been together for a while now."

I felt my eyes begin to fill, not in sadness but burning frustration.

"Yeah, so?"

"So, I'm going to want to touch your tummy."

"God. Fine."

"Oh, come on. You don't think you're being a little ridiculous?"

"Um, no. Don't you have parts of yourself you don't like?"

"I'm hairy. I don't love that."

"That's it?"

"I don't like my body hair! I have to get my whole upper body waxed just to go to the beach! It's embarrassing!"

"Well, see then?!" Point mine. Definitely.

"No, because I don't push you away whenever you come near it."

"I'm sorry. I don't mean to." I had no better excuse. "My stomach is just too disgusting."

Harry and I sat in silence for a minute waiting for someone to play the "I'm Not Crazy" card. Then, he leaned over and pushed up my T-shirt, exposing my stomach.

"Stop."

"Shhh. Just wait."

"If you're going to give me a raspberry right now..."

"I'm not going to give you a raspberry."

"I don't believe you."

"Baby, just trust me. Okay?"

It was a tall order, but I took a breath and watched as he leaned down over my exposed, lumpy belly. Very lightly, he kissed it. He kissed the spot beneath my ribs and all the way down to my navel. He kissed across my lower stomach, that wretched expanse where the stretch marks raked across my skin, then up and down my sides. Harry kissed every inch of my horrible flesh with a tenderness so great and loving, and all the while, my eyes stayed clenched tight. *I am loved*, a voice inside me declared. *Just close your eyes and get through this*, said another. *He's almost done.*

Seeing Harry so ardently love what I most loathed about myself was overwhelming. It threw my self-esteem into stark relief, exposing just how not-okay I was with me. He'd call me beautiful in the morning and I'd push my face into the pillow. Out of the blue, he'd pull me in for a kiss and I'd chalk it up to him just being an affectionate person, in general. More than once he'd tell me how happy I made him and I actually answered, "Why?" But these stumbling blocks aside, I knew that what we had was a very good and rare thing.

There was still that restless little nag in my head, always looking down the road to the next milestone and urging me to sprint for it. It only was a matter of months before we started talking about the possibility of moving in together. Well, I started talking about it. Why not? It seemed silly to take things slow when everything was so consistently rose-colored. Sure, I was struggling with some good old-fashioned self-hatred and had gained a terrifying fifteen pounds, but those things would work themselves out if I just kept plowing ahead and waited for the Love Diet to fix everything.

I was in the Buzz with someone else this time, riding even

higher than I'd been with that very first diet. I don't mean to say that falling in love was as depthless and cheap as the feeling I got from a new weight-loss plan. It was the most new and life-changing thing that had ever happened to me. But by then, I had lived my whole life in a dieter's cycle without even realizing it. I should have recognized a Buzz when I saw it, and I should have known what would come next. If I had, perhaps I could have braced us both.

Chapter 13

Hurricane Sex(ually Transmitted Infection)

The impending arrival of Hurricane Sandy, the worst natural disaster to hit New York City in centuries, sent the entire eastern seaboard into hesitant panic in late October 2012. Though many of us only half-believed in it, wondering if it was all just news hype, we still hit the grocery stores to stock up on canned goods and rushed home to fill the bathtub and hunker down. When the storm hit, I was already hunkered and my cabinets were chock-full of chicken soup. The bathtub was already full, because I'd been sitting in it for approximately three weeks.

In early October, I woke up in the middle of the night with a sore, tender feeling between my legs. I'd spent the day out with friends, walking all over Brooklyn in the Indian summer heat, so I assumed I'd chafed my skin into some kind of rash. My skin has always been fussy and delicate—the kind that welts over mosquito bites and scars if you look at it too hard. But this one was uncomfortable enough to start me Googling in the middle of the night.

Google delivered a plethora of gynecological diagnoses, including everything from Lichen Sclerosis to "swamp ass." Another word kept popping up too, over and over again, no matter how many times I rephrased my symptoms in the search box. But that couldn't be it.

Hey, can we reschedule tonight? I instant-messaged Harry the next day.

Sure, you okay? he typed back.

I squirmed around on my seat at work, trying to get comfortable.

Yeah, I'm just not feeling great.

Oh no! What's wrong?

Ugh, it's a lady thing. I'm going to the gynecologist. Plus, I think I have a cold.

Oh.

I'm not blowing you off, I swear!

Does it hurt?

It's not too bad. It was so bad that I couldn't sit for more than ten minutes.

Is it gnarly?

Oh my *God*.

Uh. I guess, a little, I replied.

What do you think it is?

Instant message or no, I could sense the tone of a fellow panic-Googler.

I don't know.

Do you think it's a thing?

I didn't need to ask what "a thing" was. Early on in our relationship, Harry and I had done the responsible-adult thing and had the brief but awkward STI/birth-control talk. I had nothing, he had nothing, and we'd both been tested just months before meeting. I'd been sort of thrilled by my first STI panel and the middling anxiety that came with it. But Jared had been the only other guy I'd had any sexual contact with that year, and he had been equally cautious, so it was no surprise that I was a-okay. Harry hadn't fooled around with anyone in between his last test and meeting me. He'd gone on a few dates with one girl, but they'd only kissed before things fizzled out, and that hardly warranted a blood draw. His sexual history was more extensive than mine, but neither of us was, ahem, worldly.

That's why I didn't believe Google or my doctor when they both told me it was probably herpes. Dr. Jameson cocked her head, all sympathy and *tough luck*, explaining that no, it probably wasn't the atomic yeast infection I'd hoped it was. She took a swab and a blood sample, but it was obvious she knew what she was looking at. Everything below the belt was simply *fucked*. It would be fucked for a week or two, she explained, in more technical terms.

"The first outbreak is the worst one. It will never be this bad again, I promise."

"But this will happen again?"

"It could. It might not. We also don't know if it's HSV1 or HSV2, yet. They can behave differently."

"I'm just confused. My boyfriend's last test was negative and so was mine."

"Well, it doesn't show up in a blood test right away. It can take weeks, months." She looked up and gestured her hand at the ceiling as if to demonstrate just how herpes works in mysterious ways.

I left with a prescription for valacyclovir and instructions to take Advil and an oatmeal bath if I got too uncomfortable. They would call me with my test results within a week. On the way home, I sent Harry the first of many grim text messages regarding the state of my vagina and told him to call his doctor.

By the following week, I didn't much care what the diagnosis was as long as this hell would soon be over. I'd taken three sick days then asked to work from home, still barely able to walk to the bathroom. I had to do something besides lying around going out of my mind with round-the-clock ruminating over what I had, how I'd gotten it, and why me? Honestly. Why me, out of all of my friends, who'd been dating for years, sowing wild oats and falling in and out of love while I went to therapy? How come I was the one who caught something the very *second* I got a sex life? I'd finally gotten the guts to put myself out there for five minutes, and this was my instant punishment for being so presumptuous. *Oh, you think you're good enough all of a sudden? You expect someone to overlook your piddling little abuse history and your neurotic personality and your big, fat, ridiculous body? Now it's big, fat, and ridiculous, with herpes. Good luck.*

As expected, my swab came back positive for HSV1 but the blood test was negative. That meant I'd definitely gotten it from Harry, and recently. His own doctor confirmed that his last result was indeed negative, but when he drew blood this time, it was positive. That girl he'd gone on a few dates with had likely passed it on to him without even being aware that she could do so just by kissing. Statistically speaking, she probably didn't even know that she had it. She probably thought she had "cold sores."

Every day, I soaked in an oatmeal bath, the only thing that took the slightest edge off. I alternated aspirin, Advil, and Tylenol so I could be on pain relievers all day and night.

"That's fine," my doctor told me. "You'll be over the hump soon."

I'd wound up in my primary care doctor's office the day after the gynecologist, when every gland on my body had swollen up and white spots appeared on my tonsils. Tonsillitis was the cherry atop this disgusting sundae, he explained. Normally, the first outbreak came on the back of some other sickness, grabbing hold of the body when the immune system was low. To me, it just felt like a secondary punishment in case I ever thought about leaving the house again.

"It's to be expected," the doctor said. "But, I promise, it will never be this bad again. Really."

Over and over, the doctors (and my old pal, Google) comforted me with these facts. It would never be this bad again, and the outbreak would be over soon.

Hurricane Sandy hit when I was on day *ten*.

You guys gonna have some hurricane sexxxxxxx? Jon texted me after the mayor ordered everyone to go inside or evacuate. No, I was not going to have any hurricane sexxxxxx. I was barely capable of peeing. But I was sick of the sight of my own apartment, so I taped up the windows, put the cat in a carrier, and transferred my sickbed to Harry's. We'd stopped talking about moving in together as soon as my crotch crisis became the sole point of conversation. He was still the one I wanted to ride out the storm with, but when I thought of the couple we were just weeks prior, fantasy apartment shopping and haggling over theoretical couches, they seemed like very different people.

The days we spent inside together during the hurricane were strange and quiet. Neither of us had been through this as individuals, let alone as a couple.

We heated soup and watched movies at night. I hugged him tight when the pain got bad and let him whimper *sorry*s into my hair. I assured him that I wasn't angry. We'd both done the responsible thing; it just happened. We stared out the window, watching the storm blow New York City apart and waited for the moment when the lights would go out.

We were so lucky. As horror stories of obliterated buildings and people drowned in their own homes came quietly through the radio, we stepped outside into a warm and humid evening in Park Slope. It was the first time I'd walked more than two blocks since the outbreak hit, but like everyone else in New York, we just wanted to see what the city looked like. The sidewalk was thick with families: children frantic with pent-up energy and weary parents who'd been cooped up with them for days, all of us pointing at every fallen twig as if we understood the devastation that had savaged those other neighborhoods and families and children in our city, who no longer had homes to go back to.

Harry and I stepped into an empty Greek restaurant and ordered some appetizers. The wallop of tonsillitis, antibiotics, and pain had killed my appetite, and for weeks I'd been nibbling on sick-day foods. *Best diet ever*, an old voice in my head chimed in from time to time. I shot back: *No diet will fix this.*

"How do you feel?" Harry asked.

"Okay." I felt sick. One bite of oily eggplant and I would vomit.

"Do you want to go home?"

"I just need to sit for a while."

"Does it hurt?"

"I mean, yeah. Of course it hurts." I looked around the restaurant and back at him with shut-up eyes.

"I'm so sorry," he said.

"Why?"

"Because we went for a walk, I guess?"

"It's fine. We just shouldn't have gone so far."

We sat in silence for ten minutes, Harry eating and me watching him eat. Normally, my chattiness balanced out his quiet nature, but I couldn't think of anything we hadn't talked about or anything I wanted to say.

That night, he scooted up behind me in bed. For weeks I'd been so raw that even the fabric of underwear felt like a serrated blade against my skin, and cuddling had been out of the question. But now I'd passed the peak of the outbreak, I was sure. Though all that meant was that the blade had finished slicing at me, and now I had to tend to the open wound that covered everything below my waist. I edged away from Harry.

"Too much?"

"Too much. I can't yet."

"I'm sorry."

"Will you stop?"

"I'm not even touching you."

"I mean stop apologizing. I'm not mad at you."

Harry didn't say anything. And I didn't fill the silence.

I want so badly to go back to that night and tell my sick and wretched self to turn around and take his hand. I want to tell her it's okay to take the space to be comfortable and to heal, but she doesn't need to do it alone. I want to tell her that sometimes you don't get the chance to jump off the cliff; that sometimes you're pushed, but either way you hit the bottom. *This part is just the falling*, I would tell her. *This part is the worst.* It would take months to heal physically. It would take many more months of shame and real hatred of my body, this spoiled, bestial thing that had turned on me again and again. It would be a full year before I decided to stop punishing my body for all its many failures: for drawing attention, for helping me hide, for keeping everything good just out of reach, even when it was lying in bed next to me.

I want to tell that girl she's just going to have to fall down through the stratosphere of all that sadness before she lands hard on a pile of leaves in East Hampton on another warm October day. Then she'll be ready for the long walk out of the woods.

Chapter 14

On Dumplings

I'd been doing intuitive eating for almost two months when I finally learned how to eat pizza. A week before Thanksgiving, Chrissy and Debbie came over to my place to eat dinner, watch a movie, and paint our nails. It was the only group ritual without Jon, who couldn't sit through a romantic drama without heckling. Often, we heckled, too, but when it was just the three of us, we took the opportunity to whip out the nail polish and take Christian Slater movies very seriously.

"What are we eating?" Debbie asked upon arrival.

Since I'd started intuitive eating, group meals had become a minefield. On a diet, I could plan out my calorie budget in advance to account for whatever cuisine we had chosen (because I had always insisted on planning in advance). I could review the menu of the restaurant or choose the recipe we made, making sure to find something on my Good list, if I was being good. If I was being bad, then we just got pizza. Now that I was allegedly allowed to eat anything, the lists were out the window. Still, every time a formerly Bad food came to the table, it was like trying to reconcile with an unfaithful lover, unpacking the problems of our past and trying to see where it all went wrong. At a dinner table, in front of all my friends.

"Could we maybe order pizza?" Chrissy asked.

And I thought, *Okay, pizza. Let's do this.*

The Christmas before I turned twelve, I opened my stocking to find a rolled-up issue of *Seventeen* along with a year's subscription to the magazine. Shortly thereafter, all the paper towels in my house disappeared.

Save an easy 500–800 calories by blotting the grease off your pizza with a napkin before you dig in.

Some people can quote Rilke from memory, or recall their favorite Shakespearean sonnets on command. For me, this remains one of the most resonant passages I have ever read. When I'm doddering around in my nineties, it won't be memories of torrid trysts or curses on ungrateful children that I mumble at the nurses all day, but rather this fat-fighting tip from a teen magazine with Jennifer Love Hewitt fake-laughing on the cover.

It was the single greatest revelation a chubby preteen could have. By simply dabbing away the grease, I could somehow make pizza "safe." It wasn't even really pizza anymore, not after ten rounds of pounding on the slice with a fistful of Bounty. Now it was simply bread and sauce and slightly dried-out cheese.

Pizza blotting soon became everything blotting. If I could perform this oil alchemy on pizza, then why shouldn't it work on every fat-containing item on my plate? Chicken breasts got the pat-down. Potato chips were lightly squeezed with napkins in between my fingers. French fries were gently smashed out of shape, but no bother. Now they were even less like French fries and I could safely eat them without the sickly fear I felt while eating an "unsafe" food in front of people. I might have looked like a malfunctioning robot, frantically trying both to clean and pulverize my food, but at least I wasn't a fat girl getting fatter.

This trick wasn't the only tip I embraced over the years in order to make food safe. I spent one weekend drinking barely diluted vinegar before each meal, then decided to make it an all-day vinegar cleanse of my own design. By Sunday, both the paper towels and the toilet paper were gone.

Over the years, I amassed a startling array of magazine knowledge. I ran bowls of ice cream under the tap after half the serving was gone. I dumped heaps of black pepper over birthday cake after I'd taken five bites. I ate apples before lunch to fill my stomach, and then finished the meal with coffee to kill my lingering appetite. I mixed psyllium husks into Diet Snapple Lemon Tea and guzzled one down in the morning and at night both to block sugar absorption and to clean out my system.

Lest you fear I'm advocating *Seventeen* as a viable medical journal, I do now realize all of this is bullshit. Psyllium makes you poop, and three cups of black coffee gives you a stomachache. And that pizza you're dabbing within an inch of its life is still pizza. You are eating pizza. Learn to live with it.

After years of reinforcement, the Good and Bad system had become the bearing wall of my eating habits. Doing intuitive eating meant it was now my job to knock this wall down. I chipped away at it with each meal, inching my way toward food neutrality like a prisoner, tunneling toward sweet freedom. One day, I would be able to eat like a human. Until then I would use all the dramatic metaphors I needed to tackle pizza. Wait, no, not pizza—my pizza beliefs.

Since I had lived much of my life in the universe of disordered eating, various foods had taken on powerful personalities and intentions of their own. Trying to see them as anything else required a kind of couples counseling between me and the meal on my plate.

Kale was the good and righteous superhero of the produce section. Whether sautéed, steamed, or raw, eating kale made me a Very Good Person. If not quite transformed into Gwyneth Paltrow, I was at least behaving Gwyn-ish. While filled with those saintly greens I could walk to work with my head held high.

"I made the best kale salad of my life last night," I told anyone who would listen.

In the old days, any poor bastard who happened to wander into the office kitchen while I made a cup of coffee got an earful of my dinner. I'd give them the full rundown on the apple, cranberry, and avocado I dressed the salad with, and how I'd only needed, like, a teaspoon of oil in the vinaigrette because I found this really nice whole-grain mustard and that made it thick enough, and oh, okay, have a good one!

Some foods, on the other hand, I never talked about. These were the burgers I ate in front of the television after having a lousy day at work. There were the brownies I baked and ate right out of the pan in my kitchen the day I found out my apartment had bedbugs. There were the egg-and-bacon-on-a-rolls that I bought outside the subway and scarfed down on my walk to work, eyes constantly scanning the street to make sure I didn't bump into a colleague. Then there were all the not-kale things I simply ate because I really, really wanted to. All those foods were without virtue, both representing my inherent lameness and further making me a Very Bad Person. No one wants to hear about those things.

Guess what? No one wanted to hear about my kale salad, either.

✳

"Was a kale salad what you wanted in the moment?" Theresa asked me one Thursday afternoon.

She'd just finished reviewing my weekly eating record. I'd finally

gotten the message that she wouldn't actually put me in a carbohydrate time-out if I reported eating baked potatoes two days in
a row, but my week still reflected a fair amount of my old Good
foods.

In my enthusiasm, the notes had become a little extreme. I
logged every detail and feeling I had about a meal—and that could
be anything from Thanksgiving dinner to the peppermint I ate
after brunch one day. I wrote five-hundred-word essays over considering oatmeal for breakfast: how I associated oatmeal with both
childhood and healthy eating, but also I just wanted it because it
was cold out, and though at first I struggled to choose between top-
ping it with almonds or raisins, I suddenly realized I could have
both, and so I did!!

"I pretty much wanted the salad," I told her. "I had some chips
afterward, but I probably could have ridden out that craving. I
know it's okay that I gave in, but I also know that I probably would
have been satisfied with just the salad, so, I'm really sorry."

She made a face as if perhaps it was strange to be apologizing for
the illicit consumption of six corn chips.

"Uh, it's okay. Why are you sorry?"

"Because I ate the chips and I didn't need them."

She pointed to my page of neatly organized notes. "Do you see
that you hadn't had any carbohydrates since breakfast? Your appetite was telling you something."

Silence. Blinking.

"You know your body and your brain need carbohydrates, right?"

"Oh, yeah. But no one needs corn chips, right?"

"Okay." She shrugged and nodded like a patient kindergarten
teacher hearing me out as I argued the legitimacy of Santa Claus.
"So, what would have been an acceptable substitute?"

"Baked chips."

✳

Here's where the bonus round of crazy comes in. By the time I landed in Theresa's office, I'd created subclasses of Good and Bad foods and the various scenarios in which they could be made Better or Worse. It was the rationale behind baked-chip logic and the formula that made a cabbage side dish cancel out a hamburger. While I've never gotten higher than a B– in any kind of math class, I'd managed to generate an internal flow chart of various food values, which I unconsciously whipped out whenever I had a menu in my hands. Brunch, for example:

The omelet comes with hash browns or salad. If one gets the hash browns the omelet must have no cheese, and there must be an additional green vegetable. The hash browns may be eaten, but at least one-fourth must be left on the plate. If one gets the salad, the omelet may have cheese *or* a meat, and one must eat the greens first while describing last night's epic kale salad to brunch companion. Two tablespoons of milk are allowed for coffee, but one must inquire if skim is available. If not, the milk ration remains the same, but one-fourth of the omelet must be left on the plate. One slice of toast is allowed if it's buttered, but two if the toast is only topped with preserves. (*Not jelly.* Preserves have seeds and jelly is purple. Jelly is for children. Gwyn-ish grown-ups eat preserves, confits, and no-sugar-added jams.) If one eats only half of the omelet, toast, *and* hash browns then one may have a frozen yogurt later and Instagram it.

Maybe most adults have instincts to keep their meals healthy and balanced. Perhaps they naturally choose between hash browns and cheese in their omelets, simply because they don't feel like quite so heavy a meal. But those people were as mysterious and unfathomable to me as child chess prodigies. I could not simply stroll into brunch and wing it without a protocol firmly in place. Even after months of intuitive eating practice, I still found myself looking around the restaurant as I ate: *Check out my toast, y'all! It's got butter and jam and I'm just eating it like whatever! They didn't have rye so I'm having wheat, but that's cool, amiright? I'm right, right?*

I thought back to the Sunday nights of my dieting days, when I'd spent hours cooking huge batches of carefully calculated recipes, sincerely intending to eat this and *only* this for the rest of the week. There were giant pots of fat-free vegan chili, giant pots of One-Point Carrot Soup, and giant pots of kale and everything. (Anything mixed with kale was made better by association.) Somewhere around Wednesday, the food would become an albatross—a Tupperware ghost haunting my fridge, shaming me for the Indian takeout I'd just ordered and the pounds of wasted ingredients I'd leave to molder in my vegetable crisper until next Sunday, when I'd finally toss it and start all over again.

And then there was the dumpling scenario. Of all the crazy, illogical equations in my head, nothing is more emblematic than the way in which I behaved around dumplings (spoiler: like a lunatic).

Dumplings were Bad, 100 percent. Thick, chewy dough, wrapped around fat-speckled meat that tasted like gristly heaven, dumplings were the first things my eye caught on any Chinese food menu. Fried was not an option. Once, my nanny Karen and I had gone to the movies at a local mall, stopping by Panda Express for a quick dinner before the film. I ate one of the fried dumplings off her plate, and then spent the rest of the night convinced I'd done irrevocable cardiac damage. I was ten.

"You're not having a heart attack."

"How do you know? Feel my heartbeat."

"It's fine, you're just amped up because you're stressing out."

"Stress causes heart attacks!"

The shushing got so bad that we eventually left the movie theater. I still have no idea what happens at the end of *My Father the Hero*.

Fried dumplings were too delicious to enjoy, but steamed dumplings were allowed for a few years. During my first round with Weight Watchers, I had them delivered three orders at a time, each with an extra set of duck sauce for dipping (duck sauce was

not listed in my Points book and therefore had no Points). I ate one
and a half orders for dinner, then pulled out the leftovers first thing
in the morning, stood in front of the open fridge, and finished the
cold, slightly hardened dumplings before anyone else woke up.

But by the time I finished college, dumplings had risen to the
top of the Bad list. They were up there with French fries and full-
fat ice cream. They were an absolute no-no, unless split with a
skinny friend and followed up with an extra workout and at least
one full head of kale, spinach, or cabbage. It wasn't just that I'd
ramped up the crazy by then, but also because I'd discovered gyoza.

Gyoza was Good. It was a diet dumpling, with a slightly thinner
skin and a little less meat inside—plus, it came in a smaller container. Fried gyoza was allowed half of the time because it wasn't
a big, fat, fried dumpling but just a small, pan-fried little nibble
of an appetizer. (Note that "pan-fried" was different from "fried"
because someone put the word "pan" in front.) Furthermore, gyoza
came from Japanese food restaurants. Japanese food was officially
Better than Chinese food, what with all the raw fish and miso soup.
Japanese lunch specials came with a side of seaweed salad, whereas
Chinese food lunch specials came with a side of an egg roll. Chinese food was for cheat days and Final Pig-Outs the night before
the next diet started. Japanese food was for light work lunches and
healthy dinners after yoga. (If you're now worried that I might be
racist, rest assured that I share your concern.)

Gyoza was Good but even Better was shumai. Shumai was basically nothing. If you ate shumai you might as well get a Big Mac
afterward, because those tiny, thin-skinned balls of steamed shrimp
purity guaranteed that you were officially Good for that entire day.
You won. By eschewing the dumplings and gyoza and opting for
the least-delicious, most miniature food option, you now had bragging rights for the next twenty-four hours, and had earned a trip
to the frozen yogurt shop. Perhaps the cashier would like to hear
about your very healthy lunch?

The dumpling revelation happened at work. A few months into intuitive eating, I found myself scanning sushi lunch specials online. But that lunch hour was an aha moment the likes of which I was not prepared for. All at once, I got it: dumplings, gyoza, and shumai are the *same damn thing*. They're slightly different shapes with slightly different fillings, but for all practical purposes, they are exactly the same. Verbal Kint is Keyser Söze, Rosebud is a sled, and I have spent twenty years wringing my hands over appetizers.

Oh, I told everyone.

"Dumplings and gyoza are the same thing. Did you ever think about that?!"

"No, not really." Harry turned around at his desk later that night. He was busy working on a freelance assignment, but by then he knew the tone that meant *Turn around so I can astound you with my latest food discovery and all my feelings about it*. It was kind of a loud tone.

"You never realized that?! They are!"

"No, I know that they are. I just never thought about it."

This is the problem with dating someone who has absolutely no food issues beyond a mild dislike of fennel.

With this first epiphany, the walls of Jericho came swiftly tumbling down. If dumplings and gyoza were pretty much the same thing in slightly different forms, then neither of them possessed the Good or Bad powers I had so fervently believed in. And if that was true for dumplings, then what other foods might be similar false idols (and demons)?

While it was thrilling to eat Chinese food without risking damnation, the miracle was unsettling. All those old rules had created a safe, knowable structure, one that I relied on to guide me through every meal and snack I encountered. They'd given me both a line to toe and a comfort zone to hide in.

One icy Sunday, I decided to poke my head out: I ordered a burger, with French fries.

I won't walk you through the advanced calculus I'd previously applied to every encounter with a fried potato stick, but not so long before, French fries had been the immortal tsar of my Bad Food list, and as such I treated them with appropriate fear and respect. Ninety-five percent of the time, I ordered a salad with my hamburger or avoided the meal altogether. If I deliberately ordered French fries, it was probably an occasion of deep despair and/or drunkenness—or the night before the new diet.

But this was a sober midday brunch with Jon at DuMont, the same restaurant from which I'd ordered my final Final Pig-Out meal. I hadn't faced that particular burger since; it felt as though I was visiting an ex-lover to pick up a box of stuff, bringing my friend along for moral support just in case the burger got passive-aggressive or tried to pick a fight with me. (*Except, no, Kelsey. It's just ground meat and potatoes. You can pick a fight with ground meat and potatoes, but they can't pick one with you. Oh God, please stop yelling at them, you're in a restaurant.*) I'd come prepared with the axioms of intuitive eating in my back pocket: I have a right to a satisfying meal; I have permission to eat French fries; eating French fries will not compromise my ethics or diminish me as a person.

"Can I get the burger, with onions and mushrooms?"

"Do you want fries, salad, or onion rings on the side?"

Oh fuck, onion rings? No. One crisis at a time.

"I will have the French fries, please."

It had taken days of preparation and a test run to let me look a waiter in the face and utter that sentence with direct eye contact. A week before the brunch experiment, determined to tackle these triggering foods, I had sat in Theresa's office and held a potato chip in the palm of my hand. The potato chip was like a less intimidating French-fry tsar—the tsarevich. It was the perfect tool for this exercise. Developed years ago by legendary mindfulness master Jon Kabat-Zinn, it was known by his students as the Raisin Meditation. Kabat-Zinn gave each of them a single raisin and instructed them first to look, then smell, then put it in their mouths. Next came the phases of feeling the raisin on one's tongue, then slowly biting it in half, and eventually, finally, chewing and swallowing. Each phase required long moments of observation both of the object itself and any mental or physical reaction the students had to the raisin. It took for-ev-er.

In my own version, I brought in a bag of Cape Cod potato chips, and Theresa guided me through the meditation over and over again. I stared at a chip, noting its bubbly surface and vaguely translucent yellow color. I smelled its salty, greasy, almost earthy aroma and felt my mouth and stomach react.

"In your mind, gauge your level of hunger and then your level of desire for the chip, on a scale of one to ten."

I hadn't eaten lunch yet. My salivary glands lightly ached behind my tongue. *I want you*, I told the chip. *I am an eight for you right now. And yet...*

"Notice any judgments you are making about the chip," Theresa prompted.

I know you to be a willful, greasy lover. You got that shiny surface in the bowels of a deep fryer. Look at yourself—you are barely potato anymore, processed into the crispy, bubbly beauty in my hand.

I placed the chip on the center of my tongue and closed my mouth around it, slowly. I felt the surge of salty flavor flare across my palate and then fade into dull, vegetal blandness. I tasted and tasted and tasted. Finally, I bit the thing in half, and held it again. I looked at Theresa, my mouth cupped around this single chip that was my current universe, and then closed my eyes. I could see it on my tongue, a crumbling heap of flakes. It tasted like nothing so much as plain potato now. Slowly, once I'd absorbed everything a person could get out of a single potato chip, I began to chew. Even then I noted subtle flavors changing, the texture evolving between my teeth, and my body's reaction to this food. Given a full six minutes to register a potato chip, my system had risen to excitement, experienced the full reality of the food, and, finally, lost interest.

It was just a potato chip. It was not some evil, greased-up bad boy calling to me from the hood of his car. It wasn't calling to anyone, because it was an inert object and not an animate being. I was the fantasist essentially playing make-believe with a snack food instead of a doll.

I ran through the meditation twice more with a chip, and by the end of the third one I couldn't have cared less about the thing.

"It's just a chip! I'm hungry, but this isn't going to do anything for me. I have no real desire for this. I desire a sandwich."

Theresa nodded, that kindergarten-teacher look back on her face.

"It's just a chip. You're right."

"I know I'm right!"

"So, what do you think about the French fries?"

I thought I was ready. Ish.

"I will have the French fries, please," I told the waiter.

When our meals came, I took a breath. Part of the intuitive eating process was starting a meal by eating the thing I wanted most on the plate. After years of opening meals with dry side salads, it still felt crazy—like ordering dessert before dinner. Oh God, would I have to start ordering dessert before dinner?

I dug into the fries while Jon chatted away, unaware of the revolutionary brunch demonstration I was leading across the table. *We're here! We like fries! Get used to it!*

They were good—certainly better than a snack-size bag of potato chips. I made a mental note that they were hot and salty, that my desire and hunger levels were both high, and that, in fact, my burger looked pretty great, too. I picked it up and took a bite. I chewed and swallowed and did it again. At one point during the meal, I was even able to engage in conversation, like an ordinary person having brunch with a friend. After about ten minutes, I looked down at my plate and realized I was done. The burger was nearly finished, but in a twist ending, there were at least twenty fries left on my plate.

I looked at them, edging on panic at the sight of this tableau. Never, not once, had I ordered fries and not finished them. If you and I were out to dinner and you ordered fries as well, I'd eat all of mine and then coquettishly ask for a few of yours. Fries on the table went into my mouth, period. But now my hunger level was nil and, though I couldn't quite believe it, so was my desire for the remaining fries. I took one last bite of a fry, just to be sure. They didn't taste the same as they had ten minutes ago. They were fine, but not great, an entirely neutral food. I was wholly sated with their crisp, salty flavor. To eat any more fries now would only take them from neutral to gross. I didn't want them. I was done.

"I'm done with my fries!" I bellowed in Jon's face. He started, looking down at the fries I was so incredibly done with.

"Okay. Well, I'm still working over here."

His mac and cheese was half finished, but this was about *my* brunch.

"Great! I'm just saying, like, I am not going to eat those fries. I could, but I don't want to."

Jon looked at my plate, then at me, with a little sideways smile. "Then, can I maybe have a few?"

As Jon picked off my plate, I came down from my not-finishing-the-fries high, looking around the restaurant, not sure what to do with myself. That's when the slightly less exciting revelation came creeping through the back door of my mind: Part of me *wanted* to want them all. Listening to my body, I could easily stop eating fries halfway through the meal. But from my brain still came a trembling whisper, breathing hard into my ear:

What are you doing? You need those fries. What if this intuitive eating thing is as strange as it sounds and this is just one long binge you haven't woken up from? What if you really can't eat fried food or hamburgers in the long run? What if you wake up one day at four hundred pounds and have to spend the rest of your life subsisting on apples and chia seeds like a macrobiotic squirrel? Surely, you will look back on these twenty-odd fries and wish you'd slapped them out of Jon's face, taken the plate, and run.

I sat in silence, telepathically apologizing to Jon, Harry, and everyone else to whom I'd flaunted all my great success. The French fries were nothing but a pantomime of victory if that voice was still sitting at the table with me. Undoubtedly, it was. And soon enough, that voice was joined by a chorus of uninvited guests, all loud and mean and drunk on mimosas, ready to trash the place.

Chapter 15

Once More, Into the Suburbs

John2John: *Ur a fat n ugly whore! time for jenny craig dumb(fat)-ass!!*

A couple weeks before Christmas, I came into work early and turned on my computer to find an early present: my very first troll. In fact, there were a handful of comments like this beneath a photo of me on the *Huffington Post*. But John2John, he had a way with words.

The night before, *HuffPo* had published a profile of me, and I'd woken up pumped. And why shouldn't I? I'd fully renounced dieting, started a successful column, and the whole world seemed to stand up and cheer every time I ate a bagel. Why hadn't I started eating bagels earlier?! Jacked up on a potent dose of self-confidence, I believed nothing and no one could get to me.

No one except John2John. And pretty much everyone else.

In the last few months, I'd shed so many of my old, destructive habits: no more bingeing, no more constant calculation, no more kale worship. I didn't miss any of that. There was only one vice from my dieting days that I secretly missed: emotional eating. It wasn't a conscious decision to stop. But eating was now about physical hunger and cravings, so when I found myself eating for reasons other than those, I just put the food down and walked away. I'd learned not to beat the shit out of myself for every "unnecessary" cookie, because that only kicked off the old cycle of resistance and caving in and, inevitably, more cookies. But that cycle, as it turned out, was half the fun of emotional eating. It also turns out that I wasn't leaning on it only for the big stuff. It didn't take a crisis to make me reach for a big bowl of Something Besides This Emotion. It just took a glance at my inbox.

Life was pretty great at the moment, but each day, without fail, I'd hit a minor snag. Halfway through a stressful e-mail at work, I'd catch myself frantically digging around in my bag for a smushed granola bar—again. I'd take a good long look at the bar and ask myself: *Wait. Do you actually want this smushed granola bar from three months ago? Or do you just want to not be reading this e-mail? If you actually desire the smushed granola bar, then, by all means, go for it. But it's not going to un-read the e-mail for you. So, what are we going to do here?* The bar would go back to the bottom of my bag, and I'd go back to the stupid, stressful e-mail and stupid, stressful reality, which I somehow had to handle without the soothing balm of a smushed granola bar to help me through.

The decline of emotional eating is one of the first recognizable perks you get from intuitive eating. But no one tells you about it, because it doesn't feel much like a perk. It feels like losing your best friend—the one that makes every situation a little bit easier, never asks anything of you, and has the Thai take-out place on speed dial just in case you should ever have an unplanned feeling. The loss isn't even voluntary; it just happens one day. When you're focused on hunger and fullness, savoring meals and tasting every bite, you can't feasibly look at a smushed granola bar the same way. You can't shove something into your face to numb out, because food is no longer numbing. In theory, I knew this was a fantastic development. But in reality, I was too busy fussing like a toddler being weaned off the pacifier. Also, masturbating.

How did the big closet-purge go? Harry texted me one Thursday night.

I looked from my overstuffed closet to the small, abandoned pile of donation clothes on the floor, and rolled over to reply with one hand:

Got distracted. Work stuff.

Sometimes I wonder if this is what everyone's doing when they're "working late."

In the absence of cookies to help me escape the uncomfortable moments (or the boring moments, or the exciting moments, or the just-okay-not-great moments), my brain sneakily sought out any other pleasant distraction it could. I was watching more television, constantly restarting familiar favorites like *The West Wing* and falling asleep to the soothing chatter of Aaron Sorkin dialogue. I was obsessively buying skin-care products, filling the bathroom cabinet with eye cream for nighttime, daytime, and absolutely no reason. And, I couldn't so much as wait for a light to change without playing Candy Crush on my phone. From a psychological standpoint, I was masturbating all over town.

Still, each day that I got up, went to the gym, and worked on my eating skills was another step out of the woods. I was doing the work. It just felt a lot like work, now.

"I'm, like, *obsessed* with Fun Size Snickers all of a sudden," I ranted in Theresa's office. "Should I just be buying the big ones? I eat like four small ones in a day! At my desk, it's Halloween forever!"

A ten-minute discourse followed, breaking down the moments in which I'd eaten each Snickers, why Fun Size was okay in my mind but full size was not, then finally addressing the monolithic specter of Snickers Ice Cream bars. No matter what the food, all of these discussions ended the same way.

"What do you need to trust this process?"

I instantly responded, "To lose weight by doing it." Obviously.

She made that universal tongue-clicking sound that means, *Sorry, kid, can't help ya.*

"Nothing is going to happen until you let go of that one."

"Okay." It wasn't.

"*Diets* are about weight loss. This is about changing your relationship with food, remember? Weight loss is a natural side effect if you have excess weight to lose, and we welcome that!" She gestured to my weekly eating record. "When all this becomes instinct, your body will settle into its normal range. But the people who can't shift the focus off of weight..." She shrugged. "Well, it takes a lot longer for the process to really begin."

"Okay." Fiiiiiiiine.

It took a few rounds of this conversation before the uncomfortable truth finally began to sink in: Just because it wasn't a diet didn't mean it wouldn't be hard. I didn't want to waste time fighting a counterintuitive battle. I'd signed up to trust myself fully, allowing for the necessary phases of rediscovering food and learning how to eat and enjoy it. If that meant I wouldn't lose any weight right away—even if I *gained* a few temporary pounds—I could handle it. But I couldn't handle much else.

Aside from the loss of my old friendship with food, there were still other challenges I had to grapple with. And by challenges, I mean, like, living.

Despite all this profound and incredible work I'd taken on, I still had to manage all the other stuff a person's expected to do in order to be a legitimate member of society. Though it seemed entirely unfair under the circumstances, the patron saint of juvenile adults did not appear to do my laundry and change the cat litter. I still had to deal with looming deadlines at work and arguments with Harry or my friends. I still had PMS and that credit card bill I had forgotten about. On top of everything else, I had John2John and his fellow idiots keeping my (fat) ass in check.

"Love the *HuffPo* piece, Kels!" my friend and fellow editorial staffer Cameron called as I swanned into the office. She got up from her desk, all bangs and leather skirt, and quickly scooted over to mine (surely, to tell me in detail just how much she *loved* the *HuffPo* piece). I smiled and shook my mouse, a window-cluttered desktop overtaking the screen.

"Just, maybe don't read the comments? I don't think they really get it."

I rolled my eyes. "It's the Internet, whatever. Everyone's ugly on-line."

"I know. But these are just stupid. There's no point in even getting into it."

"Totally. I'm too slammed for trolls today, anyway." But also, I was lying.

I skimmed the profile, taking mental note of each complimentary phrase to save for later, when the laundry pile loomed and life wasn't looking as rosy. *Remember, you are a "body-positive inspiration." You can handle this.*

Then, I clicked directly to the part that really mattered: comments. John2John's screed sat firmly beneath my grinning face. While he had his detractors, the guy appeared to being leading an entire army of me-haters. Some of them could even kind of spell:

Finally! Another excuse for being fat and lazy! Wonderful!

I'm sorry but thin is beautiful and you are just an emberassing looser.

Sad attempts at self realization. This chick is trippn.

Garden-variety assholes. I gave my screen the finger and went about my day, only pausing to think about them every twenty minutes or so.

The comments section of my own column had, for the most part, been glowing. Those were loyal readers who'd been with me from the start, the original bagel cheering section. But still, every time I mentioned something like finally being able to enjoy a hamburger *and* a side of French fries, there would always be a few folks reminding me that cavemen didn't eat burgers and fries, so maybe I wasn't eating so "intuitively" after all. These were the comments that stuck in my brain, adding fuel to the fire of my own doubts. Was I really getting better? If my old fat-girl clothes still pretty much fit, could I actually be getting healthier? How was it possible I'd begun working out five days a week and nothing that impressive had happened in the mirror? As the column got more popular, my audience grew, and I didn't really shrink. I began to wonder: *Was* I trippn?

I came home late that night, hungry for comfort food. I plated up my softly scrambled eggs and buttered bread, then sat at the table in the narrow blue hallway that served as my living room. The apartment was quiet save for the barking of my neighbor's Great Dane echoing up the airshaft. It was my first undistracted moment since I'd eaten an undistracted lunch. I allowed myself a pat on the back for giving myself this "satisfying eating experience," as Theresa would call it. It was a perfect meal for me at that moment, and I left the table full and satisfied, but not stuffed.

Worn out from a day of not eating smushed granola bars, I left the dishes in the sink and headed straight for bed. Well, TV in bed. But, before I could even reach for the remote, my heart began to race. I lay flat on the unmade sheets and quilt, placing a hand to the top of my abdomen to feel the space between the arcs of my rib cage—a habit from my nightly childhood exercise ritual. In years past, that space had been the barometer for how well my day had gone, and now I heard the same old questions come to mind. Was it convex? Could I feel the hard edge of my ribs? Or was it full and bloated, brimming with all the mistakes I'd made in the last twelve hours, the worst of which was eating dinner at all? It was almost 9:00 p.m. when I finished that last bite, and now I'd have to lie around with all this protein, fat, and processed carbohydrates lingering uselessly in my stomach. That kind of meal was allowed only in the morning, and only if I was definitely going to the gym, if not the gym *and* a yoga class. Dinner was supposed to be eaten by 6:00 p.m., 6:30 at the latest. Furthermore, it was supposed to be green.

For years, my dinner procedure was to chop up an entire head of green-leaf lettuce, add two tomatoes, throw in a soft-boiled egg, and douse the whole thing in fat-free dressing and vinegar. I'd eat the entire, enormous salad out of my largest mixing bowl, sitting on my bedroom floor, two feet in front of the television, like a ten-year-old whose babysitter had fallen asleep. Then I'd lie on my bed, bloated with the hollow fullness of raw, wet greens and not much else. On those nights, when my stomach felt achingly full, at least I knew it was full of basically nothing. But tonight, three eggs and a slice of bread had me sweating with panic as I groped at my middle.

It was full. Not rotund, thank God, but even when I sucked in a bit, I couldn't carve out that valley between my ribs. It was flat and even, filled with the dinner I'd just finished—fat fool that I was.

Right there is where it happened; I went rogue. My mind went running scared down an old, familiar rabbit hole, and I chased it all the way.

I knew weight loss was not, *could* not be my goal. But wasn't it? Really? At some point, eventually? Eventually slash soon??

Yah, John2John chimed in. *Yr lookn pretty fat n stuppid.*

But I'm trying something new. No shortcuts. Long-term. Mindfulness and stuff.

Whtvr, looser. C u at Wendys!

The next few days didn't look all that different. With my brain off and running without me, I wasn't able to see that something had changed. For three months my eating had been filled with variety: braised cabbage one day and a BLT the next. I'd been knee-deep in food exploration, relearning my own preferences, and everything was allowed—encouraged, even. But, while I'd made those choices with curiosity and excitement, I now made them with a sense of simmering anxiety. Didn't I *crave* this fat-free spinach salad for lunch? Probably. It would make me feel good and calm. Didn't *that* count as eating intuitively, too? I probably didn't need that bread on the side, but somehow I was eating it. Why? (*Becuz you an idiot. U nevr new how to eat right n u still dont. Only differnce now is everyones watchin u.*) It didn't feel like I was back on a diet. It felt like I was cheating on a diet, every day.

The holidays began to creep up. First laundry, now national holidays? I could not catch a *break*. Once, I'd been a Christmas fanatic who lightly salted batches of homemade toffee and blasted Mariah Carey so loudly that my cat would hide under the bed. Now I was one of those people upon whom the holidays "crept up." And there was one reason. Odds are, it's your reason, too. Mom.

It had been almost a full year since I had seen or heard from her. We'd had brief stretches of silence before. When I was in boarding school, some tense little telephone argument might keep me up all night for a week, stewing and refusing to be the one to call her and make up. Inevitably, I was, often sobbing for forgiveness while Mom had already forgotten the whole thing. I'd been waiting by the phone like a loser, in awe of her ability to not talk to me, and knowing I had no such stamina. In fact, she just hadn't called because she hadn't had a reason to call me.

But the fight we'd had last February was different.

Ever since that day on the porch when I'd told her about William, the truth had lurked silently beneath us like a tenuous fault line. It had taken months, but eventually she'd acknowledged the conversation. She'd even come to my therapist's office once, all apologies and woeful regret, refusing my forgiveness before I'd even offered. But the apology didn't stick. Weeks after that therapy session, she'd combusted with rage at my mention of William's name: "You just *love* to throw that in my face. Don't worry, I already hate myself even more than you hate me. Oh yes, you do."

Talking about it openly with my friends had eased the sting of her response. But I had to be cautious. There was an unspoken condition between Mom and me; I could talk about it, but never so loudly that it got back to her. My rule was no family, and none of her friends—no one who might call up and throw it in her face, too. Then, I broke the rule. One night, I'd had dinner with an old family friend, and it just came out. In the moment it was a great relief, but I woke the next morning to the sound of a ticking time bomb. I didn't have to wait long for the boom. Shortly thereafter, my mother called, screaming.

Her anger hit a tenor I'd never seen before. I was a vindictive monster bent on destroying her. I was selfish beyond measure, blabbing all over town. Who else had I told? Her parents? My siblings? Who else was I going to hurt by spreading my little sob story of "abuse"? Finally, she said, I was a liar. I'd invented the whole thing in some sort of recovered-memory therapy scenario.

It still stuns me, that terrible accusation. I believe that she believed that. Though, of course, I'd never "recovered" anything. I'd read stories about recovered-memory therapy, an early-'90s fad that was largely debunked and no longer practiced. In my own therapy, I'd never been pushed into naming "the William stuff" nor had any words been put in my mouth. That's why it took me so long to spit the truth out. Yet, my own mother was so unwilling to admit that this had happened that she'd crafted her own side of my story, in which it simply hadn't. No wonder she was furious. In her version, I really was a monster.

"My life has been blown up because of your mouth," she said, and hung up.

I gave up. There was no winning when I was fighting a genuine delusion. The best I could do was retreat and defend. I blocked her number and set up filters on my e-mail. She could keep me as the monster in her mind, but I wouldn't be waiting by the phone this time in case she changed her mind.

Since that last call in February, I tried to adjust to the idea that I might never see my mother again. On tough nights, I Googled "celebrities with estranged parents" and sent needy texts to my friends just so they knew I loved them and also please never move away. They knew what had happened, and they knew I didn't want to talk about it. Anyway, most days, I was totally fine. Most days, I was great! My biggest critic now was John2John, and I could handle that weenie. But no way could I handle Christmas.

It would be the first one I'd ever spent without her—and that meant without my grandparents, aunt, uncle, cousins, and siblings, too. Every year on Christmas Day, we'd meet at the Harvard Club in Midtown Manhattan, where my grandfather had made lunch reservations four months in advance. That place had a kind of ancient New York magic in the walls. We were still our slightly awkward selves—my mom sneaking out for cigarettes and my brother refusing to take his headphones off ("The music's off, *God!*"). But the charm of that enormous yet cozy hall, lit up with fireplaces and fragrant with popovers, trumped any lingering grump, if only for an hour. If you ran out of things to talk about, you just discussed which elephant heads on the wall Teddy Roosevelt had shot. It was like having Christmas in Edith Wharton's dollhouse, and this year I'd miss it. Rubbed raw by that silence between Mom and me, I'd never been so happy to avail myself of the divorce kid's prerogative: I booked a flight to my dad's.

Feeling my feelings felt even worse in the weeks leading up to

the holiday, as I slogged through a lifetime's worth of all the emotions I'd covered with pizza and frozen yogurt. The stressful work
e-mails were a welcome respite from the anxious grit that churned
constantly in my gut. While I didn't reach for a snack at every
flare-up, my meal choices spoke loud and clear: mashed potatoes
with a side of soup; thick-bread sandwiches and fries; egg salad on
a roll, no lettuce or tomato, and do you carry Pepto-Bismol? I'd
spend nights in, curled up with stomachaches, watching *South Park*
and Jane Austen adaptations—my recipe for TV comfort food. I lay
there, remembering how in elementary school, every bad day had
sent me right to the nurse's office, convinced it was appendicitis.
"Let her ride it out a bit," my mother would explain to her over the
phone. "Kelsey feels everything with her stomach."

Work was a respite, but only in the way that being picked on
at school is a respite for the kid getting picked on at home. As the
year's end approached, a wave of tension flooded my big, white, be-
tinseled office. If you put your ear to the lobby door you'd hear the
growing hum of whispers wondering about raises and promotions,
titles and bonuses, punctuated with the occasional secret-hallway-
crying break. Maybe every office felt like *Lord of the Flies* during
bonus season. Or, maybe it was just me.

"So, no one cries at your office?"

"No," Harry the liar replied. "Do you want a cocktail, or are we
doing wine?"

"Wine, and you're wrong."

"Kels, no one cries at my office, either. Not unless they just got
engaged or something." Jon handed me the wine list and scooted
his chair in to let Debbie pass behind him as she squeezed out of the
tiny bathroom in the back of Motorino. The tiny East Village pizza
place was the default when none of us could agree on a restaurant.

"I don't think office crying really happens after the age of, like, twenty-five." Jon turned to Harry for confirmation. They both nodded, agreeing that yes, I was a total weirdo.

I looked to Debbie, whose office was a consultation room at a psychiatric hospital, hoping for some validation.

She shrugged. "You don't do it *all* the time, right?"

No, not all the time. Just every time I thought about my family, my job, or my body. Oh, and my friends! They didn't know it but I was mad at them most of the time, too. Every day I didn't hear about a promotion or get a letter from my mom or look physically transformed, I picked a little fight with one of them in my head. Why hadn't Jon initiated plans with me in months? Why did *I* always have to reach out? Why was Chrissy texting me so much today? Does she not know I have a life and other texts to answer, too? If I have to hear about Debbie's sinus infection one more time I'm actually going to call 911 and send an ambulance to her apartment, because that's the only thing that will satisfy her. Little things that could be remedied with a phone call spun out into opera in my head. Because I didn't want to remedy them.

Occupied with their own lives, my friends somehow did not pick up on the brain waves I wordlessly directed at them: *I am having a hard time right now. I feel like a fucking motherless bastard, and my job is in limbo, and, to top it all off, I am eating and praying and loving in front of the entire world.* Well, the entire Internet, at least. I wanted them to suddenly realize the error of their ways and feel like the jerks they were. I wanted to fester. And, I wanted so, so much attention. No, never mind, don't look at me.

On Christmas morning, I flew to DC to spend the holiday with my dad and his girlfriend, Nancy. The flight was delayed about three hundred hours, and so I ended up taking sad airport Instagrams and texting with my Jewish friends in the terminal wine bar for most of the actual holiday. But I knew I'd exhale a little bit when I got to Washington, and put a few hundred miles between me and the Harvard Club.

In my dad's house, I was never a grown-up if I didn't want to be. One blessing and curse of growing up without one of your parents around is that they're always in a hurry to catch up on nurturing. My dad still struggled with letting me buy my own shoes, sure I could neither afford them nor determine my own shoe size without adult supervision. In most ways, being treated like a kid drove me up the wall, but I relished the freedom I felt to laze about and read for hours when visiting Dad's house. His couch was the only place I ever managed to take a successful nap. And, cranky fusspot that I was that December, I really needed one.

I was sick of changing my life. I was tired of having to think about this food-body-fitness stuff all the time, and I was certainly tired of feeling about it. I didn't want to do this anymore. Why did I have to "do" normal eating and exercising, when everyone else just could? Why did this problem have to be my problem? Why couldn't I have become a drunk like everyone else in my family? They make movies about people who quit drinking! No one is going to make a movie about me eating a bagel and not freaking out about it.

Oh yeah, I needed that couch.

I'd impulse-bought a stack of books at various Hudson News kiosks while waiting for my flight at JFK, including Cheryl Strayed's *Wild* and Heidi Julavits's *The Vanishers*, and shoved them in my overnight bag with my half-read copy of *Intuitive Eating*. I'd brought it along, planning to finish it over the holidays, but instead I ignored it, and dived into *Wild* as soon as I got to Dad's. Reading Strayed's memoir for three-hour stretches, I felt suddenly grateful that my own self-realization journey wasn't taking place on the Pacific Crest Trail with a hundred-pound pack on my back.

John2John chimed in: *But ur self-realization is just a sad attempt you emberassing looser.* Next to him, my mother folded her arms and said nothing.

"Any idea of what you'd like to do today?"

Dad came through from the kitchen, eyebrows raised expectantly, to find me mashed into the corner of the couch under four blankets.

"Holocaust Museum."

When I wasn't reading eating-disorder books as a kid, I went for novels like *Number the Stars*, *The Devil's Arithmetic*, and *Maus*. I was just one of those kids. I may have been an extreme case, but the volume of YA Holocaust literature out there leads me to believe there is a group of "those kids" out there.

I'd dragged my dad to the United States Memorial Holocaust Museum when I was nine, but we'd never been back. It was an intense and gutting experience that most people didn't feel the need to do twice. But after four days of post-Christmas ennui, I guess the Holocaust Museum didn't sound all that bad to him. Plus, we could go to Bertucci's after.

There's no real way to describe the experience of walking through the permanent exhibit of the USMHM, except to say that it's disorienting and transporting the way that all good museums are—but more visceral and terrifying than any other I've seen. We entered with a line of hundreds of visitors, and immediately lost each other. After five minutes of looking for Dad and Nancy, I gave up, and I knew they had, too. There's simply no way to keep an eye out for your dad while standing in a room filled with shoes stolen from prisoners upon their arrival at Auschwitz. All I could do was smell that leather and rubber and fabric in the air. I looked down at broken high heels and loafers misshapen by bunions. I knelt down to look closely at a tiny, shining buckle on a sandal strap. I thought about sandaled feet at Auschwitz. I could hardly make myself keep walking into the next room of the exhibit. It seemed too important to stand there with those shoes and really look.

Don't worry. I'm not going to draw a parallel between my diet problems and the Holocaust. Seriously, people. I'm not a fucking maniac.

Self-care is a funny thing. For some people it's funny movies and twenty-minute massages in those awkward face-holding chairs at the back of the nail salon. Some of us prefer three hours of relentless genocide remembrance. Others do the *really* healthy thing and reach out to talk about what's bothering them. I wasn't ready for the really healthy thing, but I sensed with equal dread and relief that I was on my way. I'd call a friend for the next problem (unless there would be no more problems, ever, fingers crossed!). For now, I'd at least have to tell myself what was bothering me: *I'm scared that this won't work. I'm afraid of making a fool of myself in front of everyone. I'm worried that I'm too broken.*

On the way home, I began to cry in silence in the backseat of my dad's car, feeling like a child. Crying is a good thing as long as you're crying in the right direction. I'd never been good at that, always staying dry-eyed during an actual crisis then falling apart over a typo in my essay. But, in the car that day, I knew what the tears were for. Shaken loose by an afternoon faced with true, horrific tragedy, I was having a good cry over my own, small, shitty history—and the realization that no smushed granola bar could make it better. I cried about my cross-wired brain, and how hard it would be to fix. I cried over my lousy, mean mother, because that's always a good direction to cry in. And, fuck it, I cried over John2John.

I'd never be able to stop the nonbelievers from doubting me. Haters, as the saying goes, are gonna hate. But I had plenty of ammo to toss at those doubts, whatever direction they came from. I had my French-fry success story and the Jon Kabat-Zinn meditation that worked magic on any food I applied it to. I had the fact that I had made it to the gym five days a week for the last two months without missing a single day. I had my best friends' numbers in my phone and my dad in the front seat, willing to listen to me moan for at least an hour. All I had to do was, ugh, reach out.

We got home after a quiet lunch, and after changing back into my pajamas (which I called "loungewear" in the daytime), I headed back to the living room. I looked at my book pile. I looked at my blanket pile. I looked at the butt-shaped divot in the corner of the couch. I put *Wild* aside for the time being, feeling Cheryl Strayed clap me firmly on the back, fellow traveler that she was. *On your feet*, she said with a smile. Or maybe not. I had to stop listening to these new voices in my head if I ever wanted to get anywhere. There were plenty of the old ones still echoing around in there, and I needed all the quiet I could get.

For the second time, I signed up to trust myself, and the wisdom and strength of my own body and mind. Sometimes you need to make a promise twice. I sat down and I picked up *Intuitive Eating*. There was only one road out of this mire, and it was me. Only one friend to walk beside, and it was me.

Chapter 16

"Your Image"

My trainer, Stephanie, was a nice lady, but I was pretty sure we were going to end up in a fistfight one day. There's no way you can 100 percent like the person who makes you hold a plank position at 8 a.m. while she counts down the longest minute that has ever passed in the history of recorded time.

"Forty-five seconds," she said.

I thought about my bed. I thought about my cat just lying there on top of it, starting the first of the eighteen naps he would take that day, not in the least bit worried about his core strength. I hated my cat.

"Thirty seconds."

Stephanie sat in front of me on a medicine ball, gazing calmly at her stopwatch while I panted through fluted lips, silently begging for a neck spasm or an earthquake, anything that would give me a reason to drop this plank early and lie flat on the floor until civilization collapsed and Equinox Tribeca was reclaimed by the earth. That's about how long a recovery time I would need. And after that, I wanted a smoothie.

"Twenty-eight seconds."

Now, that was just ridiculous and cruel. If she was going to give me a time check every fifteen seconds, she shouldn't be tossing out numbers like twenty-eight on a whim. How would I ever trust her again after this?

"Ten seconds—oh no, I'm sorry. Fifteen seconds."

You did that on purpose. You knew how much those five seconds meant to me. This is how it begins, Stephanie. And it ends with you and me in a parking lot, Fight Club *style, and I'm Brad Pitt except that I exist and…and, oh my Christ is it ten seconds yet??*

"Ten seconds. Why is Kevin Spacey dancing?"

Kevin Spacey was indeed dancing on the television screen above us. It was either a morning news show, or I'd slipped into in a moment of plank-psychosis.

"Five seconds."

Doesn't she know I'm not ready for this? When I come out of this plank, fall to the ground and literally expire before her eyes, she is going to feel so bad. "Cause of death: plank-related complications," the coroner will say, and then Stephanie will go to jail and I will be buried in an empire-waist dress that hides my untoned core.

"And, time."

Stephanie made me do a lot of things I didn't want to do, but *did* want to do: Cycle, power-walk, take ten thousand steps a day. When I decided to make this health-and-fitness overhaul, I knew the fitness part would take a different kind of coaching than that which I needed for eating. With eating, I needed someone to say, "Try this, and see how you feel, and let's talk about it. Then let's talk about it with your therapist." With fitness, I mostly needed someone to say "Forty-five seconds" while I gasped and struggled through a plank. We both already knew how I felt about it.

I'd become a gym-before-work person, against all odds. It was the only way to make this work without breaking the promise I made myself to maintain a social life. It was doable; I *could* get up a couple hours earlier, and moan all the way to the subway at 7 a.m. I could become a morning person, but I'd have to be a grouchy one. You know those power moms and elite businesspeople who run eleven miles before the sun comes up? No? Well, they exist. I've seen them leaving the gym, freshly blow-dried, just as I stumble in looking like a psycho in hole-worn leggings, which is exactly who I am before 8 a.m. I'd never be a power-anything at that time of day, except maybe a power-whiner. But when my early-morning rendezvous with the treadmill was over, I'd be wide awake and proud of myself for being a slightly bigger badass than I was the day before. That was the story I told myself as I left the gym and walked to work with soaking wet hair. I could work out, shower, and throw some makeup on, but blow-drying was too much to ask. *You are a badass who does not have time to blow-dry.*

Stephanie was not just my trainer in real life; she was also my trainer on TV. One morning, the *Good Morning America* team came to film me at the gym and the office for a segment on the Anti-Diet Project. A producer had spotted the column in her Facebook feed a few days prior and wondered if I might like to talk about this new-fangled "intuitive eating" thing. How was this whole "permission to eat" working out for me?

The truth was, it was working out great. For all the little bumps and even the enormous potholes, I had to admit that quitting dieting was officially not a disaster. Food was becoming simply food. Slowly, my desires had begun to balance out. As the cold weather descended, I craved rough and crunchy winter vegetables, a well-cooked steak, and Harry's hot toddies with extra cinnamon. One week I rediscovered clementines, a fruit I used to avoid, remembering the childhood Saturdays when I'd blow through an entire crate. Now, I'd have two or three as an afternoon snack and put the rest away, knowing, finally, that I could always have another later.

I still side-eyed every spontaneous craving with suspicion: *Do you really want that sashimi salad/chicken burrito/strawberry smoothie with a side of Baked Lays? Okay, your call, but I'm watching.* Watching for what, I wasn't sure, but vigilance was a dieting habit I had yet to release. That was okay, though. Kind of.

"Can you be a little patient with yourself?" Theresa asked, week after week.

"I am! I just want to stay on the right track."

"You realize that's a pretty diet-centric sentence. There isn't really a 'track.'"

"Right, of course. I know that. I get it." And sometimes I did. Then I thought of my face on television.

Here's how I looked on *Good Morning America*: fine. I was a little shiny under the hot lights and was wearing someone else's jewelry, but when I watch that video now, I can see that I look absolutely normal. I look good! I look like a fat girl who's just been let off the leash and discovered that salad isn't a punishment and French fries aren't the crime. God, I wish I had that line back then. Back then, I said something like, "Kale sometimes tastes good, did you know?!"

The story was set to air around 8:15 on a Thursday morning, when Stephanie and I had a training session. As part of the shoot, she'd taken me through a mock workout for the cameras. It was pretty faithful to our usual routine, except that I had on two inches of makeup and my hair looked *amazing*.

Midplank, I saw my face pop up on the television screen above the rowing machines.

"It's on!!!!" I whisper-screamed and hopped up to stare at myself. The opening shot had me standing in front of a counter full of food, pointing at a piece of pizza and making some kind of gesture to indicate how totally cool I was with pizza now. I watched in silence while the Closed Captioning blocks reported that I was "an Internet writer who says she's tired of being fat." Fair. The clips and sound bites were condensed in such a way that it kind of made intuitive eating sound like a diet—clapping for the kale, finger-wagging at the pizza—but that was okay, too. The important thing in that moment was that I was on TV. It actually wasn't that important to Stephanie. When the segment was over, she pointed to the ground.

"Plank, please."

✳

Back at the office, though, I was a momentary rock star—at least, in my mind. As the least fashionable person at a fashion-centric company, I'd always been conscious of myself as a slight disappointment to my coworkers. I got plenty of kudos as a good writer and resident funny-gal-at-the-office, but line me up with my flat-ironed, designer-pursed peers, and one of these things was not like the other. I had no qualms about showing up with my hair in a wet bun and a dry-clean-only sweater that I'd hand-washed in the sink. I wasn't like a hobo or anything, but if there was a hole in the armpit of my dress, I was still going to wear it. Who's waving their arms around all day, anyway?

But that morning, I felt untouchable. I left the gym and strolled into the office in un-blow-dried hair and an Old Navy button-down. I logged onto ABC's website to watch the segment again, with audio this time. That's when my heart started glugging in my chest, a sick arrhythmia begging me not to click on the Play button. When I'd first seen the clip on the gym television, I'd been stunned and giddy, but something inside me had gotten a good look at my big moon face filling up the TV screen and never wanted to see it again. *One time*, I promised. *You have to watch it one more time and then you never have to again.*

Click, and there I was: My thick thighs walking up the stairs, my chunky fingers typing on a keyboard, a double chin bulging out below my enormous melon-head as I smiled and laughed at the correspondent. *Good God, promise me you'll never laugh again.*

It was a pretty lousy five minutes. When it was over, I mentally vowed to find the best double-chin surgeon in New York City. Then I clicked away from the website, put headphones on, and shoved work into my brain. It was just another Thursday, my hair was wet, and I had trending keywords to review.

✶

When I first joined the staff of Refinery29, it wasn't as a writer but as the SEO editor, a position I willingly fell into. Since college, I'd been working in various film-related assistant gigs, while tinkering with screenplays and busting my ass on getting thin. I had far-off dreams of being an indie auteur like the female directors I assisted, but it took a few years to realize that I wouldn't just evolve into one by hanging out with them. And, if I was honest, hanging out with them was just as important to me as the dream itself. Being an assistant meant I spent all day seeking approval from cool, famous older women. It was like having mommy issues was my job.

I was assisting a female CEO in the business end of the industry when I finally decided to take a stab at writing. I had stories to tell, but finally realized that screenwriting wasn't my strong suit. If I wanted to get into print or online writing, I had to play some serious catch-up. All my peers had been cutting their teeth on personal blogs and entry-level gigs for years, while I'd been busy counting Points and fetching other peoples' lunches. So I created my own crash course, taking classes at Mediabistro, Gotham Writers' Workshop, and anywhere else with a decent reputation and discount code, scrambling to grab all the skills I'd need in order to apply for any job at any website. Next, I spent a year pitching myself to anyone I knew with a connection to the industry, picking up freelance work here and there. I got a weekly film-humor column at the blog on SundanceNow, the online streaming branch of the Sundance Channel. It appealed to the part of me still desperate for indie cool-kid credibility, and even when it became clear that approximately no one was reading the thing, I didn't care. I had an extra hundred dollars in my pocket every week and a writing gig on my résumé, and I got to work with a legitimate editor who didn't care that our audience was largely imaginary.

"You've referenced *Heathers* three times in the last month.

Moratorium on Winona Ryder movies for six weeks." He didn't let me half-ass it.

The first thing I wrote for Refinery29 was a freelance food story on easy French cooking that I'd spontaneously pitched to a friend of a friend at a Christmas party. I shot the pictures on my phone using my radiator and bedroom windowsill as a set. Somehow, they liked it. As ever, a little bit of attention just made me want more. Refinery29 kinda liked me, so I'd do anything I could to make them fall in love. I applied for three separate full-time positions at the company, all entry-level, each a major pay cut, and none of which I was entirely capable of actually doing. Still, after months of on-and-off interviews with senior-level editors, someone must have gotten tired of seeing my résumé. There were no writer gigs open, but I was decent at SEO—aka Search Engine Optimization, or the fine art of making your content super-duper Google friendly. Might I be interested in that? they asked. I was willing to make it my heart and soul if it meant getting a foot in the door at such a popular publication.

It was hard. Changing gears is always hard. I joined the company during a time of rapid growth, and every day was punctuated by some new milestone or discovery or pivot. It was technically a start-up, but it was still the biggest office I'd ever worked in, and new employees joined every week. It was both exhausting and energizing, and even if I sometimes felt like an underdressed newbie, I mostly just felt lucky to be there.

I spent my first year at the company wading through keywords, meta titles, and URL structure. It was fun sometimes, like math you do with words ("boyfriend jeans" = 6,600 average searches, but "skinny jeans" = 14,800. Just FYI). But I had a lot to learn, and taking the time to do it meant less time for pitching stories. Still, I pitched whenever I had a spare moment, offering to write a little five-hundred-word essay on my Famous Watermelon Smoothie or a DIY Shamrock Shake. All my freelance stories had been food-related, so I became the de facto Food and Drink editor in my spare time.

Slowly, my job began to evolve into something between SEO editor and food-and-funny-things writer. Gwyneth Paltrow might sell something ridiculous on her website, and I'd pitch an article to be titled, "Gwyneth's Thousand-Dollar Shot Glass and Other Things You Need This Christmas." The cronut craze swept New York City, and I spent a summer on breaking pastry news. My stories were sometimes hits but rarely flops, and so I was allowed and encouraged to keep up the dual role. Many members of the team wore multiple hats, but after a year and a half doing SEO and part-time writing at the company, it became clear which hat fit me best.

I became a staff writer in the fall of 2013, just before the Anti-Diet Project debuted. Sure, it was a title change only, but it was a win. For the time being, SEO was still my main responsibility, but I was thrilled that the higher-ups saw my value as a writer. Furthermore, I would now be included as a peer among the more senior editors, helping to develop ideas for the site. Above all, they urged, I should think about what I wanted my role to be on the team next year, because there were big things ahead, and if I kept this up I could be a part of it.

I felt recognized and welcomed. I felt like the fucking American dream. After a few years of classes and relentless self-promotion, somehow I was a working writer living in New York City. Really! With business cards and everything!

I was juggling even more responsibility, but it was responsibility I'd earned, and if I did it well, then this title-change-only would become a real promotion in the coming year. It was a testament both to my hustle and the company's faith in me that I'd gone from desperate applicant to staff writer so fast. I could not believe my outrageous luck. It wasn't until starting the Anti-Diet Project that I realized I wasn't just lucky. I was also good at my job.

✻

"I thought your *GMA* segment was great," Margaux told me one morning in the office kitchen. Margaux was a truly seasoned editor and one of the handful of senior staff who oversaw my department. She was so senior, in fact, that most of us didn't even report to her directly, but we constantly craved her praise. Sharp and glamorous, Margaux brought out the mommy issues in *all* of us. It was a pretty effective motivational tool, actually.

Though the show had aired months ago, this was the first time she'd spoken to me about it directly. I know this because I'd literally daydreamed about the scenario in which she might tell me how great it was, how proud she was, and how pretty I'd looked.

"Thank you!" I squealed, my voice coated in *love-me-love-me-love-me*. She'd come in to make a cup of tea as I stood slicing a banana onto peanut butter toast, my current breakfast phase. Something caught her eye.

"Kelsey, why are you eating this?" She picked up the loaf of potato bread I'd brought in to make the toast. "It's so processed!"

If she wasn't my boss and I wasn't so chicken I might have told her that I was eating it because: (a) I liked it. It was soft and a little sweet and reminded me of the tomato sandwiches I used to make every summer as a kid. (b) It was cheap, and I could stand to save some cash after intuitively ordering expensive take-out Vietnamese food almost every night for a week. And (c) I was a grown woman who bought whatever the hell kind of bread she wanted. Instead, I folded.

"I know. I'm sorry, you're right."

"Just eat Ezekiel bread!" She shook the offending loaf in the air to emphasize her point, then dropped it back on the counter. I nodded, rapid-fire.

"I know! I like Ezekiel bread!"

And I did! Ezekiel bread reminded me of the past as well. It was the only bread I'd been allowed to eat during the Eat Right for Your Type phase, and even then it was rationed to one slice a day. Ezekiel bread is not so much bread as it is a bunch of legumes and millet smashed into loaf form. It's hearty and dense, really good if you're in the mood for legumes and millet. But not so much if what you want is bread.

"So, why are you eating this poisonous garbage?!"

I didn't know what to say, but running away didn't seem like a move that would earn me a promotion.

"Because they didn't have any at my grocery store."

She held my gaze for just an instant while I mentally scrambled for a better excuse for eating potato bread. Temporary insanity?

"Oh, fine. I'll let you keep this." She picked up her teacup, rolled her eyes, and smiled, friends again. "Anyway, yes, congratulations on the segment. You were excellent."

Was it over? It was over.

"I'm so glad you liked it."

"You're so smart and eloquent." She pressed the hot button on the water dispenser and filled her ceramic teacup, then faced me again, her eyes now gentle and sincere. "I hope you know that."

"Thank you."

"And know that *I* know it, too."

I smiled. I did know it. And I was thankful.

"Next time," she said, eyes dropping to my shirt, "I'm styling you."

Margaux whooshed out of the kitchen in two tall, silky steps. I looked from my half-sliced banana to the criminal loaf of potato bread and took a few deep breaths. It felt as if I'd just been fired but still had to go to work.

From then on, I tried to eat out of sight. It wasn't just Margaux; many of my colleagues were gluten-free or Paleo or on Day 300 of a nine-year cleanse. The fridges were filled with dark green bottles, marked up with initials so no one would accidentally drink someone else's green juice and incite a knife fight in the office. There were a few rogue eaters. My desk-mate kept boxes of Easy Mac under her desk, and everyone's diets went out the window if someone suggested getting Chipotle for lunch. This was a unique and innovative team, no question. But, in terms of food, it fit the fashion-website mold to a T. Staffers dressed well and ate weird. And then there was me.

There were few food rules in my new routine, but undistracted eating was one of them. Removing work, GChat, and Internet gossip from my lunch hour was a pain in the ass, but it did help me to taste food more, sense fullness approaching, and learn to actually *eat* rather than shove a burrito into my face until it was gone. At work, however, it served another purpose: hiding.

Yes, it was a healthy habit, taking the bowl of udon away from my desk to find a little nook in the lounge area where I'd sit quietly for ten minutes, engaging with nothing but lunch. But it also kept me hidden from the casual glances and commentary of colleagues. Someone might see me slurping up noodles and say, "Oh my God, *what* are you eating?" and I'd freeze, waiting for another potato-bread lecture. But, more often than not, they'd follow up with, "It looks incredible." I'd watch them walk away in cool shoes to eat a cool lunch, then look at my delicious noodles and wish I'd been craving something more on-trend. Maybe *raw* noodles.

Nobody else ever picked on me for eating anything, but my self-consciousness knew no boundaries. Neutral or not, any comment on my meal made me feel like that little kid, caught in the pantry with a handful of chocolate chips. Enjoying food in public was strange, to say the least. Here I was, eating udon noodles, devil-may-care. What a pioneer I was: a fat girl in Keds, having lunch in front of God and everyone.

Except the "fat girl" part seemed to be changing a little. The same old digital scale still idled under my bureau, though I hadn't stepped on it in months, knowing what a seductive little trigger it was. When I was dieting, my whole day had been dictated by those numbers, and in my self-conscious state, I could easily slide back into that old habit. Stephanie did routine physical assessments of me at the gym, but I just looked at the ceiling while she recorded my weight. Whatever the number, it wouldn't be right. I wanted to be the kind of person who wouldn't be thrown into a tailspin by the bathroom scale, but the best I could do was acknowledge that in fact, I absolutely was. So, I looked at the ceiling then stepped off the scale, trying to read a number in Stephanie's face.

There were numbers I could enjoy, though. In the few months since I'd quit dieting and begun a regular fitness routine, my blood pressure had normalized, my resting heart rate had dropped, and my body fat percentage had taken a serious hit. To the naysayers, the diet peddlers, and the nasty voices in my own head, I said: *How do you like them apples?* Those stats were a balm on my anxious doubts and a real piece of proof that intuitive eating hadn't led me to overdose on pizza.

I wasn't trying on my skinny clothes yet, but my wardrobe had nearly doubled as I began to fit into my slightly-less-fat clothes. It was such a subtle shift that at first it barely registered. When it did start to sink in, I actively tried not to get too excited about it. Excitement lives right next door to anxiety.

"You look great, dude!" Chrissy announced one night when we met up for dinner at a little Williamsburg bistro tucked under the Brooklyn-Queens Expressway. She'd been away for over a month, overseeing her work in a group art show.

"Aw, thanks," I demurred. Compliments were the worst.

"Seriously!" she added with a double thumbs-up.

I thanked her again, and then ducked my head into the menu, a little nameless knot of something curled up in my chest. I couldn't decide what to get. If I got the pasta, I wouldn't have any protein and would probably need a snack later. Steak frites sounded great, but it also sounded really heavy, and it didn't come with greens.

I needed greens, suddenly, urgently. The spiral commenced: Why did the scallops come with béarnaise sauce? Scallops were supposed to be clean and light, not drowned in buttery goo. Maybe I could get the scallops but with the sauce on the side and greens instead of potatoes? Would they do that in a place like this? This looked like a no-substitutions kind of restaurant. God, fucking Williamsburg. Why did I live here? The waitress approached with a friendly hello and I almost jumped out of my chair.

I ordered the steak frites and ate every bite in under five minutes.

"Congratulations, you have been named a Body Image Hero of 2013!" The e-mail press release detailed an eleven-person list of women who'd "spoken out about how we treat women's bodies, and why standard beauty ideals are failing us." I'd come in at number nine, right between Jennifer Lawrence and a plus-size Barbie doll.

By mid-winter, a lot of things seemed to have happened at once. The Anti-Diet Project had been written up by a handful of media outlets, I'd been interviewed about my revolutionary decision to eat like a normal person, and now I was a hero. Those first few instances of praise and recognition were thrilling and novel; I could post them on my Facebook page, accompanied by some self-deprecating witticism, and not look like a total braggart. But seeing my name next to the word *hero* made me feel like the nerd who gets named prom queen as a joke. I wasn't a hero, and I wasn't trying to be. I just didn't want to be such a loser.

Still, some part of all this illustrious ass-kissing must have sunk in, because it wasn't just the Anti-Diet Project that was getting all the attention. In recent months, I'd begun to pitch bigger, more ambitious stories. I wrote more and more first-person opinion pieces, grabbing at any opportunity to take a stance on something. Writing the column, I'd realized it wasn't just talking about weight and body image that made it successful, but the way I talked about it. I had a big mouth, and a lot of people seemed to like it. Even those who didn't sure seemed to like disagreeing with it. I ventured out of my comfort zone, pitching in-depth stories on men's rights activists, the college campus rape crisis, and other things that really pissed me off. I still enjoyed writing the Anti-Diet Project and the occasional watermelon-smoothie stories, because everyone loves a good smoothie. But it was thrilling to discover I could write about something other than food and my relationship to it. Why not? If the press, the readers, and my colleagues thought I was smart, maybe I was. Maybe I could speak up, have an opinion, and ask for things—and maybe I deserved them?

✶

Margaux and I sat in a conference room one frozen January morning. After half an hour of deep breathing and pep-talking myself, I'd called the meeting to discuss my future position, promotion, and, maybe, a raise? Months had passed while I'd waited for all those things to spontaneously happen, before it occurred to me that wishing only works if you have a genie on hand, so perhaps it was up to me to *ask* for them.

I'd thought it over and come up with what seemed like a perfect-fit title for me: lifestyle editor. It was a hypothetical role that had been floating around in the ether of the company, so I decided to nominate myself. I'd proven a valued member of the team and had as much of a presence on the site as anyone else with "editor" in their title. I'd been there even longer than some of them, so seniority wasn't an issue. I didn't know if I was "lifestyle" enough, but I was *something* enough to have been given the same responsibilities as those peers. It was time to jump off the fence and into the role I'd been unofficially playing for months.

"Okay," Margaux replied after I delivered the pitch. "That's an interesting choice."

"It's broad, and that allows for flexibility in the role," I explained, reading not-so-discreetly from my notes.

"But you're a writer."

"Of course, but I think I could still write in a role like this."

She nodded. "I suppose you could. And it covers a lot of your territory."

OH MY GOD, IS THIS ACTUALLY WORKING?

"This is a senior editor role, of course." Margaux raised her eyebrows and locked eyes with me. "That means a lot more than just writing and editing."

"Oh, absolutely."

"When you're in a role like that, you need to project an image."

"I understand."

"And I think we need to talk more about *your* image."

"That's fine. That'd be great."

"Being our lifestyle editor means you'd need to be out there and visible. It's about being a representative. It's not about wearing flip-flops and sitting slumped over your desk all day."

I felt the urge to sit up straighter in my chair. Did I *slump?*

"If you want to be on that level, I need to see something aspirational."

"Okay. I hear you on that."

"I'm glad you brought this up. Never be afraid to call these meetings."

"Thank you for taking the time." I looked down at all my notes. All those ridiculous exclamation points.

Margaux cocked her head to grab my gaze again, and smiled. "Listen, this isn't a no. We just want to find the role that fits you best."

"Of course. Got it."

"I hope you do. And, in the meantime, I want to see you project an image. I want you to inspire."

I left the meeting feeling less like a hero than ever before. Margaux wasn't entirely wrong. I'd never worn flip-flops to the office, but I didn't look like anyone worth aspiring to. A more secure woman might not take it so personally, but she probably wouldn't have to eat lunch in hiding, either.

I love a good makeover montage. Sitting at my desk, clicking glumly through e-mails, I made a decision. I could mope and cry and feel put upon, or I could montage myself. I didn't have to go full-blown *Grease*, strutting into the office wearing leather pants and swinging a loaf of Ezekiel bread. I'd just start to step it up a little: get my boots shined and throw on some lipstick. I liked having shiny boots and lipstick—I just never took the time to actually have them. It never occurred to me that they were deal breakers.

Fashion was the only topic I didn't cover at a largely fashion-based publication. People often asked me why, and I'd reply that I never got interested in fashion because fashion wasn't interested in me, which was true. High-end designers didn't consider bodies like mine to be of any value. Nor did many mainstream stores, which didn't carry anything over a size 10 or 12. My first year at Refinery29, I received a gift card to Madewell for my birthday. I left the Soho store empty-handed, having found nothing over a size 10 on the racks. I was shopping with five-one, pixie-weight Debbie, my tiniest friend. Walking down Broadway, I attempted a joke to shake off the embarrassment I imagined we both felt:

"I guess I shouldn't expect Madewell to carry monster-size." Then I cried like a monster-size baby. (It's really good to have a friend who's a shrink.)

It wasn't just the issue of availability that made me the kind of woman who didn't care about clothing. In fact, I did care about it. From the first time I saw Ali MacGraw in *Love Story*, I've coveted camel coats and bell sleeves. For years, I collected Victorian nightgowns off of eBay—the kind you might wear while dying of Spanish flu. And, of course, there was my bulging closet full of skinny clothes, ranked in order of their resemblance to anything Claire Danes wore in *Romeo + Juliet*. My taste was almost unreasonably feminine. But all those things looked hideous on my body, because my body was hideous. You just can't put a monster in a baby doll dress.

Still, I would give "aspirational" a shot. One Sunday night, I combed through my wardrobe, making piles for Cute, Boring, and Can I Get This Stain Out. I tried wearing actual shoes to work instead of sneakers. I spent the extra ten minutes to blow my hair dry instead of letting it freeze into dreadlocks on my five-minute walk from the gym to the office. When I had an interview or a photo shoot, I tiptoed up to my stylish colleagues for advice, all but begging for them to montage me. It wasn't *Grease* so much as *Cinderella* I was going for, and what a relief to have an office full of on-trend birds and well-coiffed mice who were happy to teach me how to knot my belt and roll up my sleeves just so.

"You're looking good, you know," Stephanie said with a smile, watching me go through my warm-up at the gym one morning. At the time, I was midsquat, a resistance band wrapped around my thighs for stability. Trust me when I tell you that no one looks good in this position. I sputtered out a laugh.

"I'm serious," she continued. "You've come a long way since the fall."

"Yeah? Then why are my knees still shaking?" They were trembling lightly in the resistance band as I finished the twenty-fifth squat.

"Because knees are tricky and Rome wasn't built in a day. But, come on, look at the progress you've made."

I shrugged, trying to duck out from underneath her compliment.

"I'm serious. Look at yourself."

She pointed to the mirrored wall in front of us. During workouts, I routinely stepped to the side or faced the other way to avoid
watching myself. It was hard enough to walk past a plate-glass
window in my favorite outfit; staring at my lightly dimpled ass in
profile as I wobbled through a set of backward lunges seemed like
borderline masochism. Still, she pointed, so I looked. In the mirror
I saw a tilted, round face, craned upward to hide a potential double
chin. I saw legs placed wide apart, with one hip jutted out so the
thighs didn't touch. I saw hands on hips and elbows yanked back to
narrow my broad shoulders. I saw everything I did to avoid seeing
myself. It was full-body duck face. It was the only way I knew how
to look in a mirror.

I left the gym with Stephanie's encouragement ringing through
my mind like a catchy tune. I was "looking good." I was "getting
better." I was also starving after she'd kicked my ass up and down
the StairMaster, and couldn't wait for breakfast. On hard-core
workout days, I almost always craved an omelet from the deli in
our office lobby. That morning I wanted it with extra broccoli and
spinach, a little American cheese, and a side of potatoes.

As I was waiting in line to order my breakfast, a wave of anxiety
hit me right in the gut. *Do I really need all that fat? Maybe I should skip
the cheese today—no, maybe I* want *to skip the cheese today. And the potatoes would be overkill. I always end up throwing out the last few bites, and
isn't that wasteful? Would I even eat any of them if they weren't there? How
about I just get oatmeal today? Or oatmeal and a hard-boiled egg. That'll be
just as satisfying as the omelet. I just want the omelet because it tastes good,
but my body doesn't need eggs and cheese and the oil they'll cook it in. It's not
that the omelet isn't allowed, it's just that I don't actually want it.*

I ordered the oatmeal and a hard-boiled egg, both of which were
a little on the slimy side. It didn't matter, though, since I rapidly
gobbled up the whole meal the moment I sat down at my desk,
anxious to finish before anyone could see me. My throat burned,
scalded by the hot oatmeal, and I took enormous gulps from my

water bottle, a splash of water dripping off my chin and onto my crisp, striped dress. I wasn't eating like a normal person anymore. I was eating like a cartoon—a Looney Tune.

That night I lay in bed, grabbing the flesh of my stomach in an effort to ascertain my weight. In theory, I didn't care about it, or at least I shouldn't care about it, and up until this week, I thought I'd pretty much stopped caring about it. But my hands sure did. They were frenzied and filled with panic at the new fullness in my middle—and it was new. That morning, I'd put on the jeans that had fit three weeks ago and found them newly snug. Something had changed.

For months, I'd been casually conscious of a slow but steady weight loss, but it had seemed like small potatoes next to the progress I was making with everything else. Intuitive eating had been life-altering in a way that no diet had been, but every diet had promised to be. I was far less focused on food, naturally inclined toward balanced eating, and, finally free from juggling calories and carbs, my life had suddenly cracked wide open with possibility. After a lifetime of pouting in the shadows, I'd made myself a spotlight. Ugh, and now I had to stand in it, belly flab and all.

I stop reading any sentence that starts with "Last night I dreamt..." unless it ends with "...I went to Manderley again." As a device, it's indulgent and easy, and I don't believe the writer anyway. That said, believe *me* when I say: That night I dreamt I went to Walnut Hill again. It wasn't an entirely unexpected jaunt into the past, since every challenge in my adult life seemed to send me right back to high school, and my ickiest self. The dream was a re-creation of a real-life scene I'd trotted out many times for sympathy from friends. But really, it only hurts because it's true:

I was sixteen and it was the fall of my junior year. By then, I'd slowly begun to find my little niche. My friends were real friends now, I had a lunch table, and though I was by no means top of the heap, there was a certain confidence that came with knowing that at least I wasn't a new kid anymore, simply because there were even newer kids now. I'd even been cast in my first play, as a female police officer, though getting the role still felt like a sneaky trick I'd pulled off. Before I went in to read for the director (my acting teacher, Henry), I'd seen another girl practicing her audition in front of her friends. She'd lowered her voice to a guttural bark, plainly doing the stereotypical butch lady cop. Kat was older than me, and part of a group that was decidedly top of the heap. Her friends laughed as she puffed up her chest, stood with her legs apart and even thrust her belly forward trying to thicken up her slender frame.

When she went into the audition room I overheard how Henry guffawed with laughter, applauding as she went more and more over the top, going from stereotype to caricature. It was so gruff, so entirely macho that I sat agape, listening outside the door. She exited the room, a slight, wavy-haired goddess again, smirking with the confidence of someone who knows they've gotten the role.

At once, I realized that was how the part had been written, and why it had never occurred to me to read it that way. It was too obvious. I didn't need to stick out my stomach or toughen up my girlishness. I already fit the bill all too well. I looked exactly like the character described in the Xeroxed summaries handed out to us with audition material: "butch, no-nonsense, hot-tempered, and can take a punch." But I had been at Walnut Hill for a year and had yet to be cast in a show. I was not a bad actress, but maybe, *maybe*, I was hesitant. So, if I could get a part by playing the fat girl like a fat girl should act, then I couldn't be afraid to try.

In my audition, I stood with legs splayed wide and fists on hips, long hair hidden in a bun behind my head. I barked through the monologue and paused as Henry laughed maniacally, wiping tears from the corners of his eyes as I threw in a spontaneous armpit sniff. It was a comedy after all. And fat people were supposed to be smelly. Of course I got the part.

But three weeks later, he'd stopped laughing.

"Chest voice, please!" he called to me as we rehearsed on stage. The three other cast members stood quietly as he gave me the same note I got every day. I cleared my throat, husky from yelling, and delivered my line again.

"Kelsey, go deeper," he coached. "I know you've got that voice in there somewhere."

I did it again. Henry jumped up from his seat and came up to the stage. I looked over at Kat, who'd been cast in another role, and rolled my eyes. We weren't friends, but we'd become friendly enough to roll our eyes at each other whenever Henry gave an annoying note during rehearsals. This time, however, she just folded her arms and looked away, as sick of this as I was.

"What's going on, huh?" Henry asked. I could tell that he was trying to walk the line between frustrated director and empathetic teacher.

"I don't know. I'm trying to project."

"You've got to practice and train your voice. Have you been doing those exercises?"

"Yes, every day." Well, every other day–ish.

"I can't stress enough how important this is for you. You've *got* to develop your lower register."

"I know."

"You can't be all the way up here," he squeaked in a mock-girly voice. "That lower register is going to be your best friend. If you want to do this for a living"—he gestured around the stage—"then you've got to understand that."

"I do understand."

"No, listen. You're never going to be Juliet, honey."

At this I felt the rest of the cast turn, pretending not to look. I was suddenly, horribly visible. Henry kept going.

"Never. *Maybe* you could do Lady Macbeth someday, but I don't know. Come on, you know you're not the ingenue. These are the roles you need to get good at." He pointed at my boxy police-uniform costume. "This is who you are."

You're never going to be Juliet, honey. That's the phrase I really lean on when I tell this story. When I dreamt of it, I mostly dreamt of that sentence and the silence that came after. But when I woke up that morning back in my apartment, I finally had a comeback: Fuck. That.

Fuck that attitude. Fuck shitty teachers who dare to tell sixteen-year-olds who they are. Fuck anyone who looks at your stomach or your arms or your perfectly human body and says you better quit trying to look like a girly girl and act like the fat, sexless, support-ing role you were born to be. Fuck people who'd rather you look like what they want to see or else not be seen at all. *Yes, please, oh please, just don't make us look at you.* Fuck that nonsense because it's too late. I exist. Sorry, sucks for you.

I lay in bed thinking in "fucks" for a while when I finally thought: *Fuck flip-flops!* Margaux had told me that if I wanted to be a senior editor then I had to stop "wearing flip-flops and sitting slumped over your desk all day." And for weeks I'd been playing dress-up, all the while thinking, *But I don't wear flip-flops! I may wear Target dresses, but I'm not such an urchin that I'd wear shower shoes to work!* That anger had felt good—righteous. I was beleaguered and oppressed, a victim of workplace fashion harassment. In my at-tempt at a makeover, I'd applied more lipstick over gritted teeth and tottered around in heels, all the while knowing the promotion was lost and it was all just because I wasn't pretty enough.

Wasn't that a seductive little story? And how long had I been telling it to myself?

Henry was right; I am no Juliet, nor am I ever going to be. Juliet is a suicidal teenager who married the first guy she kissed and then faked her own death when her parents kind of freaked out about it.

The only thing we have in common is that we're both total drama queens. But that doesn't mean I can't wear lacy dresses and delicate bracelets and long, wavy haircuts. It doesn't mean that I'm not worthy of playing the lead. What the hell kind of life am I living if I cast myself as the sidekick?

I wasn't an editor, either. As the weeks went on and I awaited word on my new position, I finally heard what Margaux had said in that first meeting: *You're a writer.* Yeah, I had plenty of other skills, but this was the one I'd hitched my wagon to. It was the job I wanted. So why was I running from the career I'd worked so damn hard for? Because *editor* sounded more prestigious? Because it would make me feel equal to my stylish, skinny-girl colleagues? Was I trying to Juliet this thing?

Here's another thing I'm not: in high school anymore. At sixteen, a teacher's flippant remark could crush me. But I was twenty-nine and still desperate to play the victim. No one should be picked on for the bread they eat or the shoes they wear, but what was stopping me from saying, "Thanks, I got this!" and walking away? Why did I persistently see things through a lens of meanness, filtering out any praise or respect? How come I chose to believe only the bad things people said about me?

I didn't have the answer, but I suspected it had something to do with that scared little kid in the pantry. I'd known from that first meeting with Theresa that she wasn't quite done with me yet. If I was ever going to shake her, I had to quit listening so hard to other people and their rules. I'd learned to turn inward and listen to my body, but my mind was still a sieve of rejection and criticisms, and everyone who ever told me I wasn't Juliet, but a big, fat slob in flip-flops, slouching on the sidelines. There was such a pitiful ease in believing them, too. As long as I was officially unworthy, I could stay safe and invisible, dreaming of my bright, thin future while never actually trying because, y'know, they'd never let me play anyway. But in the last few months, I'd stepped into that future, regardless of my size, and now my life was bigger and better than I'd ever expected it to be.

I was, as Margaux had urged, projecting an image. But it was *my* image, and maybe not her ideal. Maybe it wasn't yet my ideal, either, because when I look back at *Good Morning America*, I see a girl who wanted nothing more than recognition—except to go hide under the bed all day. Faking confidence had taken me a long way toward actual confidence, but I had to take the last step myself. That was the step out of someone else's opinion of me, and into my own, true skin. Maybe a baby doll dress, too.

There's a popular self-helpy quote that says you teach people how to treat you. I think that's true, but you also teach them how to look at you. Margaux taught me that, when I finally learned the right way to hear her. She, as much as anyone, nudged me out of my shell and into the world: *Here I am, like it or not.* She also soon promoted me into the senior writing position where I belonged.

It wasn't just criticisms but also compliments that I had to learn how to hear. All those you-look-great (read: you-look-skinnier) comments had sent me right back into diet mode. The second people started noticing the subtle changes in my body, I'd wanted to accelerate the process, keep going forward, better, right to the top of the heap and the low end of the scale. That's what got me panicking over omelets and gobbling down my dinner. I'd been overthinking and eating with anxiety again, looking up for those approving faces rather than in at my own hunger. I lost touch with my body for a moment there, and now my jeans were snug again. I'd forgotten the primary step in intuitive eating. Once again, I gave myself permission to eat, to stop eating, to buy potato bread, and to wear the clothes that made me feel good. Only then did my mind quit racing at mealtimes, allowing me to start eating like a person again.

It is easy to say that people are good or bad, because villains and heroes make for great stories. But that's rarely true. Villains are almost always phantoms of our own making, and real heroism happens when you stop repeating that same old story and start telling the truth.

In reality, I wasn't an ingenue or a teenager or a fan of high heels. Once, I'd been a kid in a pantry, but I wasn't her anymore, either. As long as I clung to those identities, I would never find my own. I had to quit trying so hard to become something else—I just had to quit trying so hard, period. If I wanted to move forward, I had to get good and comfortable with who I really was: a writer, a woman, and kind of a drama queen.

Chapter 17

Someone Else's Story

How are things different now that you've given up dieting?"
The question sounded garbled through the conference-room speakerphone, but I didn't need her to repeat it. The nineteen-year-old interviewing me for her student newspaper was not the first to ask me this. Almost every day the topic came up. I sometimes imagined this must be what it felt like to be Jennifer Aniston, constantly having to tell reporters that she was fine, just fine, thanks, and she promised to have a baby ASAP. (Except, I wasn't Jennifer Aniston and this wasn't *Vanity Fair*. It was a bi-monthly insert in a free campus newspaper; more copies would be barfed on than actually read.) Still, I let myself have the self-important daydream as I answered the same old queries: Had I lost weight? Was I in better shape? Those answers I'd gotten down pat. Then came that last question and I choked, every time.

"It's nice to be able to eat pizza without freaking out," I replied. Groundbreaking, I know.

I wrapped up the interview and headed back to my desk, grabbing my lunch out of the office refrigerator on the way. I was on a purple cabbage kick, so I filled a plate with the crunchy salad and leftover chicken thighs I'd baked with apples and onions the night before. The office seemed more occupied than usual, as everyone

had skipped their Starbucks runs and off-site lunches to huddle inside against the endless winter, now bleeding into spring. Rather
than find a free corner for a distraction-free lunch, I decided to eat
at my desk, utilizing the original site blocker: a scarf over the computer screen. But first, I Instagrammed it.

It's virtually impossible to succinctly summarize the transforma-
tive joy that begins when you jail-break out of the cage that's kept
you anxious and miserable and self-defeating for your entire conscious life. So when pressed for a straightforward answer about how
quitting dieting had changed my life, all I came up with was the
pizza quote.

I don't know when or why I picked that food as my personal
emblem. It was my first instinct, but it wasn't the whole truth. I
said "pizza" because I was fairly certain that no one wanted to hear
the real answer: mindfulness. That's what I talk about when I talk
about pizza. If it sounds boring, it's because it is—atomically boring. It was that extreme boredom that turned my whole life upside
down.

People often conflate "mindful eating" with intuitive eating, but
that's just because they both sound kind of Zen and tedious. Intuitive eating is a multilayered approach that helps maniacs like
me learn to eat like normal people. Mindful eating plays a role in
that process, but it is simply the practice of eating mindfully. And,
when I say simple, I mean the hardest fucking thing I had ever had
to learn.

In my early days of intuitive eating, it was simple. It meant
turning off the television, taking out my headphones, or stepping
away from the computer for at least one meal a day. The difference
there was instantly apparent: I tasted more, I needed less, and I actually felt the experience of satisfying hunger and fueling my body.
On the one hand, it was incredible! What a novel experience, being
so singularly focused and aware. On the other hand, it was awful.
And, soon, that hand balled into a fist and banged onto the table,

making a racket throughout every damn dinner. I was antsy and irritated, every single time. I forced myself to slow down and chew
with consciousness, but it took all my effort not to shovel down
the food and get back to *anything* else. How about picking up that
essay I'd started writing two years ago? Or I could change the litter box! My kingdom for a credit-card charge to dispute. But I'd
strong-armed myself into this promise to eat just *one* meal per day
with only myself for company.

Anyone who's ever meditated understands the importance of riding out that itchy restlessness. But I'd never lasted for more than
one meditation class, and I'd never met an itch I hadn't scratched.

I did my best. For months, I sat there with my plate and breathed
through the irritation. Wasn't it worth it for all the benefits?
Without mindfulness, I'd never have been able to neutralize French
fries in the great Battle of Brunch. But by now, it had become routine and boring. My lunch break had become less break and more
just lunch. Looking back on the one hand—the rational one—I
knew that was the whole point of this undertaking. But on the
balled-up-fist hand, that didn't mean I had to like it. That didn't
mean I couldn't sit down with my steak salad, furious with it for being nothing but meat and spinach—a lunch I desired but still nothing more than lunch. And after each of those quiet, conscious meals,
I got a glimpse of something unfamiliar and inevitable: Mindfulness
was sneaking off of the plate and into the rest of my life.

People say that food is the good girl's drug. Certainly, I'll own up
to my decades of addictive, disordered behavior around food. But
now I realize it was just one particularly cheap and sticky strain of
my real drug of choice: distraction.

It was easy to see how it slipped by me for so long. When I was
a little kid, it just meant I was daydreamy, or imaginative, running

around performing whole musicals and movie scenes for the cat. When I grew up into a voracious reader, then great! Who would discourage a twelve-year-old from rereading *The Catcher in the Rye?* In high school, I was a devoted theater student, and in college I was serious about film study.

All that was true. Then there's the truer version.

I wasn't just rereading *The Catcher in the Rye.* I was rereading everything, constantly: in the car on the way to school, at recess, waiting for Karen to come pick me up, and then all the way home. When I got home, I shoved a book on tape into my boom box and listened to another story until I fell asleep. Once, I discovered there was no audio version of *Just As Long As We're Together* (the Judy Blume novel I just couldn't grow out of), so I spent a weekend making one by reading the book aloud into a tape recorder. Then I just sat down and listened to it, playing Free Cell on the computer, for an entire summer.

Those teenaged nights I spent alone in my dorm at Walnut Hill singing along to CDs weren't just about musical appreciation. They were about not being there, not being me. I was long gone, deep in my head, buried in the drama of "Someone Else's Story" (from the original Broadway cast recording of *Chess*).

Then I'd gone off to spend college in one long movie binge under the auspices of "studying." True, I did honestly love the medium, but part of what I loved about it was sitting in the dark watching other people live their lives. (And it's not as if my taste was strictly highbrow; for every Andrzej Wajda film in my repertoire, there was a *Garden State*.) No matter what the quality, any film was better than my own life. I much preferred staying in to watch *Reality Bites* rather than going out and experiencing just how much reality actually bit. But that was just the mildest symptom of my distraction habit.

Driving back from BU sophomore year, I got pulled over by a state police officer going ninety-four miles an hour while listening to a particularly tense and thrilling chapter of *Harry Potter and the Order of the Phoenix*. Later that summer I totaled my mother's minivan in my first and only car accident. I wish I could tell you I was drunk, but the truth is I was singing at the top of my lungs along with *Joseph and the Amazing Technicolor Dreamcoat*, completely shit-faced on Andrew Lloyd Webber.

Not once did it occur to me that this might be a problem. How could it? I'd built a wall of sound around myself so loud that nothing could get in. And I damn sure didn't want to get out. It wasn't until I started sitting through those quiet, mindful meals that the truth began to dawn on me.

As an unhappy kid, I'd let distraction swallow me whole, and that was fair. Children have no control over their own lives, caught in the wake of grown-up reality. But even as I grew into a teenager and adult, the fantasy was all I needed, and all I could handle. I'd handle real life later. When I chose a story to escape into, it was always about someone a little bit older than me—nothing too relatable. In high school I watched *Love Story*, imagining how much better life would be when I got to college. In college, I watched *The Last Days of Disco*, thinking how sophisticated and social I would be once I got that first job and cramped but well-decorated apartment. My dorm room was a sty, but the second I got my degree I'd transform into the kind of person who vacuumed.

Then, there I was, an alleged adult with the cramped apartment and cat hair all over the floor. The more real my life became around me, the harder I read, sang, watched, and of course, ate.

When I was being good, I'd spend weekends chopping up heaps of greens for those virtuous pots of healthy soup, listening to David Sedaris read essays on a CD player, then an iPod, then an iPhone. When I was in between diets, I'd pull sheet after sheet of chocolate chip cookies out of the oven, then eat a stinging hot plateful in front of *When Harry Met Sally*. Fine, my twenties weren't going as planned, but I would make lemons into lemon bars and remember that everything would become better, brighter, and funnier when I hit my thirties. Thirty was the new twenty, the part where everything got good. So said every women's magazine: *By thirty, you know what you want, you're making more money, and you're finally comfortable in your own skin.* Really? Great! After spending a decade in my aimless, broke, uncomfortable twenties, thirty sounded like a blast. Until then, I'd just watch a movie and wait to grow up.

I was twenty-nine when I sat down for that first distraction-free meal. I didn't know then, but each time I came to the table I took another step out of the daydream and into reality.

"How are things different now that you've given up dieting?" they asked, and I'd give them the pizza quote. It was true. Then there was the truer version.

Chapter 18

The Truer Version

Heading out the door one steel-blue winter morning, I did the usual routine: zip the coat, scan the room, earbuds in, gym bag, handbag, keys. I locked the door and shook it in the jamb, just to be sure, then lumbered down the stairs making a swishy racket in all my winter gear. Outside, I waved at my early-morning neighbor friend and his rambunctious golden retriever. We'd never exchanged names, but Friendly Glasses Man and I saw each other most mornings as I headed to the gym before work. I liked to think he called me Cool Sneakers Lady.

A busy Thursday lay ahead, but I had a whole two hours between me and my to-do list. Blustery though it was, this little walk to the subway was my peaceful interlude before the day got hold of me. I flexed my toes inside my sneakers, breathed in deep swallows of ice-water air, and guffawed as I turned onto the avenue and got smacked in the face by wind. Everything felt more awake, somehow. There was a new vibrancy to my neighborhood, as if someone had come in and polished all of Brooklyn overnight. I turned my face up toward bright spots of sunlight cutting through the cold.

9/11.

It occurred to me just as I made it to the subway entrance. *Oh right, 9/11. That's what this morning reminds me of. Clear blue and cloudless. People always talk about how gorgeous the weather was that day, and it was remarkable. I remember sitting on the porch outside my dorm at Walnut Hill, under the same crisp, blue sky, redialing my grandparents, then my mom, then Dad, and then my stepdad. With each unanswered line or busy signal, I grew more certain that all of them were dead. And, even after I had ascertained that everyone I knew was alive, I knew they would be dead soon, and so would I if I wasn't careful. Each night for months, I patrolled the dorm, slamming every window and laying my towel down to block the air gap under my bedroom door, just in case the terrorists returned with crop dusters, scattering anthrax up and down the eastern seaboard. I slept with the radio alarm clock turned on and tuned to the twenty-four-hour news station, quiet enough to appease my roommate, but loud enough so I could listen to all the updates on the end of the world.*

The J train arrived, interrupting my trip down terrible-memory lane. That was when I realized what was different. I'd put in my earbuds before leaving the house, but hadn't turned anything on. I'd walked five and a half blocks without any distraction, and now 9/11 had occupied my head.

Motherfucking mindfulness.

That was the culprit. This ridiculous commitment to growth and change and "mental health" had ruined absolutely all the fun. No, it was more serious than that. I didn't listen to audiobooks and musicals for *fun.* I listened to them in order not to think, because look where thinking got me. I needed those thought-killing distractions to get through the day, and clearly I wasn't ready to go cold turkey. That kind of detox is dangerous for any addict, and I had almost thirty years of using to my name.

Sure, someday I'd like to be able to walk five blocks in silence, but I had a lot on my plate, so to speak. So, for now, I just wouldn't push it. Not yet. I'd still be twenty-nine for a few weeks. It would be easier when I was thirty.

Mealtime rules remained. I'd turn off the television or cover the computer screen and squirm through a mindful turkey sandwich until I felt full and satisfied. Then, I got back to the noise. I couldn't enjoy distracted eating, but I went whole hog on distracted everything else. I could navigate my entire commute without employing the senses of sight and sound, occupied as they were with the Twitter app on my screen and the podcast in my ears. I blew out my phone data plan every month, downloading new episodes on the go, simply incapable of riding the subway without Marc Maron or Ira Glass for company. If I spotted a friend, I turned away and looked at my phone, preferring to hang out with the people I could hit Pause on. The TV went on the moment I got home. Swinging the door shut, I grabbed the remote before my shoes were even off, like a kid who gets twenty minutes of television before her parents get home and make her empty the dishwasher. I didn't turn the screen off until the last possible second before bed, and then came the audiobook to read me to sleep.

I fell back on my high school cast-recording habit, loading up my iPhone with *Wicked* and *Spring Awakening*, but only the biggest, belt-iest numbers. Because I no longer lived in a musical theater prep school dorm, I quit singing out loud with the windows open, lest I incur a noise violation for waking up all of Williamsburg. Instead, I just mouthed along with the lyrics—which made it even better. Now, I didn't even have to hear my own voice; I could just borrow Idina Menzel's or Audra McDonald's!

Next, I invented a new way of lip-synching without even opening my mouth. All I had to do was put on some headphones and let my facial expressions do the singing. Walking down the street or hiking up the StairMaster, I could face-sing along with "Defying Gravity," my eyebrows and forehead contorting through emotional beats of hope, excitement, vengeance, and, at last, triumph. This, by the way, is a *great* way to appear completely unhinged in public.

Grocery shopping was made all the more dramatic as I sang the first act of *The Last Five Years*, in my head, in the produce section, never once making a sound. I wasn't putting apples in a bag. I was packing up clothes to leave my husband, remorseful and crying over our shattered marriage. In New York, no one is fazed by seeing a lunatic in the supermarket. I just had to resign myself to being that lunatic and I'd never have to suffer the monotonous reality of grocery shopping again.

On the treadmill, I went back to my childhood obsession, *The Secret Garden*. Being almost thirty, I decided I was *almost* too old to fantasize about playing an eleven-year-old, so I just started face-singing along with the older female characters. Progress! Adulthood! Normal! Right?!

In those final, sweat-soaked minutes, I'd reach for the good stuff. I needed something really potent to get me through the last push. But first, I took a quick look around the gym, just to make sure my middle-school crush hadn't suddenly turned up at Equinox Tribeca to catch me working out to *Newsies*. The movie.

The closest comparison I draw to this experience is "smiling with your eyes"—that bizarre photo trend that Tyra Banks made famous, inspiring a generation of slightly-too-wide-eyed selfie takers. But instead of smiling with my eyes, I was high-kicking down nineteenth-century New York streets, tryna sell more papes. With my eyes. I'd unconsciously throw back my head, "hitting the high notes" and punching the air while holding my phone, triggering Siri to interrupt and ask me if I needed help. Only then would I notice the alarmed gaze of the woman jogging next to me, alerting both me and Siri to the fact that yes indeed, I needed serious help.

"What do you mean by *everything?*" Theresa asked during one of our weekday sessions. I'd forgotten my headphones back at the office and arrived a twitchy mess after having to endure a fifteen-minute subway ride without a podcast in my ears. One raised eyebrow from Theresa, and I cracked.

"I mean, I do every single thing with a distraction. I feel like I'm not even in the world, just in my head. Also, I think I'm addicted to multitasking."

Theresa gave a light chuckle at what she must have assumed was sarcasm. It was not sarcasm.

"I can't even walk to the train without headphones. I can't watch TV without playing a game on my phone."

I felt like a deviant teenager. I wanted her to ground me with no TV and no phone.

"Maybe you could try reading?"

I nodded. I listened to audiobooks every day, but couldn't remember the last time I'd read words on paper.

"Just a suggestion. It's totally up to you. I'm just saying, it might be worth a shot. Think about what mindfulness has done for you with food."

"Yeah, I know. I enjoy food more, and I don't eat past the point of fullness," I grumbled, really leaning into the sulky-teenager bit.

"Cool. What else?"

I shrugged. She shrugged back. No dice.

I left Theresa's office and headed out into the ceaseless gale blowing down Madison Avenue. This season had been record-breaking in its miserableness. Months of relentless, bone-deep cold had turned throngs of commuters into huddled masses yearning to break free. The wind itself felt like a perfect excuse to hop in a taxi and go home to watch movies in bed. But I'd just spent forty-five minutes talking about how I wanted to grow the hell up and quit escaping reality. Responsible adults didn't hail cabs they couldn't afford and go home to watch *Sliding Doors* on a weekday afternoon. They walked to the subway and went back to work.

I instinctively reached for my headphones before remembering I had left them at the office. *You can do this*, I ordered myself. *Jesus, you can make it fifteen minutes without* This American Life *to entertain you.* I turned onto Forty-Second Street and headed toward Grand

Central, hearing snippets of conversation as bundled-up tourists stopped on the corner to admire the big old train station. The air was so frigid that prickles of pain blew across my face, but they didn't seem bothered. It was all I could do not to shake their shoulders and tell them to get inside, get out of this horrible day, that Grand Central wasn't going anywhere and they should come back in the spring, when everything would be better.

Without any available entertainment, I decided to go ahead and think about Theresa's question. What *had* mindfulness really done for me with food? The answer came so quick and simple that I actually rolled my eyes at it: everything. Fine. I admit it. While I couldn't quit distraction all day, quitting it at mealtimes had changed every single thing about food and the way I ate it. It wasn't just about feeling full faster or tasting more flavors. I didn't even like the same foods anymore.

It started with soda. I'd been a Diet Coke junkie for years, downing two to four (to five) per day. I used to get a kick out of horrifying colleagues when I cracked a cold can first thing in the morning. "It's the same as you drinking your latte," I'd say. "Except it's fat free!"

Sometime in the past few months, though, I'd stopped drinking soda like water. Now, I could hardly drink it at all, grossed out by the bitter film of aspartame that lingered on my tongue. With every sip I was suddenly conscious of the not-realness of it: fake flavor, fake sweetness. Each time I popped into a bodega for a beverage on my way to the subway, I wound up dawdling in front of the soda section, staring at the plastic bottles like a visitor at a particularly dull zoo. *You can eat or drink whatever you want*, I reminded myself. That was rule #1 of this no-rule system. But, I just didn't want it. For the first time, drinking soda felt like pouring a can of chemicals into my body for no discernible reason. It didn't feel like a Bad Food so much as a pointless one. It was something I'd gotten used to over the years as a legal indulgence. On a diet, I couldn't eat popcorn at the movies, but I could suck down fifty-four ounces of Diet Anything, guilt and worry free. Now that guilt and worry were off the table, I didn't need soda as a defense. I just needed something to drink.

Another spooky shift came as I watched the food on my plate gradually become more seasonal. All winter, I carted home great gourds and squashes for pots of pilgrim-y soup. I roasted every root I could find and threw pomegranate seeds and orange zest on top, never once thinking of mangoes or tomatoes.

"My body is psychic!" I told Theresa, imagining that I'd reached a mythic upper echelon of intuitive eating where cravings became magically aligned with mother earth.

"I think it's just that citrus fruits taste really good right now," she countered. "Plus, they're on sale."

I paused to think about all the people I'd already told about my psychic stomach.

Okay, but so what if it wasn't actual magic? Mindful eating had worked more wonders than any diet had. All they'd done was teach me to ignore my dumb-ass body with its fat-ass desires and just eat what they told me to eat. Now that I'd flipped the switch, bringing consciousness to every bite, my body seemed to desire only the best, the freshest—and frankly, the cheapest. That, too, was a relief. Had I been craving daily avocadoes that winter, I would have gone broke by March.

Other cheap foods, however, had lost all their guilty pleasure. Running errands one Sunday afternoon, I dashed into a Midtown deli, hungry for lunch and overwhelmed by a PMS craving for salty, fried meat. I hit the hot food trays in the back and loaded up my plate with spare ribs and chicken fried rice. Scooping on a modest side of green beans, my ovaries screamed *"More meat, bitch,"* but I told them to watch their language and remember that they could always go back for more.

Yanking out my earbuds, I sat down at a sticky table in the back.

It took a few minutes of consciously (quickly, but consciously) chewing through tough, gristly bites before I looked up from my polystyrene plate and realized I was eating a stomachache. A year earlier, this food might have been my secret treat—a prime selection for a Final Pig-Out. Now, it tasted like fishy, reheated oil and the freezer. It tasted like almost-garbage, and as I sat there thinking of all the times I'd impulsively binged on a plateful of heat-lamp food, the meal turned rotten in my mouth. My salty-fried-meat craving wasn't so much satisfied as it was trumped by the greasy churning in my stomach. Had I scarfed it down while reading a magazine or clicking through Twitter, it might not have registered. But now I knew I'd never be able to eat this food again—certainly not for fun.

Once I started paying attention while eating, so many things were not fun anymore: fast food, soda, stale Halloween candy. No wonder I didn't want to pay attention to the rest of my life. That was the sneaky magic of mindfulness, I realized. One plate at a time, it was dragging me, kicking and screaming, into adulthood.

Chapter 19

Thirty

Life as it was on the day I turned thirty could not have been more impressive to my twenty-something self.

Harry asked me to meet him on the corner of Ludlow and Broome Street on the Lower East Side. Walking from the subway, I turned off my musical theater mix and clicked on the next episode of the *Radiolab* podcast, trying to calm down. I was far too nervous-excited to take off my headphones. Tomorrow I would try again to be a grown-up, but not tonight. I spied Harry outside a deli, looking down at his phone.

"Where are we going?!" I rushed up to him with a quick kiss, bouncing around on the slushy sidewalk. He took my hand and shook his head, suppressing a pleased-as-punch grin.

For my birthday dinner, he had planned a mysterious restaurant hop around downtown Manhattan. It was one of the most romantic, thoughtful things anyone had ever done for me. But that was just dinner. My birthday *gift* was flat-out ridiculous.

Harry had always been the better gift giver in our relationship, plotting creative and personalized presents months in advance. For his thirtieth, I'd taken him out to a dinner that cost my rent and a half. Not so creative, perhaps, but he'd been trying to get reservations for months, so for once I thought I'd nailed it.

"How am I ever going to top this?" he'd asked at the end of the meal.

"I'm sure you'll think of something," I replied, smug with the certainty that I'd won this round.

A few months before my own birthday, he asked if I could put in for some vacation time in the summer. I thought maybe we were going to the beach. Then he asked if my passport was up-to-date.

I'd taken him to a restaurant, and Harry was taking me on an international, three-city mystery trip tailored specifically to my tastes and interests. I mean, *okay*, show-off.

He'd been plotting the itinerary for months but refused to give me a single clue until my actual birthday. Each stop in tonight's restaurant hop corresponded to one of the locations we would visit. As we turned the corner onto Orchard Street, my heart thudded with anticipation. Harry stopped us in front of the door to a small, woodsy restaurant called Café Katja.

"Austria?!" I cried out. He smiled and shrugged.

Harry spilled the beans over plates of braised cabbage and thin, crispy pork cutlets. Salzburg would be our first stop. He'd used my childhood obsessions as inspiration for the trip, and Salzburg represented two of them: *The Sound of Music* and Mozart. On one of our first dates, I'd trotted out the story about my memorizing scenes from *Amadeus* as a kid, and (as I intended) he thought it both precocious and adorable. Many months later, when he officially loved me, I'd persuaded him to host a *Sound of Music* viewing party at his apartment, with the understanding that I would be singing along from start to finish. This, he found less adorable, but it had given him the idea to put Salzburg on our itinerary. From there, he explained, we'd hop a train to Vienna, where Mozart had lived and died. In between, we would stop in a spa town to eat cake and float around in saltwater pools.

"I love salt!"

"I know you do, baby!"

I had the sensation of being in a dream, bouncing around the city with my boyfriend as he teased me with more details of the magical adventure he had planned. Harry was an amateur travel junkie, so I knew this trip was as much of a treat for him, but still—this was movie-level romance. This was like *Gone with the Wind*, but without slavery, rape, or dead children. I'd known Harry was thoughtful and generous, but it was as if he'd remembered every anecdote I'd ever told him, every book I'd ever liked, and all the strange childhood interests I'd mentioned in the year and a half we'd been together. One interest in particular, it seemed.

In retrospect, I should have seen it coming. But when Harry stopped us in front of the Polish bar, I was still imagining us swimming through saltwater pools at a mountainside spa in Austria.

"What?" I asked.

He hesitated in front of the door. His face turned nervous; it was the expression of someone who just realized they were about to make a mistake.

"I—I'm taking you to Auschwitz."

I froze. "Oh."

"I mean. I know you always wanted to visit the memorial. So..."

"Are you serious?"

He opened the door to the bar. "Yeah?"

I followed him inside, still stunned.

"Oh no," he moaned, sliding up beside me in a booth. "Did I do the wrong thing?"

"I'm just surprised," I answered, trying to smile.

"That would just be part of it. We'd get to see Krakow, too, and I know how much you love Polish history and movies and everything."

He was right. He knew me well.

"But we don't have to do the Auschwitz tour, okay? We don't even have to go to Poland if you don't want to. It's just—you always said how important it was."

"Just give me a second, okay?"

Harry's face deflated. My heart crumpled. He got up to order the beers.

It was true; I had always talked about visiting Auschwitz. It did feel important. Come on, hadn't I been the kid who dragged her dad to the Holocaust museum? Hadn't I been the one who went to Amsterdam for the Anne Frank House rather than hookers and weed? And wasn't it incredible that my boyfriend, who would rather spend his vacation days, oh, *anywhere* but a concentration camp memorial museum, had made this incredible gesture?

Until this part of the evening, the trip had been a fantasy vacation. Now, it was all too real. Something about this announcement had yanked me back into reality.

I looked at Harry, waiting patiently for the bartender's attention. It wasn't just where we were going, but that we were going together. He was my real, live boyfriend. We were a grown-up couple going on a trip, with passports and everything. This wasn't a frivolous, romantic getaway. At least, in part, it was going to be an experience neither of us would ever forget, and we were going to have it together. It was the most uniquely generous and personal gift I would ever receive. Holy *shit*, this guy loved me.

I felt unsettled and disoriented. The bar smelled rank and unfamiliar. I felt stuck to everything. Watching Harry order our beers, I started gaming out the possibilities. What if we get in a fight on the trip? Will he get pissed if I'm jet-lagged and cranky? What happens if I cry at Auschwitz and he doesn't cry? Can you get mad at someone for not crying at Auschwitz? Would I have to break up with him if he didn't?

I wanted to be home, in bed, playing Words with Friends and rewatching *The Office*. It would be perfect, so cozy and quiet and under my control. I could ignore my texts, pretend I was asleep, and just deal with it all in the morning, when everything would be better.

Stop. Please, stop this.

It wasn't a thought, exactly. It was almost a voice. It sounded like the same internal voice that sat me down to eat at the table instead of on the floor in front of my television. I thought of it as the forty-year-old version of myself—the mythical me that was always just a few years down the line. Now, she came and sat beside me. She'd had it with this nonsense.

I had thought that when you hit bottom it was, like, the bottom. Meaning, your worst possible moment, definable and whole. I thought that if you did it right you didn't have to do it again. And I'd done it exactly right. I'd crushed my bottom and turned it into a career.

But what happened in that bar—and again and again in the months to come—was another kind of bottoming out. Back in those woods, I'd finally stopped running, scrambling toward the next diet or the new fitness fad that would lead me to skinny nirvana. All fall and winter, I'd taught myself to be present with the food on my plate and the flesh on my body. Suddenly, though, it wasn't just about the physical—the things I could taste and feel and see in a mirror. What did it matter if I was present in my body if I was so willfully absent from the world? I wanted to taste and feel and see all of that, too. Somehow, I had to quit running from my real life and give up on nirvana, period. It couldn't wait until I was older or not so scared, because I'd just turned thirty and that meant I'd probably die someday.

With every story I escaped into and each commute I spent staring at my phone, I skipped out on seeing the people around me. Who knows? I might have passed by a celebrity! Those times that I nearly walked into traffic while performing a song in my head, I wasn't just lost in the music, I was *walking into traffic*. All those movie plots I held up for comparison left my own precious life more lacking in my eyes. Every year I told myself that things would be better when I was older, when I got it together. Every year, it got harder to see that things were damn great just as they were.

My apartment would never be as nice as Sally's, and my own Harry never raced to crash a New Year's Eve party at midnight and deliver a dramatic monologue. I probably would have been kind of annoyed if he had. Instead, he was going to whisk me away on a trip around the world. He wanted to be with me for the fun and the hard parts. And, here I sat, pining for Netflix.

My existential crisis was winding down by the time Harry got back with the beer. I thanked him again for this evening, and for the astonishing gift he'd created for me. Life was ruthless and death was inevitable, but there were magic moments, and this was one of them. I wanted to feel it, through and through. We didn't have a Zeffirelli score or Nora Ephron dialogue, only "Thank you" and "I love you," and his hand squeezing mine back under the table. I had to pee and the music was loud. I was a little anxious and tired, and Harry kept blowing his nose. The bar was overheated, but when he scooted closer, I didn't move away. Runny nose or not, you just don't scoot away from the man who always squeezes your hand back. I took a breath in and let it out, tasting and feeling and seeing the moment, just as it was. I wanted, so badly, not to miss another.

Chapter 20

Still Thirty

Any good novelist would leave us there at the bar, holding hands and lesson learned. But that was just the decision to learn it. It was the first of many deep-breath moments, and one of the best. Mindfulness isn't for wimps. When you decide to take off your headphones, relinquish future thinking, and let the real world flood your fantasy, there's no telling what you'll get. The only guarantee is that you get little say in any of it. That spring, as I learned to stand still for the first time in my life, eyes open and ears alert, I got a lot of good. I got lucky.

At first, I got quiet morning walks to the train, overhearing the funny little conversations of moms taking their first graders to the elementary school around the corner. I got long nights with Debbie and Chrissy, loafing on my cat-scratched sofa with no pizza, no wine, no movie to keep us company. What a wonder to realize we didn't need dinner to hold our friendship together. All we needed was something to talk about, and there was always something to talk about. What a wonder, too, to spend Sunday mornings with Harry, having nothing much to say.

"How cool is this?!" I'd shout from the other end of the sofa, making him jump.

"What?"

"Just...this!" waving my arms around in what used to be our cozy silence.

I decided to wean myself off constant narration and background noise. I made a project of it with tiny, bite-size goals. I could listen to whatever I wanted at the gym, but had to walk to work afterward headphone free. I set a timer and taught myself to read books on paper again, twenty minutes at a time. I would not turn on the television as soon as I walked in the door, even if it just meant standing around chewing my lip for one deliberate minute, and then turning it on. That was one more minute in the real world, and that was where I wanted to live, even if life on *Downton Abbey* was a lot more interesting than mine on a Tuesday night. Like, a *lot* more interesting.

That was the other side of living consciously, and the truth I'd been fudging with fiction all these years. My life was not what I'd imagined it would be by this point. True, I had imagined it as some hyperbolic wonderland based on all the best parts of every movie I'd ever seen. That was a ridiculous expectation—a fact that everyone else seemed to have figured out a long time ago. Where had I been? Playing Candy Crush?

Facing real life for the first time at thirty, I sometimes sounded impossibly naïve, asking myself things like *Wait, what if I don't become famous?* or *If I don't have sex with Harry on Valentine's Day, does that mean I don't really love him?* In the past, I'd patched over all these worries with a quick hit of distraction. *Don't think about it!* 30 *Rock's on! You'll be just like Tina Fey! Later!* Now, I'd turned off the television and ripped off the bandage to reveal a host of untended wounds and stark realities. Without an arsenal of cheeseburgers and musical theater to manage them, every underlying issue came to the surface and demanded my attention.

There was the day in April, when I could not stop crying over a story that came back from my editor bleeding with the red ink of her edits. I spent the entire morning fake-sneezing into a tissue, hoping to explain away my red face. By afternoon I realized no one was buying it and spent the rest of the day openly desk-weeping in silence. I was raw to every criticism and flinched when I received anything but gold stars for my work. Silver stars were a slap in the face. *Useless*, something whispered inside me. *Why do you even try? You're only embarrassing yourself. It's time to quit and move away to start over someplace where nobody knows how awful you are.*

I left for the gym one podcast-free morning, observing with mild horror as I locked, opened, and relocked the door three times in perfect succession. I thought back to the night before when I'd checked the same lock three times before bed, then my bedroom lock, then the windows, and then the living room windows. I stood there in the hallway, suddenly flooded with the nagging worries and unspeakable thoughts that had kept me up every night that week, my mind scrambling to solve a puzzle but only finding more loose pieces.

It had been years since I'd thought about my knee-banging and prayer rituals. I had long ago outgrown the childhood demon that had kept me bruised and terrified for years. Or perhaps I had just quieted its waspish little voice. Maybe I'd learned to drown it out by singing at the top of my lungs, filling my brain with other stories, and stuffing my mouth with anything, anything to stop those desperate prayers. Now the voice was back, furious for all the years I'd hushed it, and finally free to scream me into submission. I let go of the doorknob and walked away from it.

Then there came the night in Salzburg on the second day of our trip, when the voice shrieked so long and loud that even Harry heard it. It had been a jet-lagged, rainy day. The quiet between us was no longer warm and comfortable as we trudged around the city, soaked and chilly. He wanted to wander aimlessly down alleyways, and I wanted to know exactly where we were going, how long it would take, and if there would be a bathroom nearby. He wanted to hit every conceivable café and castle, and I wanted to read *The*

Fault in Our Stars and take a nap. But neither of us seemed capable of saying those things, let alone admitting our own grumpiness—not on the Perfect Birthday Trip. My feet got sore, his camera got wet, and the voice got louder and louder, filling our silence. That night as Harry fell asleep beside me in the luxurious bed of our vacation rental apartment, it reached full volume:

This is wrong.

You aren't right together.

This vacation is a sign that you should break up right now and stop wasting both your lives. Do it, do it, do it, now.

A scalding flush of blood rushed up into my head as I careened into a full-blown panic attack, shaking Harry awake so he could have it with me. The voice was *my* voice now, and with it I pummeled him with all my enormous fears and worries and every reason that added up to the inevitable end of a relationship that had been the greatest blessing of my life.

"Aren't you scared, too?" I demanded of him in a ragged gasp.

"Yes, this is really scary right now. You're scaring me."

"I'm sorry. I had to say it out loud."

"Are you breaking up with me?"

"No! I love you. I'm just worried."

"Well, I'm worried now, too."

"I don't know what to do."

"I don't know, either."

And there was nothing to do. It wasn't until we got home weeks later that the panic fully receded enough for me to see what needed to be done. By then, the voice was tired out, having run its big, fat mouth every day of our trip. I didn't have another panic attack on our vacation, but I lay awake each night, waiting for one. The voice whispered meanness into my ear, even on our most fun and beautiful days, of which we had many. All I could do was squeeze my sweet man's hand, a real and tangible thing that pulled me back into the moment, if only briefly. Why he still wanted to hold my hand after that awful night, I really don't know.

There is a terrible selfishness to anxiety and obsessive-compulsive disorders. The voice could distract me from the world more powerfully than food or fiction ever could. It berated me as we wandered through Hapsburg palaces and bullied me into silence on Krakow's bustling city squares. Even on our visit to Auschwitz—a place where one can hardly think at all, so blunting and unspeakable is the experience of standing on that ground—the voice was with me. The catastrophic shame I felt, unable to escape my own mind on that day, was what made me realize how much help I really needed. At last, I saw how deep a hole I'd dug, filling it with all the things I had not wanted to deal with just yet. I thought that I'd hit bottom? Ha! I didn't have a clue where the real bottom was.

"Fuck this," I said to myself, aloud and clear, one Wednesday morning in my bedroom. It wasn't directed at anything in particular; some mornings I just woke up with a mouthful of expletives. Maybe it was wet and dreary outside, or perhaps I was anxious and occupied with the looming to-do list burning a hole in my day. On those mornings, all I wanted to do was turn on a funny movie while I got dressed, and then plug into my headphones for a five-minute sing-along while walking to the subway.

"Fuck this bullshit, I wanna sing show tunes," I whined to the cat, watching him blink back at me.

Loud swearing was a habit I picked up shortly after starting cognitive behavioral therapy. I'd made the appointment just days after we landed back in New York, both of us frazzled from my Perfect Birthday Trip Freak-Out. Soon, I was elbow-deep in the process of learning to live with my unquiet mind, without the dulling filter of distraction. Without a constant stream of Oreos and noise, the voice in my head would have plenty of room to make a racket, and I'd just have to let it. And, some mornings, I let it out loud.

"Fuuuuuck this mindful, shrinky, bullshiiiiiiit," I sang, wrestling myself into a sports bra.

It helped to make the voice my own. Though, really, it had always been mine. It was my voice in the bar, urging me to slow down and enjoy the life I had, rather than escape it through every possible hatch. And, it was my voice, my anxiety, my obsessive, whirring brain that turned on me when I took away those hatches. Both times, it was my voice that eventually led me in the right direction. There's a lot we can learn from the worst sides of ourselves.

Even if your boyfriend orchestrates a perfect birthday evening and gives you the perfect gift, there's a good chance you might ruin it. Even on your dream trip, there's no avoiding jet lag. The bad news is there is no avoiding any of the ugliness in life. The even worse news is that whether you're standing in an imperial palace or a Holocaust memorial site, you cannot escape the ugliness in yourself.

Here's the only slightly better news: When you quit trying to escape your ugly truth, it's not so hard to live with. Same goes for the ugly truths about your body, your relationships, and your stupid, small apartment. Some things are fixable and others are just there. But if you hang around waiting for it all to turn perfect, you're going to miss out on all the fun parts. You'll still get in on all the *not*-fun parts, though!

"Sometimes food is disappointing," Theresa once told me. I'd written it down in giant block letters, utterly astounded by the revelation. Even when you order exactly what you want, there's no guarantee it will satisfy you perfectly. Sometimes the cupcake is stale or the apple is mealy. Sometimes it rains in Salzburg, and yet the world keeps spinning.

I didn't have to break up with Harry just because we had a seriously imperfect day. I needed to accept that we would have bad days. What would have happened if I'd just stopped in the middle of that rainy street and said, "Well, this sucks, huh?" Maybe he would have laughed or maybe he would have been pissed, but at least I wouldn't have walked around stewing while the molehill became Mount Everest.

I had to get comfortable with uncomfortable thoughts, worry, and doubt. To expect uncompromised happiness was as unreasonable as looking for solutions at the bottom of a bowl of ice cream.

And I didn't. That's one part I can be perfectly proud of, amid everything I'd rather forget about those rocky months. Not once did I find myself standing in front of the fridge, halfway through a mixing bowl of leftover pasta, nauseated and numb. Even on the days when I was jittery with sleeplessness or tangled up in the gnarled forest of my own anxiety, I would not dampen it with food. It was the first promise I made myself that I never even tried to break.

I thought about it, though, remembering my slightly younger self. On bad days back then, it was an icky thrill to cancel plans, buy a bottle of wine, and bake sweet potato fries. I'd eat them on my bedroom floor and watch *The Great Gatsby* with a roll of paper towels beside me to wipe my greasy fingers. Finally, I'd fall asleep with a stomachache so acute that I could think of nothing else.

That was the recourse of a sad kid, one who didn't have the guts to grow the hell up. It was like the behavior of a twenty-eight-year-old who still partied like a college kid. In fact, I *was* that twenty-eight-year-old, because sweet potato fries were how I partied in college.

I got home from work around seven that Wednesday, no longer swearing a blue streak. Heating up a plate of chicken and pasta leftovers, I still felt the lingering rumbles of my morning grump. How easy it would have been to just turn on the television and drift away from the day. But I wasn't that twenty-eight-year-old anymore, solitary and bloated on the bedroom floor, lost in unreality. I was right here in my thirty-year-old life, eating dinner at a wobbly IKEA table. It wasn't amazing or terrible. It was just Wednesday, not the Wednesday That Changed My Life—and there was nothing wrong with that. I'd get pretty exhausted if every Wednesday was *incredible*. It took me thirty years to realize it. But when I did, finally, thank God, everything was better.

Chapter 21

The End (Just Kidding)

Good-byes are not my strong suit. Whether it's leaving a wedding or quitting a job, I'd rather just do it over e-mail. Trust me, it's better for everyone that way.

I watched the last episode of *Friends* in my college dorm room with a group of other girls who lived on my floor. Jenna had a tiny TV that sat on top of our rented microfridge, making us extremely popular during Thursday night primetime. Jenna, of course, was already popular, and I spent the entire hour on my side of the room, watching a pile of girls on her bed go through the five stages of grief as we said good-bye to the TV show that defined our formative years, God help us. Jenna had teared up as soon as the theme song began, kicking off a chain reaction of eye fanning and quiet awe.

"If I order Cinnastix, will anyone else have some?" The entire group turned to me, the heathen on a cell phone. Who called Domino's at a time like this, such an important historical moment? Me. That's who.

I just don't cry at finales—film, television, or otherwise. But dry eyes notwithstanding, when *Friends* ended, I was panicked and devastated as any red-blooded American would be. If I didn't care so much, I would have eaten fat-free popcorn! Watching Monica and Chandler pack up and move out of that big, purple apartment, leaving nothing but a soundstage, was so emotionally shattering that I needed immediate and plentiful Cinnastix.

The same thing had happened a few months earlier, when *Sex and the City* aired its series finale. At the time, my high school best friend, Sydney, was a student at the nearby Boston Conservatory, and she invited me over to the apartment she shared with two other musical theater majors. Rolling my eyes at their hysterics, I worked my way through a pile of pad thai, all the while thinking: *This is the end of an era and the end of your youth. Remember what you are wearing right now so one day you can show your grandchildren this BU hoodie. And, yes, I said, "grandchildren," because you were a child when this show began and now you are twenty and basically dead.* By the time Big professed his tearful love to Carrie, I'd eaten everyone's forgotten leftovers and the entire party was clutching hands in a spontaneous support-group circle, weeping vodka-drunk tears. That time, I succumbed to the peer pressure and decided just to fake it.

Most TV series finales soften the blow by oversweetening the story; they pump us full of high-potency nostalgia, and tie things up with a bow so neat we'd never tolerate it if it weren't the last hurrah. But the embarrassing truth is that we want that bow, so badly. It is our reward as loyal acolytes. When the screen goes black on Tony Soprano midmeal, we riot. That shit is just not fair. We need to feel safe and secure knowing all the brass rings have been caught: Carrie gets Big, Ross gets Rachel, and then everyone goes to the coffee shop. Only after that cure-all finale can we have our cathartic cry and get back to chasing our own brass rings, assured that we will get them, too.

Jon and Chrissy moved out of their big, white loft one gray morning in June. All of us—the VIP friends—came over to haul boxes and sweep floors. There was a fair amount of hugging and staring out of windows, talking about how far we all had come. It's easy to turn moving day into a finale of sorts, and this one was already gooey with sweetness. "Reel it in, guys," the director would shout. "I'm not buying it."

It was Jon's big move, really. Three weeks prior he'd suddenly announced he was moving in with Ben, his boyfriend of almost a year. We'd all seen it coming, of course. This was the Age of Engagement, when every other weekend was devoted to house-warmings and weddings and pretending none of it fazed us at all. But Jon was the first of our inner circle to break ranks and join the cohabitators. And, true to form, he'd done it perfectly. In quick succession he'd gotten the European dreamboat, the whirlwind romance, and finally, the Fort Greene brownstone.

"When it's right, you just know," he told Debbie, Chrissy, and me over pizza one night. I felt my smile turn to smirk, but then I realized he wasn't quoting the Nicholas Sparks movie we'd hate-watched last month. He meant it. I'd never been so sure about a lunch order, let alone another person. If Jon could be reduced to such unabashed sincerity, then this must really be it. So, in a slightly jealous show of support, we came to pack the boxes that would go in their new home.

That moving day was top-heavy with milestones. By odd coincidence, it was my and Harry's two-year anniversary, Chrissy's thirty-first birthday, and the week Debbie got her master's degree. Never before had we been such a sitcom.

"Are you excited, Dr. Debbie?" The floor was still covered in bottle-cap litter from the farewell party the night before. Outside we could hear Harry, Jon, and Ben having the very specific conversation of three dudes negotiating a mattress into a U-Haul, and decided not to help. Debbie and I stood in the empty living area where Jon and Chrissy's couch had been, bopping a balloon back and forth to each other.

She smiled. "Not a doctor yet."

"Half a doctor?"

"Yes, I'm excited to be half a doctor."

Chrissy came down the dark, skinny hall to join us, the clunk of her boots echoing off the suddenly huge and empty space.

"Is that everything?" she asked.

"Think so. You need help up there?" Still scrambling to find a new roommate, Chrissy had moved into another apartment on the second floor.

"No, I think I'm all good."

"So, are we doing drinks tonight, birthday girl?" Debbie asked.

"Oof, I don't know. I'm already beat." I bopped the balloon to her.

"And who knows if Jon will be around?" She flicked it toward Debbie, who let it fall almost to her feet before kicking it back up to me like a soccer ball.

"Right, I guess they have to unpack and everything," I mumbled, hitting the balloon just past Chrissy's shoulder. "Wait, get it!" I yelped, as she crouched down just before it hit the ground, scooping it back up into the air.

The balloon floated back and forth between us for a silent minute and then another. Jon came striding in, all bubble and fizz now that the truck was full.

"Wait, I wanna play!"

"This is a very complicated game," I said, knocking the balloon toward him with my forehead. "It's like Quidditch."

"I don't know what that is."

"Never mind, shut up." For another few minutes, we stood in the empty apartment, completely absorbed in the balloon-bopping game. Then Jon aimed for Chrissy and bonked the balloon way too hard, sending it out of the circle and onto the floor.

"Oh my God, I dropped the ball! I ruined everything!"

I swear to God, this happened. There was a literal ball and Jon dropped it and said, "I ruined everything." Believe me, I'm a sap but even I could not have scripted such a painfully obvious metaphor. I have witnesses.

The highly symbolic game was over and I leaned over to pull Jon in for a sideways hug. He hadn't ruined anything, of course. He was simply moving forward into his own life and that meant stepping outside of our shared past. Even the fucking *Friends* couldn't live across the hall from one another forever. They had babies to raise and spinoffs to tank.

Jon had a brownstone apartment to remodel, but we all seemed to be spinning off into a more adult adulthood. Debbie was still only half a psychologist, but she'd already treated patients in some of New York's most renowned and/or terrifying hospitals. Chrissy had defied every possible statistic, forging a successful painting career (not successful-for-a-painter—successful, period). And Jon hadn't just lapped us on the relationship front—he was probably going to be famous. After years of beating down doors in the television industry, they had finally begun to open for him.

Oh, right. And *I got a book deal, bitches.*

For the first time, I could appreciate my friends' successes without being swallowed up by toxic envy. I had my own bright, tangible milestone within reach. Not only did I have a book to write, I was ready to write it. I had a story to tell and, at last, the courage to spit it out. Later that afternoon, I'd go back to my apartment, put up my hair in a getting-shit-done ponytail, and sit down to work on my next chapter. But first: high fives, all around.

"Nothing else is allowed to happen this summer. Cool?" I demanded. By now, our circle had closed into a quiet group hug. It was tense with a kind of loaded affection, all of us feeling The End coming fast, and none of us wanting to cry at the finale. I didn't have Cinnastix to call attention to anymore, so instead I just called it to myself.

"I'm serious. This is it. I have to write a book this summer, so no more big life changes, okay? No terminal illnesses, no one can get hit by a car 'til next year."

All three of them chuckled and nodded, accustomed to this after fifteen years of my moment killing.

"It's a deal," Debbie said quietly. I heard something close to tears in her voice and shone a big, loud grin in her direction. She didn't smile back, but nodded.

"We have a lot to celebrate."

Two weeks later, I sat in Theresa's waiting room, scrolling through notes on my phone. Ordinarily, I got the ball rolling in our sessions with a new success story ("I declined a cupcake at work because I didn't feel like it!") or else a pressing food crisis ("I *only* want to eat cupcakes, help me, oh God"). Either way, we always had something to hash out. But, that week, my chipper little Notes app was full of only story ideas or anecdotes I wanted to remember for the book. They looked like the jottings of someone who didn't think about food all that much, someone who had bigger fish to fry than lunch.

I'd quit recording my meals two months prior. It didn't seem necessary to manually write down every feeling, desire, hunger pang, and degree of fullness anymore. Those things were still important, but they'd become a natural part of the process—thoughts I didn't really think about. It was almost as if...but, no. Shut up, don't scare it away.

"So. Any challenges in the coming week?" Theresa probed after we'd passed fifteen minutes of food-related small talk.

"Um, nothing major. Fourth of July is coming up."

"Okay, and what do you usually do on the Fourth?"

Normally, I went to a friend's rooftop in Greenpoint, the northernmost neighborhood in Brooklyn. From there, my friends and I could usually catch Manhattan's fireworks and even the edge of

New Jersey's. We'd drink plastic cups of spiked lemonade and eventually run out of buns, but eat the hot dogs anyway. I'd always looked forward to these food-focused holidays, knowing everyone else would overeat, too. I wouldn't be the anxious fat girl, forever clutching a plate in her hand. I'd just be celebrating like everyone else, and then we'd all spend July 5 nursing bloated hangovers. But thinking about it this year just felt like a stomachache I'd once had, or a virus I'd cleared and was now immune to.

"What would success look like in this scenario?" Theresa asked, as usual.

"Just enjoying the party, I suppose."

"And, in regard to the food?"

"Success would be not leaving the party uncomfortably full, for once."

"What do you think you need to achieve that?"

In truth, I didn't know. Let's be clear: It wasn't as if I'd become a socially comfortable, panic-free barbecue wunderkind. If it weren't federally mandated that we, as a nation, put on shorts and stare at the sky together, I would just as soon spend Independence Day independently. Maybe with a magazine. The only difference now was that hot dogs no longer had the power to assuage my party nerves. All they could do was assuage my hunger, if I was hungry. If I wasn't, they were just there. So was my anxiety, but that was my issue, not the hot dogs'.

"I'll just eat what I feel like eating, I guess."

"Okay." She shrugged. Again, I noted her lack of note-taking and wondered if I was just being lazy.

"I might still overdo it. I mean, I know that's definitely possible. But I guess that'll just give us more data?"

She smiled. "Well, don't do it just so we have something to talk about."

"Of course not! I'm sorry! I just don't know what's going on with me. I'm feeling pretty good."

At last, a confession: I was feeling good. *That* must be the problem. "What's wrong with that?! That's great!"

I looked to my old friend, the tissue box. I hadn't cried in this room for months. After all that drama, the novelty of normal eating had begun to wear off. If it wasn't quite instinct then it had become habit. I applied my new eating skills without much conscious effort, like the novice driver who suddenly finds herself shifting into third without even looking down at the gearshift. Oh, I still stalled out frequently enough, but that was just part of the deal. Cars stall sometimes. You don't call AAA for such a minor incident. You sit there for a second, trying to figure out what happened, and then you restart the engine.

For instance, earlier that week, I'd been lying in bed at 11 p.m., thinking about Oreos. It was an odd but nagging yen, and so I padded to the kitchen for the box of cookies in the back of the cabinet. I stood at the counter, eating them in the dark, noting how fast I chewed and how much I wanted a third, a fourth, a fifth Oreo. They were tasty, but not *that* tasty. They were as good as stale Oreos can be, so what was going on? Hormones? Stress? What was I missing? Oh, right: Dinner.

I'd come home from work still pretty full from my late lunch and decided to skip the evening meal entirely. Why eat if I wasn't really hungry? Intuitive! Cut to: four hours later when I intuitively shoved a bunch of cookies in my face. But it wasn't some crisis of binge-eating backsliding. It was a normal, biological instinct given that I hadn't eaten since 3 p.m. and set myself up for a late-night blood sugar crash. The lesson was simple: a late lunch doesn't mean skipping dinner. It means eating a later dinner. This was one of those stall-out moments that made me stop and pay attention. It's how I learned that intuitive eating wasn't just about listening to my gut. I still had a brain, and I should listen to that, too. Since I didn't have to punish myself for eating anymore, I could be curious about why, when, what, and how I ate. Thinking about dinner in terms of nutrition (rather than net carbs) and satisfaction (rather than cheating) meant I could have Oreos when I wanted them, but never wind up in a situation where I *needed* them.

Wow. Did I have my shit together, or what?

"So, am I like...Am I official?"

"An official what?" Theresa asked.

"I mean, am I an intuitive eater? Officially?"

She raised her eyebrows like I was a child suddenly asking to sleep in a big-girl bed.

"What do you think?"

"Come on."

"I don't have a certificate, if that's what you're asking for."

That was definitely what I was asking for.

"Look," she conceded. "I think you know this work takes time, right? Did you expect to be all done in, what, nine months?"

"Not *done* done."

"You're in a boring phase right now. Consistency is boring, but it's a good thing. How much are you thinking about food these days?"

Aside from the occasional Oreo incident, I only really thought about food as long as it took to realize I was hungry and decide what I wanted to eat.

"Not much."

"Good," she said. "Right?"

"Right."

"How would you feel about taking a break from our sessions for a while? Just to see how it goes?"

I froze. Was she dumping me? The Oreo story wasn't that impressive. I wasn't done! Fuck this big-girl bed!

"Oh. We could try that."

Theresa and I picked a date six weeks down the line, and I managed to leave without hugging her.

"Okay, off you go!" She waved as I headed for the elevator. "Have fun with boring consistency!"

*

Theresa hadn't stamped me on the forehead and declared me finished. But, after that session, I had to admit to feeling done-ish. The peaks and pits of those early stages had passed, and now the only task was to keep walking on this long, level ground. I knew too that there was no going back. I would never diet again. I'd never even want to. I'd known from the beginning that this would be a lifelong process, but it was strange to see how different I suddenly was from the person I'd been less than a year ago.

That sounded like an ending, of sorts. And what a relief, because I had a story to tell. All along, I'd known it wouldn't conclude with me striding out onto a stage in a brand-new bikini and highlights, revealing myself shiny and new: the "after" shot.

The whole point was to quit trying to get to that perfect "after" and deal with my food issues in reality instead of on a reality show. Still, a book needs an ending, so I had to find a finale somewhere. And, this moment, with my friends and I moving on with our lives and Theresa taking off my training wheels—it felt just right. Handling change and boring consistency: That's pretty much adult life, right?

My perfect finish would be even better for its imperfection. No bullshit. No convenient sunsets or last-minute epiphanies where it turns out that what you needed was right in front of you, all along. No neatly tied-up ending, but a nice bow nonetheless. Had I not been so preoccupied with my lovely little analogy, I might have remembered that bows are made to be yanked loose.

Chapter 22

The Sucker Punch

I got the first text about an hour after work. Standing in my kitchen, I chopped cool chunks of mango, waiting for the air-conditioning to cut through eight hours of clingy heat trapped in my airless, top-floor apartment. All week I'd been making big bowls of mango and avocado salsas for dinner, resentful of my stove's very existence. My phone began to chirp in the living room. It was one of those rapid series of text-message pings that usually signaled an engagement or break-up announcement.

Oh my God, did you hear from Jon?! It was Chrissy. I wiped my hands on a dishcloth and began to type back. Before I even got the *No* out, Jon's face popped up on my screen as the phone began to ring. It was a heavily filtered picture of him dancing in my kitchen two years earlier, back when we could hardly fathom the novelty of making your phone photos look like real photos.

"Hi," I answered, guts in a preemptive knot. "What's up? Are you okay?"

"Ben just broke up with me."

"What? When?"

"Just now."

"Oh my God."

"Yeah."

I looked up at a dusty shelf in my living room and stared at a used-up Anthropologie candle I hadn't yet bothered to throw out. I didn't know what to say, and what came out of my mouth sounded something like a 911 operator script:

"Are you alone? Where are you right now?"

"I'm walking down the street. I literally just walked out the door." He sounded dazed and hoarse.

"What street?"

"Uh, Clinton Street."

"Okay, are you all right?"

"No, Jesus. No, I'm not."

I flinched at my own idiocy. Obviously, he wasn't all right. "Okay, just tell me where you're going and I'll meet you there."

I scooped a few mouthfuls of mango and avocado into my mouth, stuck the bowl in the fridge, and headed out the door.

I'd seen Jon cry a handful of times in the fifteen years we'd known each other. Most of the time it was at the end of some campy tearjerker like *Steel Magnolias* when I'd catch him dabbing quickly at his eyes. But that night at Chrissy's house, he sat on the sofa wracked with the kind of sobs that bring no catharsis. They didn't end so much as ebb and then surge out of him again. Soon, Debbie came over, and the three of us sat in uncertain silence around our friend looking at each other and thinking of how useless people are at a time like this. At least, that was what I was thinking.

I went home that night, rattled and angry on Jon's behalf. Breakups happened, of course, but this was a bad one, and he'd need extra support. Tomorrow I'd ask him over for dinner; I'd make a vegetarian pasta while he sipped wine in my kitchen and gave me the latest updates. Then we'd watch something silly, with no discernible romance (*Showgirls? Romy and Michele's?*), before he'd doze off on my couch. Our friends would close ranks around him, help look for apartments, sit and talk on each other's couches until he felt better.

I pulled the half-made mango salsa out of the fridge and sat on my bed, ravenous and sleepy. I hadn't let myself get this hungry in a long time, but hey—life intervenes. I sat in quiet, itching for sound and wanting to shake the night out of my brain. But, no, I would be mindful. I'd get this one thing right. In silence I ate every bite of my chilly dinner and went to sleep, leaving the dishes for later.

Jon didn't come over the next night. Instead, he asked me to come to his place.

I'm coming from the doctor. Might be 5 mins late, he texted, as I dashed into the subway, dodging an ominous sprinkle.

The doctor? I thought.

By the time I got aboveground, the rain had turned biblical. It was the first of a dozen treacherous rainstorms that flooded the city all summer, as if June and July had to one-up winter. I trudged toward the brownstone Jon had lived in for less than a month before the breakup, and waited in the wide, prewar door frame. As miserable as it was, it felt right to be cold and bedraggled in the rain. Jon showed up ten minutes later with a bandage in the crook of his elbow, wet and shaky as a cat.

"Are you all right?" I asked. Again, the answer was obvious.

I'd thought I'd come to help him pack up his boxes and get him drunk while he cried over Ben. But an hour later, the bottle of white wine sat sweating and unopened on the kitchen counter. Jon picked at the bandage on his arm from where they'd drawn his blood sample, and told me the rest of the story. Weeks ago, he'd felt the pain in his groin. He didn't go to the doctor, because he never went to the doctor. Then the pain got worse.

"Then this happened." He gestured around his newly broken home. When he'd finally gotten checked out, the mass had gotten even bigger.

"Hey, you don't know if it's a 'mass' yet," I cut in.

"Right," he murmured, still staring at the bandage.

"It's probably just a cyst. I'm 99 percent sure." Of course it was. It had to be. "Listen, we're thirty! This is normal! It's just wrinkles and cysts from here on out!"

Jon laughed a little, but didn't meet my eyes.

"Dinner?" I asked. And, he looked up at last.

No, I realized. It's not bad breakups that render friends useless. At least then there are bags you can carry and Unfriend buttons you can hit. Cancer makes an idiot of everyone.

It took weeks to get a diagnosis and even longer to find a surgeon. Getting cancer in the movies always seems so formal: The doctor comes in with a file in his hand, smiles, and tells you the plan. But the first thing we learned when Jon got sick is that no one's got the plan. You can get all the files and smiles you want, but it takes a village to find a specialist.

The period that followed was a whirlwind of text messaging and irresponsible Googling. Jon soon told Debbie and Chrissy, and then we started the group texts: The girls and I kept our anxious worrying to one chain and included the upbeat, informational updates on the chain we shared with Jon. After a few days of cold-calling hospitals, he eventually wound up at Beth Israel Medical Center, officially diagnosed with testicular cancer.

That was the scariest part of that mean, relentless summer: the casual chaos of it all. What if the Affordable Care Act hadn't passed and he hadn't been forced to get insurance, finally? What if Google had gotten him the wrong doctor? What if he'd ignored the pain for another week? In just the five days between his diagnosis and surgery, the tumor had grown even larger.

*

What do you want for dinner? Harry's text popped up as I climbed the stairs out of the subway. It was a Tuesday evening in July, and so hot that the idea of cooking sounded like a punishment.

Let's order, I replied. *Whatever you feel like.*

We'd fallen into a habit of weekly work nights at his apartment. Harry would sit at his computer, plowing through graphics for his latest freelance project, while I sat on the couch behind him tapping sporadically at my laptop. It wasn't exactly romantic, but neither was the prospect of going out to dinner when all I had to talk about was my friend, his breakup-cancer crisis, and all the work I wasn't getting done because of my friend and his breakup-cancer crisis. It felt wormy, being so stressed out by someone *else's* personal disaster, but the fact was I could barely concentrate at the office, forever waiting for the phone to ring and the bad news to get worse. And, when it did, what could I do but get up and go? There are people in your life whose hands are yours to hold, no matter what, and Jon was one of those in mine—even if I had specifically asked him *not* to get cancer this summer.

I stopped into the gourmet grocery downstairs from Harry's studio for a bottle of seltzer before heading up to our super sexy work date. Hit with a blast of deep-freeze air-conditioning, I spent ten minutes wandering up and down the aisles in delicious procrastination. Suddenly, I had the best idea ever: ice cream. Oh my God, did ice cream sound good. Every inch of my body still tacky with sweat, I beelined for the freezer aisle.

For most of my life, real ice cream had been out of the question. It was for birthdays and cheat days and national emergencies. I'm pretty sure I bought a newspaper on 9/11, but I'm positive that I bought a pint of Häagen-Dazs. Aside from those circumstances, no way. If I wanted cookie dough ice cream, I got low-fat cookie dough frozen yogurt. That was indulgence enough, but real ice cream, without a good reason, was simple hedonism.

But I'd already worked through ice cream in Theresa's office.

It was up there with French fries in terms of Bad foods that I'd wrestled into neutrality. Now it was just something I enjoyed on occasion. Ice-cream-flavored frozen yogurt had fallen into the realm of diet soda; it tasted like a chemical facsimile of something real. Now I understood that a real craving could be satisfied only by the real thing. And this was an extremely real craving.

"Ooh, you got a little work-night treat, huh?" Harry spotted the pint of Coffee Toffee Crunch I'd left to soften on the counter. He passed me a take-out box of cold shrimp summer rolls from the Vietnamese restaurant down the street.

"It's not a *treat*. I don't do food treats anymore," I replied in a fake-smug voice, trying to hide the actual smug.

"Okay," he said with a shrug.

"God, shut up! I just felt like it. Intuitive ice cream!"

"Got it! Do I get to have some, too?"

"No, I'm going to eat the entire pint."

He shrugged again. I put down my summer roll. "Did you think I was going to eat the whole thing, like some monster?"

"Nope, just wanted some ice cream. Didn't mean to call you a monster."

We finished dinner then worked until almost midnight. Rather, he worked, and I rewrote the same paragraph eight times, then scrolled through Twitter for an hour. Before bed, we took two spoons and dug into the pint of Ben & Jerry's, trying to think of things to talk about besides cancer.

The day of Jon's surgery, I slow-cooked a giant pot of ratatouille. True, food can't solve a crisis, but people still need to eat during one. Making a decent meal is one of the few ways to feel less useless in the face of serious illness.

At five o'clock, I pulled the pot off the stove and went to get dressed. I threw on a short, airy summer dress and took a quick glance in the mirror. It was a basic, blue babydoll frock I'd purchased years ago, cut loose in the middle so I could comfortably wear it during fat and thin-ish times. My gaze paused on the short, cap sleeves pinching slightly into my upper arms. I turned sideways and, holy shit. I looked pregnant. I looked swollen and sweaty and twelve months pregnant.

I yanked the dress over my head and opened the closet again. As ever, the thing was messily jammed with decades of clothing, most of which I never wore. In recent months, I'd branched out and begun wearing more than the same five items, but all of a sudden, nothing looked right. That blouse was too tight around my breasts and that skirt always made my hips look even wider than they already were.

Ten minutes later, half my closet lay heaped on the bed and I still wasn't dressed. I was, however, late. Giving up, I pulled the old blue dress back on, grabbed the pot of summer stew, and headed out the door, feeling my inner thighs brush lightly against each other with every step.

When I arrived at the apartment, Jon was a dopey, slowed-down version of himself. I hugged his parents and sister, who'd flown in the day before the surgery to help him through the recovery. Soon, a gang of friends descended and we all clustered around him on the couch for the weirdest dinner party any of us had ever been to.

"Dude, you're totally high. I think your parents can tell."

Jon smiled through a codeine haze. "Shhhh, be cool."

"You need anything?"

"Ugh, yeah. I need to call Ben."

"Whoa, no you don't. What?"

"Not today, but I gotta call him. I have to forgive him, or something."

"Yeah, or something. I thought we were going to give him bedbugs."

He looked at me, squinting, trying to find the thought. Finally, he gestured at the ice pack in his lap.

"It's too much. I can't deal with being mad anymore. I've got to make some peace, even if he doesn't deserve it. I mean, *I* deserve it, right?"

"Okay. Right."

God, he was high.

The air was still thick with muddy heat when I left just after sunset. Still, I decided to walk the forty minutes home, because I hadn't been to the gym all week. Twice I'd canceled training sessions with Stephanie, needing to squeeze in an extra hour at the office, or sit through a bad night with Jon. Walking home was good enough, I told myself. Life gets messy, and there are far worse messes than having your *workout schedule* interrupted. Besides, I would be half asleep at the gym. Most nights I patched together just a few hours' sleep, lying awake and worrying about all the things I couldn't control. Next, I worried about the things I could control, but wasn't: the week-old dishes in the sink, the unread e-mails stacking up no matter how many times I flagged them, and the laundry pile slumped over in the corner of my room like a body that I just didn't have time to bury. One morning, while yanking my hair into an unwashed ponytail, I noticed my armpit fuzz had grown to making-a-statement lengths, simply because I'd forgotten to shave for a month. I looked down at my legs, covered in light blonde down, and decided maybe I was making a statement after all: *I am busy.*

Nearing home, I wandered into the bodega down the block from my apartment to buy cat litter, congratulating myself for remembering at least one thing. Then, I remembered another thing: ice cream. Like all the twenty-four-hour delis in my neighborhood, this one kept two things well-stocked: loose cigarettes and a freezer drawer jammed with rock-solid pints of ice cream, absolutely none of which were low-fat frozen yogurt.

This time, I paused. An ice cream craving was fine, of course. But this was no isolated incident. First, there was the Ben & Jerry's that night at Harry's. Then, earlier this week I'd gone to the deli downstairs at work to buy a turkey sandwich for lunch, and noticed the gelato stand in the corner. The whole sandwich idea seemed idiotic all of a sudden—too dry, too salty. It wouldn't be remotely satisfying, and true satisfaction was the most important thing, right? I ended up having two scoops of strawberry gelato for lunch, chasing it with a handful of almonds to make it more arguably a meal, should I be called upon to defend it in a court of law.

I'd popped downstairs for gelato most days for the last two weeks, usually just having one scoop as an afternoon snack. I'd always thought it ludicrous that a half cup was the recommended portion on the back of every pint. But I had to admit that when I ate the real-deal, cream-based stuff with mindful attention, it didn't take much more than that to fulfill the craving.

Then there were the days when I wasn't so mindful. Sometimes I ate my afternoon ice cream while browsing through Sephora.com's latest facial serums that might be worth incurring a little credit card debt. Sometimes I scraped the tiny plastic spoon around for one last bite while watching *Saturday Night Live* clips on YouTube, promising myself that I'd watch just one more, just until I reeeeeaaallly finished the ice cream. Then I'd get back to writing this tricky paragraph, return my dad's phone call, and shave my armpits.

Now, here I was, walking home from my best friend's cancer party. And fuck it. It was hot. It was July, when you're supposed to want ice cream. If I was craving fresh baked brownies, then sure, we could call that an instance of emotional eating. But what could be more instinctive than following a light summer-vegetable meal with a scoop of mint chocolate chip? Also, it had protein!

Upstairs, I grabbed a spoon, took off all my clothes, and sat on my unmade bed, reaching for the remote. I thought about Jon, likely nodding off into twelve hours of painkiller sleep. I remembered how, earlier that evening, he smiled when I walked through the door, then winced, hard. But still, he leaned up from the sofa to hug me with the arm that wasn't holding down the ice pack.

"Hey, MG," he said.

✳

"MG" was our shared nickname, created the first year we met at Walnut Hill. It began one Friday night, when we rented a video of *Breakfast at Tiffany's* and got permission for Jon to stay late in my dorm's common room to watch it.

Neither of us had seen the film before, and both thought we were in for some gentle, old-timey comedy. But when Mickey Rooney appeared on screen as Holly Golightly's "Japanese" neighbor, we were struck dumb. When the movie came out in 1961, reviews described this character as "broadly exotic." Today, we might call him "so fucking racist." We're talking buckteeth, taped eyelids, and an inability to pronounce the letter *L*.

On screen, Rooney started screeching "Missa Go-right-reee!" and Jon and I turned to each other, agape. Then, we exploded with teenaged outrage. What should we do? Call the police? Write a manifesto? How did this film become so universally adored? The movie-watching night was over. We were too busy exclaiming "Missa Gorightry?!" at an ever-more loud and flabbergasted volume. One of my dorm-mates emerged in the doorway, pissed off and half asleep, clearly having been awoken by our spontaneous antiracism demonstration (which probably looked more like two white kids screaming racial slurs at each other). We stopped yelling and burst into unstoppable laughter.

We never saw the end of *Breakfast at Tiffany's*. But that night,

the "Missa Gorightry" screaming match became the inside joke
that Jon and I never got over. We'd called each other "MG" ever
since. When new acquaintances asked where the nickname came
from, it was virtually impossible to explain without making us
sound like racially insensitive idiots. That's why you keep old
friends around. In a crowd of strangers, they're the ones who know
your true heart. And that you're not a racist.

A car alarm bleated beneath my window and I fell out of the memory. All of a sudden, I was back in my apartment, tired and hot.
Jon was sleeping somewhere, full of stitches and medicine. When I
looked down at the pint of ice cream, half of it was gone.

Chapter 23

Ice Cream Revisited

L et's talk about this for a minute. Do you have time?"
Stephanie looked up from my chart, having just recorded all my measurements.

"Sure."

It was an early Friday morning in August, and this meeting would be our last. The gym had been incredibly generous in letting me temporarily train with her for free, but Stephanie no longer had room in her schedule, and I just didn't have the cash flow that would allow me to pay for a new personal trainer. Besides, it was never my intention to have one forever. I'd learned my way around the gym and gotten used to being a regularly active person. Before my gym schedule got thrown out of whack in the last couple months, I'd even come to like jogging. I kind of hated myself for admitting it, but I suppose begrudging progress is progress nonetheless.

"Your blood pressure's a little higher than last time."

"Oh?"

"Yeah. Any idea why that might be?"

"I have a little too much on my plate right now, I guess. And I'm not sleeping much."

"Okay. Well, keep an eye on that. The other thing is your body fat."

"What about it?"

"There's been some change." Stephanie pointed to the graph where she'd recorded all my numbers after pinching my upper arms, lower belly, and other fatty spots with measuring calipers.

"See, your abdomen is down, but your arms are actually up a little."

"Ah." I couldn't think of anything else to say. Maybe *sorry?*

"Same thing here. Your calf measurement is down, but your thighs haven't changed at all. And your subscapular is up a bit as well."

"Is that unusual? To fluctuate?"

"No, it's not uncommon. But I mention it because you've been a little inconsistent this summer."

Right. All those mornings I'd canceled. All those weeks I'd worked out three days instead of five, either occupied with Jon, catching up on work, or too exhausted from my cool new insomnia habit.

"I have had a lot going on." I heard defensiveness creeping into my voice.

"I just hope you're not quitting this thing."

"I'm not. Of course I'm not."

"Good. Because you've come a long way."

"I know that. And I'm not done."

She looked down at the numbers and shook her head. "I wish we weren't finishing on this note."

I looked down at the page. I saw the months of Stephanie's diligent recording, noting my resting heart rate, my stamina on the treadmill, but mostly all those little pudgy spots she pinched with calipers to track my body fat. On paper, that was all that mattered. On a deeper level, I knew there was a more important story the calipers couldn't tell. But, sitting there with Stephanie's mild disappointment, it was hard to hear.

"Stephanie, thank you for everything."

She smiled and reached out long, strong arms for a hug.

"You helped me change my life," I told her.

It was true. She'd pushed me as far as I could go. Now, it was up to me to stay there. If I could do that by myself, I wouldn't need a piece of paper for proof. I wasn't quitting anything.

I headed upstairs to the treadmills and power-walked through a quick workout on my own. Disappointment was okay. I could have a little pout, right? I reached for my phone and the particular form of validation one can achieve only through social media. People talk about how social media keeps us isolated from one another and unable to fully process our feelings. But if I ever needed a reality check on my emotional stability, all I needed to do was open an app. The more needy I was, the more I Facebooked, Instagrammed, and tweeted. *Did you guys see the moon last night? So crazy!* (Please say yes, for I am so alone in this world and need the solace of knowing that someone else looked up at the moon and thought it was so crazy.) *Can you believe how huge my laundry pile is?!* (*Can* you believe it? Is it unhealthy? Am I a hoarder? What do you think?)

Stomping uphill at 3.1 mph, I tweeted something about watching *Law & Order* at the gym. Everyone watched *Law & Order*, and surely one of those fans would click the little Favorite button under my tweet, giving me the gold star I needed. No, not "needed." Not anymore. Now, I just really, really wanted it, and that was different.

I forgot to eat lunch until almost four. Somewhere around midday, I'd had a few low-grade hunger twinges, but mostly, I just felt tired. The night before, I'd found myself thrashing around in Harry's bed, hurling my face into the pillow and ordering myself to sleep. He'd recently bought an ultrathick foam mattress cover to try to alleviate one of the five thousand things that suddenly kept me up all night. Now I watched him sleep soundly through my insomnia tantrum, completely undisturbed. He was the wineglass and I was the lady jumping on the bed, or rather, kicking and moaning on the bed. Those commercials aren't exaggerating. That space foam is good.

For most of the night, I just stared at the ceiling, reprioritizing my to-worry list; there was one item slowly creeping right to the top. Ever since Jon's post-surgery party, I couldn't get his words of codeine wisdom out of my head. *I can't deal with being mad anymore,* he'd said about his brutal dumping. *I've got to make some peace, even if he doesn't deserve it.*

She didn't deserve it, either. But maybe I did. If Jon could forgive the guy who'd broken his heart, maybe it was possible to forgive the woman who'd broken mine. I sat up in bed and grabbed my phone, looking through my contacts just to see if it was still there. It had been almost ten years since I'd lived in that house, but the number was still labeled "Home."

The next day, coffee was my first priority. Numb with sleeplessness, I hurried through a decent breakfast, knowing that without protein and carbs in the morning, I'd be half asleep at my desk all afternoon. Next, I drank as much coffee as I could stand before noon (the caffeine cutoff time in my new Get Some Fucking Sleep plan). I'd never been a committed coffee person, but now that I was a zombie, I found it made me a slightly more productive zombie. The only issue was that coffee turned the volume on my appetite way down. Most days I reminded myself to listen for it anyway, but other times, screw it. That day was a "screw it" day. Eating well was a priority, but so were things like unfinished work, friends in crisis, and staying awake.

In lieu of lunch I took a bag of stale almonds out of my desk drawer, dumped a small heap next to my keyboard, and clicked to the comments of my latest Anti-Diet Project post.

Catybaby: *This is so stupid. You're saying we should eat whatever we want? It's okay to be fat and lazy? What if I "intuitively" want a pound of bacon every day? That's how this country became a bunch of disgusting, diseased morons. If I accepted myself as a weak fat-ass I'd kill myself.*

YES. Jerks and idiots. This was also a priority, and my favorite kind. I replied:

Kelsey Miller: *Wow, sorry to hear that! If you check out the rest of the column you'll see fitness is a big part of it, and it's not quite as simple as eating pounds of bacon. Intuitive eating encourages people to honor hunger and enjoy food with mindfulness and self-respect. Hope that helps clarify!*

Catybaby never replied, but someone else did:

DaniellaB: *Show me the studies that says this works. Bet u have none.*

I grabbed some bookmarked studies on the benefits of intuitive eating and diet-failure stats, pasting them into a reply. Then I launched into a chipper tirade about how "working" meant different things to different people, and mine didn't mean getting skinny. Thnx!

I clicked deeper into the comments, thanking the supporters for their support but keeping my eyes peeled for what I really wanted (the critics!). Then, out of the clear blue Internet, came the name I hadn't seen in months.

John2John: *Lol, fatso loves bacon nom nom nom. ur still ugly.*

I could hardly believe the prickly glee that filled me from head to toe upon seeing this comment. It was perfect, pure dumb-assery, and mean as any insult I'd ever gotten. I mean, "fatso." It took confidence to whip out an old-school "fatso." My hat-tip to you, John2John. How I missed your ugly mug.

What trolls like John2John didn't realize was that, as much as they wanted to make me feel bad, I got a gross and secret thrill from their nastiness. It satisfied the part of me that was used to being bullied—comfortable even. And I loved to see other readers come to my defense, like an army of usernames and avatars. The only downside was that I couldn't really reply, the way I did to other criticisms. There was no valid argument I could negate, and to acknowledge him would just make it look as if I took the term "fatso" seriously. I'd just have to enjoy watching his comment get pushed to the bottom, buried by all the nice ones. But that was not what happened. Instead, someone backed him up.

TomatoPlant: *I don't know that I'd call her ugly, but she's definitely irresponsible. She just wants everyone to be fat like her because losing weight and getting healthy is too much work. It's pathetic. She's desperate. Sigh.*

This, I could not abide. How could someone both agree with a troll like John2John and do it in correct grammatical format? TomatoPlant was obviously a real person who knew how to use commas when calling me a loser. I went into personal PR overdrive, replying with something like:

Kelsey Miller: *Hi there, TomatoPlant! I'm actually in the best shape of my life these days. And, in fact, it's been even harder than dieting, but the difference is that this time I'm actually getting healthy and happy. Doesn't feel so pathetic! Thanks for reading!!*

TomatoPlant: *So, that's why you've replied to every single negative comment on every single story? Okay, honey.*

When I looked up from the screen next, half the office was gone. It was like one of those nights when falling asleep and waking up feels like merely blinking. I'd waded belly-deep into the comments on each and every one of my Anti-Diet Project posts, and then dozens of other stories I'd written in the last two months. Every four-hundred-word post, every personal essay—I combed them all for negative comments and saw that somewhere, someone who called herself "TomatoPlant" was exactly right about me, at least in one regard. I'd never once let a negative comment go unanswered. I'd defended myself against legitimate critics, juvenile jerks, and people who'd clearly not read past the first paragraph of the story.

Looking at Twitter, I saw that negative tweets about my work were met with aggressively positive replies. Almost every time, my response was longer than the critical comment itself. In the last year, I'd made my tiny mark as a writer who broadcast a message

of confidence and self-acceptance. I could click on any interview I'd
given or any piece I'd written and see myself as the poised, kick-ass
woman I wanted to be. That was the real story. But scroll down to
the comments or check my Twitter feed, and there I found it punc-
tured with a million tiny holes.

You busy tonight? Jon's text buzzed my phone to life, interrupting
the great TomatoPlant revelation.

Approaching the bodega on my way home that evening, I didn't
have to wait for a craving to arrive. It was a constant, low-grade
ice cream fever now, and one that could only be cured with more
ice cream. I didn't even pretend to ask the guy behind the register
how much. I just plunked down five bucks for a pint of AmeriCone
Dream and told him I didn't need a bag.

"Spoon?" he asked.

"What? No."

I could have picked the same argument I'd had with Harry, demanding if the cashier thought I was the kind of wildebeest that
ate Ben & Jerry's by the pint, and what made him think that, and
what right did he have to offer me a spoon in that tone? But I
decided one cliché was enough for today. Right now only my jam-
packed freezer knew what a Bridget Jonesian mess I was. I wasn't
even the flawed but charming book version of Bridget Jones or the
flawed and slightly less charming movie version. I mean the movie
sequel version where she cries in the street and exclaims things like,
"Oh God, I'm *never* going to get married!"

Two hours later, Jon and I sat watching *Pretty Woman* and passing pints of ice cream back and forth across my cat-hair-covered
sofa. This scene wouldn't even have made it into the movie. My life
now looked like something *cut out* of *Bridget Jones's Diary.*

Lying in bed that night, awake again, I thought about the

radical eating coach I'd interviewed earlier that summer on the subject of *"emotional eating."* That's how she put it—*"emotional eating,"*
in highly italicized air quotes.

"I don't really buy into the idea of it," she told me, going on to
say that every person eats *"emotionally."*

"But, obviously, a person should feel their feelings rather than
eat over them constantly," I replied.

She shook her head. "You can still feel your feelings and eat. Dieters call it *'emotional eating,'* but regular people just call it *'wanting
a cookie.'* I don't think *'emotional eating'* really exists."

A *"radical"* concept indeed, but she had a point about the
cookie. Even in childhood, no Nutter Butter ever fully prevented
me from feeling the shit I didn't want to feel. But that never
stopped me from throwing more cookies at the problem. Cookies,
or ice cream.

It took approximately two more nights of ice cream and romcoms
before I gave in and went full-blown Jones, street-crying and all.
Harry and I were walking to a birthday party on the Lower East
Side when our casual conversation took a turn. All he did was
ask how the book was coming along, and my eyes filled with hot,
ridiculous tears.

"Let's go find a place to talk," he said, taking my hand and
pulling me out of the Friday night foot traffic heading down Orchard Street.

"No, we have to go to the party. Let's just go!" I wiped at my
eyes, so embarrassed.

"We can be late. What's going on?"

Here's where I needed the monologue. This was my chance to
unleash a summer's worth of cathartic sobs. (Only then could I begin my redemptive late-night-walking-around-the-city-thinking-

about-where-shit-went-wrong montage. With original scoring by Aimee Mann.) If I'd been able to speak, I'd have started with how scary it had been to see my friend laid low, and how the tiny, vanishingly small chance of his death made life feel at once precious and pointless. I'd talk about how stressful writing this book was and how monstrous I felt to be stressed over something like that when cancer stress should be the *only* stress. I'd throw in something about my mom and how I'd stared at her number in my phone four times that day, unsure if I should dial or delete it for good. I'd finish by saying that I was a fraud. I walked such a good walk, telling readers how well and joyous I was now that I'd gotten free of all my food issues. But TomatoPlant and the deli guy knew the real me: a sad, frightened, dependent thing with a freezer full of *"emotions."*

I couldn't say any of that, though, because I was crying too hard to talk. Harry stood silent, rubbing my back lightly, while the Lower East Side went on about its Friday night. I sobbed into his shoulder, completely unable to care who saw. Once you start street-weeping, you just need to keep going until the fadeout.

It took a month. I spent the rest of the summer crying all over the city, making up for lost tears. I listened to what could only be described as a fuck-ton of Aimee Mann. Harry got good at talking me through sleepless nights, and I got *slightly* better at talking about the things keeping me awake. I bought ice cream and I ate it, sometimes because I wanted it and other times because I really, really wanted it. All the air quotes in the world couldn't make this any less real.

I knew ice cream wouldn't make things less stressful, keep my friend's cancer from returning, or un-feel my fear about it. I went back to *Intuitive Eating* and reread the chapter on emotional eating. One of the goals of the program is to learn how to cope without food, but the book stressed how important it was to recognize the "perks" of emotional eating. It wasn't a symptom of failure, but simply "a sign that stressors in your life at that moment surpass the coping mechanisms that you have developed," the chapter explained. "Overeating becomes a red flag to let you know that something isn't right in your life." *No shit*, I thought. *Thanks for the heads-up, Häagen-Dazs.*

This was a habit I didn't want to have. But maybe eating some emotional ice cream wasn't a deal breaker. Maybe it would take more than ten months to get over a lifelong toxic relationship with food. And maybe it would take even longer to get over my mom.

Here was the really scary thought: *What if I never got over it?*

*

We met at Grand Central. I spotted her first, standing in front of the clock in the middle of the bustling great hall. I raised my hand in a little wave as I approached.

"Can I give you a hug?" she asked.

I nodded and stepped into her familiar arms, both of us hesitant, but trying.

"Hi, Mom."

We walked to the nearest exit, swarmed by Saturday tourists, and I aimed for Bryant Park.

"I don't really know what to say," she said, as we sat down at a spindly green table by the lawn.

I couldn't think where to begin. *Do you still think I made up that whole molestation thing to ruin your life? Hey, I'm writing a memoir, and you're gonna be in it!* There was nothing we could resolve in an hour in the park. Even if there was, I hadn't come for resolution, only peace. It didn't really matter what we sat there and talked about, or even that we talked. The most important thing was that we sat there, together, for a while.

That night, I recounted the Mom meeting to Jon over bowls of cold, late-summer pasta at my little dining table. In the last few weeks, I'd watched as he went through a posttrauma montage of his own. (His was more of an early-morning, take-on-the-day montage, with Janet Jackson in the background.) He'd rented a gorgeous high-rise apartment with a two-bridge view. He'd forgiven Ben and bounced back from both the surgery and the breakup in record time, suddenly taking up jogging and dating a new guy we called "Harvard Penis." Having hit my own bottom less than a year before, it was stunning to see my friend rebound from his own, and a lot more quickly than I had.

"And, that's the magic of cancer!" he tilted his head and smiled a real-fake smile.

"Here's lookin' at you, cancer." I extended my tumbler of Prosecco toward him, and we toasted to cancer like two old friends at the end of a long, lesson-learning movie. Ah, sure, there'd been some hits, but the important thing was everyone was alive, happy and better for the journey. And, it was over.

Except no, of course it wasn't. Five minutes later, Jon was in hysterics, enraged at his ex and terrified that every flicker of pain in his body was the cancer coming back. In that moment, none of it felt *over*. The cold pasta sat between us getting colder, and the only sound to score his sadness was the light fizzing of a cheap sparkling wine. By now, even I'd run out of platitudes. This time, I'd have to improvise.

"You know what I heard on a podcast this morning?" I asked, the way all good speeches begin.

"What?" He looked up from under a single, trembling hand.

"So, I was listening to *WTF* at the gym this morning. You don't listen to that, right?"

"No, I don't listen to any podcasts. I know, I know."

"Right, no, that's not the point. Anyway, Rosanne Cash was on."

It would have been a nicer moment had these words of wisdom come from my own well-earned experience. Even if I'd pulled them from a favorite old book, that might have given them more gravitas. But I'd take an epiphany wherever I could get it, and this one came courtesy of a celebrity interview I'd heard on the treadmill one morning.

"She said this thing about how 'closure' doesn't really exist."

"Okay." Jon raised his eyebrows, unimpressed.

"Think about it, though! It's amazing."

"Yeah?"

"Yeah, we all talk about 'closure' as if it's mandatory."

"Right, so you can move on."

"Exactly! But when has that ever happened? When it counts, I mean."

He sniffed and shrugged.

"What if closure is bullshit?"

"It's all bullshit."

"I'm serious. What if we never waited around for this mythical feeling, and just moved on without it?"

He shrugged again, then nodded in the way that means: *I love you and I get it and you can stop talking now.*

The best part of going on a diet is knowing it will end. I don't mean the part where the whole thing falls apart and you find yourself whispering on the phone with the Chinese place, calling in dumplings like a mob hit. I mean the "after" shot. We think we're running toward a goal weight, but really, we're not running toward anything so much as running away from that "before."

"Before," I was fat. I was fearful and embarrassed by myself. I was too damaged by everything that came "before": the pantry full of chocolate chips, the late nights lurched in front of the toilet, the looking and touching I could never hide from as a kid, and all the other looks and touches I'd missed out on, hiding as an adult. The failure, most of all, is what defined "before." Not since that first diet at age eleven, when I'd lost thirty pounds in two weeks by subsisting on green beans and mania, had I ever hit a goal weight. I lost so much, but never enough. If I went from a size 16 to an 8, then that was half-way to a 4. And when I hit 160 after losing fifty pounds, I was that much closer to 120, when I would finally leave my room, buy all new clothes, and start my life, for real. Until then: reruns and crunches on a floor that I should probably vacuum. That was before.

The day I quit dieting was the day I gave up on "after," and what a great relief it was. But it took almost a year for me to realize that there's no escaping my "before." All that history is in me. The people who hurt me and the ways I've hurt myself— they are part of the messy, awkward truth of who I was and who I am now.

I am better, but I am not done. I no longer have a clear picture of what being done looks like, and I think, more than anything, that's the change that's made me better. When I stopped trying so desperately to starve and burn "before" away, I finally got to par-ticipate in right now. That baggage wasn't going anywhere. So, I'd just have to bring it with me.

Here's the uninspiring truth that I learned one uneventful morn-ing while climbing up the treadmill: Endings are baloney. You can look at any day of your life and call it an ending, a beginning, or a Tuesday. That doesn't mean that every day will be the same, only that there's no point in standing around screaming at the sun to set. There is no such thing as real closure the way we typically define it. It's not a gift someone else can give to you. The apology will never erase the argument. The good-bye kiss won't make you miss them any less. The diet may help you drop the baby weight, but you still had a baby. You'll never un-have it, no matter how much dressing you order on the side.

I didn't want this story to end in a bikini, but fine—I wanted the beach. I probably imagined applause and bowing at some point, too. But in fact, it ends at my IKEA table with my hair blowing in the breeze of a secondhand air conditioner. We don't get montages or grand finales. We just eat dinner and do the dishes, and absolutely no one's going to clap their hands about it.

With or without a diet, life had intervened. Sometimes, reality just smashes like a brick through your bedroom window and wakes you up in the middle of the night, even if you're supposed to get up and go to the gym in the morning. On those days, I will be exhausted and snappish and maybe I'll want to eat some fucking ice cream, and so what? Neither ice cream nor the gym matters as much as cleaning up the glass.

Part of being better means having bad days. Man, I wish it hadn't taken me thirty years to just have bad days. On a diet, those days will ruin your streak, urging you to cheat until you find yourself clawing through a loaf of Wonder Bread because, fuck it, you'll have to start over again tomorrow anyway. In the real world, there's no starting over. Those days are just days in your life. They will suck, and there's no guarantee that tomorrow won't suck even worse. Still, every morning you wake up is another you get to have. Whether it's a good day or a bad day isn't so important. The only part that really matters is that you get up.

For the record, I have a hard time believing this bullshit on the bad days, too. That's why I wrote it down.

Another End

November 2014

Last week, I went apple picking with my three best friends and
Harry. For the last seven years, my friends and I have kept up
the tradition, jamming ourselves into a rental car and driving up to
the Hudson Valley, hoping there will still be apples on the trees. It
was Harry's first time joining us, and he brought along his fancy
camera. For once I didn't complain about the constant snapshot-
ting. I'd asked him to bring it, because this apple-picking trip
would almost certainly be the last. In fact, it would be the last day
my friends and I would have together for a very long time.

Four months and two hundred pages ago, I wrote that my deepest fear was one of my friends moving to another borough—and I
was just barely exaggerating. But that was back before I understood
that there were far worse ways to lose someone. Back then, I really
thought that untangling my relationship with food, my past, and
my body was the hardest thing I'd go through. Idiotic as it sounds,
those were the things that had derailed me at every turn thus far
in life, and I was *pretty* sure that if I could just get that situation
under control, then every other challenge would be cake. Maybe

there would be no happily ever after, but as long as I still had my best friends right around the corner and nothing else changed ever again, then I'd be content.

"Jesus Christ, I'm not dying." Jon dropped his head back and rolled his eyes for the hundredth time that day. "I'm *just* moving to LA!"

Once again, I welled up and threw my hands around his middle like a kid refusing to let daddy leave for a business trip.

"Take another picture?!" I called to Harry, who turned his lens on the two of us standing in a row of overpicked Cortlandt trees. In the photo, I do indeed look childish, gawking up at my tall, old friend, both of us on the verge of laughing. In all the photos from that day, my friends and I look a little silly and wistful, but not nearly as silly and wistful as we felt.

"This time next year..." we kept repeating. This time next year, where would everyone be? What would our lives look like? We all knew better than to answer these questions, but it was hard not to ask them.

Personally, I try hard not to divine my future too specifically. This time last fall I'd decided that the year ahead would be the Best Year of My Life, and I wasn't quite wrong. But "the best" looked a lot different than I thought it would. I suppose that's the truth about most things in our lives, and fine—I guess that's okay, too. If everything turned out the way we imagined it, there'd be no surprises. Even after seeing how rotten surprises can be, I think I still prefer a life with them in it. Good thing I don't have a choice.

But certain things I'm pretty sure of about this time next year. I'll be in better health and shape than I was for most of my life. My recent annual physical reports that this is already true. While I'm not going to take any "after" photos, I will disclose that my blood sugar and blood pressure are normal, my cholesterol kicks ass, and my doctor says that all those other hormones and bodily statistics I don't understand are equally thumbs-up. My weight is no longer my concern, and though I let him weigh me, I ask him to keep the number to himself. It's not just so I can keep the focus on health instead of weight loss, but because part of being healthy is knowing what my triggers are. Like an old, vicious lover, that number on the scale still has a seductive pull. I could probably handle seeing it, but why would I, unless some part of me wanted to get back together?

That's one more thing I know with certainty: There's no going back. No matter what happens down the line, I've clawed my way out of the proverbial cave, seen the real light of day, and felt the cold, wet morning grass beneath my feet. I'm staying right here.

I know I still have work ahead of me, and that I will next year, too. This is a process, but so is, like, being alive. Fingers crossed, I'll still be forging ahead with both for a good long time.

I know this, too: I will still have stupid arguments with my friends. I'll still cry at the office every once in a while and pretend that no one saw. I will still panic a little when my dad asks if Harry and I are going to get married, and then I'll yell at him about feminism and generational biases. I will always love my mother and hope that she loves me. No matter how painful our past or uncertain our future, that much I know is true.

A couple years ago, those things would send me crawling into bed with a glass of wine and a sleeve of Thin Mints. Now, I know there is no avoiding the hard times, and there are no guarantees about when the good times will come around again. The Thin Mints can't help me there. But getting out of bed might.

I know that giving up diets means I never get to be done with one. Changing your life means you're never done changing it. Just like when you fall in love, you're not "done" falling in love, nor are you wholly cured of all relationship neuroses. And just because you turn thirty, that doesn't mean you're finished being a twenty-something idiot. Getting older doesn't mean I'm a grown-up. Certainly, no one who's seen the state of my closet would argue that.

People talk about late bloomers like they're somehow handi-capped, but I kind of like being one. This is not a bad place to be: a thirty-year-old writer with rock-solid friends, someone to love, try-ing to do the work of being happy and maybe finding a slightly less crappy apartment.

At the end of this path, I find I'm still on it. No matter where I am, I'm on it. Climbing that windy orchard hill, and reaching up to yank a Braeburn off the tree, I felt a rush of knock-out joy, so grateful that I'd finally gotten up and started walking, with the ones I love beside me, and each on their own path.

I'm not done. I don't want to be done.

Discussion Questions

1. As a child, Kelsey was constantly bingeing in secret as her mother pressured her to diet and lose weight. Do you think these early habits led to her adult yo-yo dieting? To what extent do our parents help shape our relationship with food?

2. In talking about all the diets she's been on, Kelsey identifies the "New Diet Buzz," a high that accompanies every new diet, making you think that success is inevitable—and therefore making the diet failure all the more crushing. Do unrealistic expectations set us up for failure? Do you recognize the Buzz in other areas of life?

3. At one point, Kelsey's intuitive eating coach, Theresa, says, "No one is broken. I've never met anyone who was broken." Do you agree? Are some people too far gone to be able to change their behavior? How does the idea of being irreparably broken make it more difficult for you to achieve your goals?

4. At a young age, Kelsey blamed her own body for tempting family friend William into touching her inappropriately. How did these feelings of guilt over something she couldn't control translate into her feelings about her body later in life? How was she ultimately able to combat the guilt this abuse created?

5. When Kelsey reaches the age of twenty-six and is still a virgin, she jokingly declares it "a national emergency." How is the pressure to become romantically and sexually

active different in your mid-twenties than it is when you're a teenager? In what ways has the sexual freedom of the millennial generation contributed to or taken away from this pressure?

6. When discussing the way the media portrays female celebrities and their relationship with food, Kelsey points out "I've never read a male celebrity profile that opens with a line about how amazing it is that he ordered whole milk in his latte." How does this media treatment of celebrities' bodies affect the relationship we have with food and our own bodies? How is this different for women than it is for men?

7. Throughout her life, Kelsey always seems just one diet away from her perfect life—when she's finally thin she'll have the perfect college social life or win her dream job or meet the perfect man. How did this illusion that thinness is the key to happiness keep her from pursuing her dreams? Why is she finally able to chase her dreams without necessarily achieving major weight loss?

8. It takes Kelsey a while to fully accept that her career success is a result of her talent and hard work, and not just random luck. Why is that? Do you sometimes have difficulty believing that your success is deserved?

9. Kelsey claims that distraction is her "drug of choice" and points out the ways that she uses podcasts and music to keep her mind occupied as she moves about her life. How does technology keep us from being more mindful? Do you find yourself constantly distracted or are you able to have small moments of reflection throughout the day?

10. One of Kelsey's big revelations is that there's no such thing as real closure. Do you agree? Why or why not?

Many Thanks

First of all, I must thank Grand Central Publishing for making this book a reality, and embracing it with such excitement and warmth. You made me feel as if I'd been invited to sit at the cool kids' table, and was somehow now a cool kid myself.

Thanks to my editor, Emily Griffin, for your truly incredible guidance and vision. You saw the things I couldn't or didn't want to see, and told me so with sensitivity and patience, and more than anything, I'm grateful for that honesty. I also want to thank Sara Weiss, the first editor who championed this book in the early stages and guided me through my first draft. I honestly didn't know if I could do it, but you did, so I believed you. Thank you for that.

To my agent, Allison Hunter, I can hardly think of how to thank you adequately. A pony? A unicorn? I give up. Your wisdom and support throughout this process have been invaluable, and I am forever grateful.

On that note, I must thank Andy Ward, who introduced me to Allison, and Susan Kaplow, who introduced me to Andy. I also gratefully acknowledge Susie Duff, who first gave voice to the thought I was too scared to say: *You should write a book.* Without these people all of this would still be a daydream. Thank you.

I am endlessly grateful to Refinery29, not just for giving me a job, but for giving me the right job. Writing at this publication has taught me to work harder than I ever have, because the work is worth it. Thank you for allowing me to take risks, having my back, and reminding me that my voice is of value. My special thanks to

Christene Barberich, who urged and empowered me to be the best, brightest version of myself, every day.

Thanks to my writing teachers—thanks to *all* writing teachers, in fact. In particular, thanks to Julie Faulstich, my high school English teacher, who created a safe, exciting space to try and fail and try again. I hold that space within me whenever I sit down in front of a scary blank page. And, thank you to Jack Murnighan, who said that I could be a writer and I should be. I don't know if I would have tried if you hadn't flat-out told me to.

Thanks to Theresa Kinsella, who so patiently guided me back to my senses and taught me how to eat like a human again. Thank you to Stephanie Irvin, who showed me how truly capable my body was. Thank you to my therapists, because without therapy I would never have had it in me to start this journey, let alone stick with it. Of course, huge thanks to Evelyn Tribole and Elyse Resch, the authors of *Intuitive Eating*. These are the people who gave me the tools to change my life.

Thank you to my family, especially my parents, who always, always believed in my ambitions, even when my ambition was to be a Broadway star / screenwriter / indie film "it" girl / David Sedaris. You never once told me it was impossible. You never urged me toward something more practical. You gave me an education, and you never made me feel like an asshole when I needed help making rent. Regardless of anything else, you taught me to believe I could do it. Thank you so much.

Thank you to my dear and understanding friends for sticking by me, even when I am a frazzled, unwashed mess, as I've been for much of this last year. Further thanks to those friends who have lent me their lives for this book. In particular, thanks to Jonathan Parks-Ramage, whose story smashed into mine as I was writing. Thank you for your great generosity in letting me use your personal crisis as third-act material. I'll try to time my breakdown for when you're writing your memoir. Deal?

Thanks to Kelsey Osgood. There are some things I can vent about only to another writer, and you always let me do so with such patience and empathy. Thank you to Cheryl Strayed, who reminded me to be brave, compassionate, and wholly honest with myself in these pages. And thank you for reminding me that in the end, it's all probably going to be okay.

Finally, thank you, Harry Tanielyan. You have borne the brunt of me, riding out sleepless nights and whole months of crippling anxiety. You celebrate my successes, and more than that, you remind *me* to celebrate them. You make me want to do the work of being better, and this book is the brightest reflection of that. I am so grateful for you I can hardly believe it.